WOMEN'S FICTION
BETWEEN THE WARS

WOMEN'S FICTION BETWEEN THE WARS

Mothers, Daughters and Writing

Heather Ingman

Edinburgh University Press

For my mother, in memory of her mother.
And for my father.

© Heather Ingman, 1998

Edinburgh University Press
22 George Square, Edinburgh

Typeset in 11 on 13pt Monotype Bembo
by Hewer Text Composition Services, Edinburgh,
and printed and bound in Great Britain by
Cambridge University Press

A CIP record for this book is available from the British Library

ISBN 0 7486 1002 2 (hardback)
ISBN 0 7486 0940 7 (paperback)

'My chief memory of the catechism was a little girl who persisted obstinately in saying "My mother!" "No dear, that's not the answer. Now think – who made you?" "My mother," the stolid girl replied. At last the nun, exasperated, banished her from the class.'

(Jean Rhys, Smile Please, 1981: 78)

Contents

Acknowledgements

My very great thanks go to Marion Shaw for her judicious comments on this book throughout its various stages, for many interesting and pleasurable discussions and for her unfailing support. Her considerable knowledge of the inter-war period has been a constant safeguard and stimulus to the project.

My thanks also go to Patsy Stoneman and Angela Leighton for all that they have taught me through their teaching, writings and conversation. This book could not have been written without the help of their dear and careful expositions of many aspects of feminist literary theory.

I am indebted to many students of the MA course in 'Women and Literature' at Hull University. Their insights and enthusiasm have been an additional source of encouragement.

I would like to thank Ferdinand von Prondzynski for his financial and emotional support during the writing of this book and for so wholeheartedly sharing with me in the mothering of our two sons.

Abbreviations

Primary works are given in parenthesis in the text.

ELIZABETH BOWEN

H: *The Hotel*, Harmondsworth: Penguin, 1987.
HP: *The House in Paris*, Harmondsworth: Penguin, 1976.
DH: *The Death of the Heart*, Harmondsworth: Penguin, 1989.
ET: *Eva Trout*, Harmondsworth: Penguin, 1987.

VERA BRITTAIN

TY: *Testament of Youth*, London: Virago, 1978.
TF: *Testament of Friendship*, London: Virago, 1989.
TG: *Testament of a Generation. The Journalism of Vera Brittain and Winifred Holtby*, London: Virago, 1985.

IVY COMPTON-BURNETT

Dol: *Dolores*, Edinburgh: Blackwood, 1971.
BS: *Brothers and Sisters*, London: Victor Gollancz, 1954.
FF: *A Father and His Fate*, London: Victor Gollancz, 1972.
LF: *The Last and the First*, London: Victor Gollancz, 1971.
MW: *Men and Wives*, London: Eyre and Spottiswood, 1948.
EB: *Elders and Betters*, London: Victor Gollancz, 1944.
PC: *Parents and Children*, Harmondsworth: Penguin, 1984.
DS: *Daughters and Sons*, London: Victor Gollancz, 1961.

SIGMUND FREUD

SE: *The Standard Edition of the Complete Psychological Works of Sigmund Freud*, vols XXI, XXII, London: Hogarth Press, 1961.

ROSE MACAULAY

P: *Potterism*, London: Collins, 1920.
DA: *Dangerous Ages*, London: Collins, 1921.
NC: *Non-Combatants and Others*, London: Methuen, 1986.
KUA: *Keeping Up Appearances*, London: Methuen, 1986.
WW: *The World My Wilderness*, London: Virago, 1983.

JEAN RHYS

VD: *Voyage in the Dark*, Harmondsworth: Penguin, 1969.
AL: *After Leaving Mr Mackenzie*, Harmondsworth: Penguin, 1971.
Q: *Quartet*, Harmondsworth: Penguin, 1973.
GMM: *Good Morning, Midnight*, Harmondsworth: Penguin, 1969.
WSS: *Wide Sargasso Sea*, Harmondsworth: Penguin, 1968.

DOROTHY RICHARDSON

RL: *Revolving Lights* in *Collected Edition* 4 vols, London: J. M. Dent and Sons,
    1967.
D'sLH: *Dawn's Left Hand* in *Collected Edition*.
CH: *Clear Horizon* in *Collected Edition*.
MM: *March Moonlight* in *Collected Edition*.

MAY SINCLAIR

HF: *The Life and Death of Harriett Frean*, London: Virago, 1980.
MO: *Mary Olivier: A Life*, London: Virago, 1980.

VIRGINIA WOOLF

RO: *A Room of One's Own. Three Guineas*, ed. M. Shiach, Oxford: Oxford
    University Press, 1992.
VO: *The Voyage Out*, London: Granada, 1981.
ND: *Night and Day*, Harmondsworth: Penguin, 1992.
J: *Jacob's Room*, London: Granada, 1976.
D: *Mrs Dalloway*, London: Granada, 1981.
TL: *To the Lighthouse*, London: Grafton, 1988.
W: *The Waves*, London: Granada, 1980.
Y: *The Years*, London: Granada, 1985.
BA: *Between the Acts*, London: Grafton, 1978.

Prefatory Note

Because the relationship with the mother is so central to a daughter's sense of identity, and therefore so personal, accounts of fictional mother–daughter stories inevitably become entangled in autobiography. I have not been able, nor have I wished, to avoid reference to these writers' historical relationships with their mothers, but these have been dealt with separately at the end of each chapter. They are not intended to be full-scale biographies since for each of these writers there is at least one up-to-date biography; instead they deal simply with the mother–daughter relationship in the context of the daughter's life as a writer. Priority is always given to the art: these writers are not recounting their actual relationship with their mothers; they are reinventing it, departicularising it, turning it into a metaphor.

1

The Historical Context

Far from being inborn and unchanging, mothering is shaped by the society in which mothers live and in turn daughters are brought up by their mothers to fit into their particular society's understanding of womanhood. Given that motherhood and daughterhood are not stable concepts but socially constructed, we need to set this study of mothers, daughters and writing in the general context of women's lives during the inter-war years in Britain. Let us imagine the life of a woman born, like Winifred Holtby and many of the other authors discussed here, in the late 1890s and grown to adulthood by the end of the First World War. Let us call her Olive, in honour of Olive Schreiner whose book, *Woman and Labour*, published in 1911, was sometimes referred to as 'the Bible of the woman's movement' (*TG*: 314).

If, like most of the writers discussed in this study, Olive belonged to the middle, or upper middle class, she would have experienced the type of Victorian upbringing common to almost all of them. There would have been a strict division still between the outer, public, 'masculine' world and the private, domestic, 'woman's' world, the kind of divide described by Richard Dalloway in *The Voyage Out* (1915):

> It is impossible for human beings, constituted as they are, both to fight and have ideals. If I have preserved mine, as I am thankful to say that in great measure I have, it is due to the fact that I have been able to come home to my wife in the evening and to find that she has spent her day in calling, music, play with the children, domestic duties – what you will; her illusions have not been destroyed. She gives me the courage to go on. The strain of public life is very great. (*VO*: 62)

So was the strain of private life, as we shall see.

As a daughter, Olive would be expected to conform to her society's construct of femininity. In fact she would have been socialised into the female role from the day she was born: in Sylvia Townsend Warner's novel, *Lolly Willowes*, we are told that Lolly's father 'was in love with her femininity from the moment he set eyes on her' (Warner 1926: 13). At an early age she would be expected to shoulder her share of domestic responsibilities. 'I had mended my own clothes ever since I was eight, but now I had to help my mother to mend the household linen and all the "men's" underclothes . . . for some – to me inscrutable – reason boys were not expected to help with it' (Swanwick 1935: 58; ellipsis mine). Olive would soon see that the household revolved around the wishes of an often absent father and pressure on daughters at home would be increased if, as in the Stephen household, their father was left a widower. Stella and then Vanessa were expected to supply their mother's place and wait on their father. Such circumstances could well, as their sister was aware, cut off a woman writer's career before it had started: Woolf noted in her diary that if her father had not died 'his life would have entirely ended mine. What would have happened? No writing, no books; – inconceivable' (Woolf 1978b: 137).

Olive would quickly become conscious of her inferior status as a daughter. When her brother falls ill with rheumatic fever, eight-year-old Mary Olivier overhears:

> Jenny saying to Mamma, 'If it had to be one of them it had ought to have been Miss Mary.' And Mamma saying to Jenny, 'It wouldn't have mattered so much if it had been the girl,' (*MO*: 67)

Olive would be taught, like Harriett Frean, not to grab at things for herself. ' "Well, I'm glad my little girl didn't snatch and push. It's better to go without than to take from other people. That's ugly," ' says Harriett's mother when she learns that her daughter has gone away hungry from a tea party (*HF*: 14–15). May Sinclair's novel *The Life and Death of Harriett Frean* (1922) is a potent analysis of the destructive and infantilising effects of Victorian ideals of self-sacrificing womanhood and the part mothers play in transmitting those ideals to their daughters: Harriett knows that when she is grown up 'she would be like Maman, and her little girl would be like herself. She couldn't think of it any other way' (*HF*: 11).

Even if Olive was fortunate enough to have spent a relatively carefree childhood like Rose Macaulay who, between the ages of six and thirteen, lived in Italy and thereby escaped many of the restraints of a late Victorian childhood, she would not be able to avoid becoming a young lady in the end. On their return to England, Rose Macaulay's father told her firmly that there must be no more talk about growing up to be a boy and joining the Navy. Becoming a young lady before the First World War meant leaving off 'tomboy' habits, wearing long skirts and putting up one's hair. Laura Willowes's legs are 'very slim and frisky, they liked climbing trees and jumping over haycocks, they had no wish to retire from the world and belong to a young lady' (Warner 1926: 18). Nevertheless, putting on her new clothes, 'Laura accepted the inevitable. Sooner or later she must be subdued into young-ladyhood' (*ibid.*)

The Fisher Education Act of 1918 provided elementary schooling for all children up to the age of fourteen but if Olive belonged, like the majority of our novelists, to the middle class, she would have been educated at home, like Virginia Woolf and Rosamond Lehmann. Or had a governess for her early years and then gone away to a private, fee-paying school, like Ivy Compton-Burnett, Dorothy Richardson, Vera Brittain, Winifred Holtby, Elizabeth Bowen and countless others. For a young girl who wished to be a writer, or indeed pursue any kind of career, her governess might well be yet another obstacle in her path for many of the women employed by the middle classes to teach their daughters had received no proper education themselves. In 'Journey to Paradise', Dorothy Richardson wrote of hers: 'if she could, [she] would have formed us to the almost outmoded pattern of female education: the minimum of knowledge and a smattering of various "accomplishments" . . . for me . . . she was torment unmitigated' (Richardson 1989: 134; ellipses mine).

If Olive was lucky she might, like Virginia Woolf, Rose Macaulay and the fictional Lolly Willowes, be allowed the freedom of her father's library. Even with this little bit of education, she would in all probability outgrow her mother intellectually at an early age, like Joan Ogden in Radclyffe Hall's novel, *The Unlit Lamp*: 'Joan was fourteen now, she was growing – growing mentally out of Mrs Ogden. There was so much these days they could not discuss together' (Hall 1924/1981: 54). She might find, like Mary Olivier, that her mother resisted the idea of her learning certain subjects because they were the preserve of boys:

> There was something queer about learning Greek. Mamma did not actually forbid it; but she said it must not be done in lesson time or sewing time, or when people could see you doing it, lest they should think you were showing off. You could see that she didn't believe you *could* learn Greek and that she wouldn't like it if you did. (*MO*: 78).

Her education would be neglected in favour of her brothers'; after all what was the point of educating a daughter when her real task in life was to get married? In *The Crowded Street*, Muriel Hammond's father expresses indifference to his daughters' education: ' "Do what ye will with the lasses. If they'd 'a been lads, I might ha' had sommat to say" ' (Holtby 1924/1981: 26).

Ivy Compton-Burnett and Virginia Woolf were more fortunate. Compton-Burnett shared her brothers' Greek and Latin lessons and continued to have extra coaching in Greek when she went to school. Her biographer, Hilary Spurling, remarks: 'Such a thing, for a nicely-brought-up girl who had no need to earn her own living, was almost unheard of: history and literature, a little French, music lessons and sums were as much as was generally considered advisable, or even decent' (Spurling 1984: 53). Woolf was allowed, at the age of fifteen, to attend Greek and history classes intermittently at King's College, London and these classes were supplemented by teaching at home by Janet Case, one of the first women to pass through Girton College, Cambridge. Nevertheless, educating herself at home was a solitary process and Woolf envied the opportunities of her brother Thoby, then at Trinity College, Cambridge, for intellectual debate:

> I don't get anybody to argue with me now and feel the want. I have to delve from books, painfully and all alone, what you get every evening sitting over your fire and smoking your pipe with Strachey etc. No wonder my knowledge is but scant. There's nothing like talk as an educator I'm sure. (letter to Thoby Stephen, quoted in Gordon 1984: 83)

Olive might attend one of the public schools for girls where the curriculum was modelled on the education available to boys (Beddoe 1989: 40). The teachers in such schools concentrated on academic achievement and on forming a new generation of career women. One such school was Cheltenham Ladies College which both May Sinclair and Margaret Kennedy attended. Girls' schools were not necessarily feminist institutions but being educated in one would give Olive confidence and self-respect, for she would see a world where women were in charge. Such a world is depicted in Holtby's novel, *South Riding*, where Holtby underlines the lack of real interest in girls' education at the time. Kiplington Girls' High School owes its existence to 'masculine pride rather than to educational necessity,' (Holtby 1936/1988: 21): it is thought that the daily journey into Kingsport, whilst acceptable for boys, would be unsafe for girls. The school is housed in grim apartment houses bought on the cheap and run on a shoestring. Out of this unpromising material ('Four wretched houses. A sticky board of governors. A moribund local authority'), Sarah Burton must endeavour to give her girls a sense of self-worth: 'She wished to prepare their minds, to train their bodies, and to inoculate their spirits with some of her own courage, optimism and unstaled delight' (*op. cit.* 48). Sarah is an inspiring role model for her pupils and, in her influence on their lives, a not untypical example of many women teachers of her day. Vera Brittain has described how she was first influenced in favour of feminism by one of her teachers at St Monica's, Miss Heath

Jones, 'a brilliant, dynamic woman who had been educated at Cheltenham and Newnham' (*TY*: 32).

In F. Tennyson Jesse's novel, *A Pin to See the Peepshow*, Julia Almond's education comes to an end when she is sixteen: 'the Almonds could not afford to go on indefinitely with the education of a daughter' (Jesse 1934/1979: 49). John Stevenson comments: 'Women . . . were the group least likely to receive higher education. Less than a quarter of English university students in the mid-1920s were women' (Stevenson 1990: 257–8; ellipsis mine). If Olive did go on to higher education it might well be against her mother's wishes. Joan Ogden's mother hopes ' "that neither of *my* girls will want to go to a university, they would never do so with my approval" ' (Hall 1924/1981: 60). In *Testament of Youth* (1933) Vera Brittain recounts her struggle to get her parents' consent to go up to Oxford (they automatically expected her younger brother, Edward, to go). Winifred Holtby comments: 'I am one of the very few women I know who went to Oxford because my mother wished it' (*TG*: 273). Not many daughters were blessed with a mother like Storm Jameson's:

> My mother was zealous for my future. Was it she or I who discovered that three County Scholarships – worth sixty pounds – were awarded yearly, in each Riding, on the results of the Matriculation examination? . . . It was my one chance. Sixty pounds would cover the fees at a provincial university – to our innocence all universities were equal – and she could, she said, find another pound or thirty shillings a week for my living expenses. It occurred to neither of us to ask my father for help. (*Journey from the North* vol. 1 1984: 46; ellipsis mine)

This was in 1910. Storm Jameson's autobiography is particularly valuable as a record of life at a co-educational school in the North of England just before the First World War and at a provincial university (Leeds) during the war.

Let us suppose Olive goes to one of the Oxbridge colleges or perhaps, like Ivy Compton-Burnett, to Royal Holloway College, London; what will she find there? Depending on her background she might, like Virginia Woolf, be discouraged by the austerity: 'One cannot think well, love well, sleep well, if one has not dined well. The lamp in the spine does not light on beef and prunes,' says Woolf in *A Room of One's Own* (*RO*: 23) and contrasts the poverty of her imaginary women's college, Fernham (based on Newnham College, Cambridge), with the luxury of the men's colleges. Judith Earle, the heroine of Rosamond Lehmann's novel, *Dusty Answer*, comes, like Woolf, from an upper middle-class background and feels similarly disillusioned: 'Trips. Labs. Lectures. Dons. Vacs. Chaperons. The voices gabbled on. The forks clattered. The roof echoed. "Ugly and noisy," muttered Judith. "Ugly and noisy and crude and smelly" ' (Lehmann 1927/1936: 110). She, too, contrasts this Cambridge with that of her father: 'If he could have known how very unlike his Cambridge this place was!' (*op. cit.* 116). Students at Royal Holloway fared better: the college was centrally heated, had its own kitchen gardens and 'in sharp contrast to other impoverished and comfortless women's colleges of the day, was celebrated alike for its good living and excellent food' (Spurling 1984: 131).

Despite the poor food and uncomfortable accommodation, most women delighted in the chance to escape a narrow home life, make new friends and get involved in new activities: 'Why do male reviewers believe that life in a woman's college is gruesome? . . . Friends, work, games, the river, rooms of their own, comparative grown-up freedom, the University atmosphere – those who enjoy none of those things should not have come up, but have come out instead,' declared Rose Macaulay (*Spectator* 5 April 1935; ellipsis mine). At Royal Holloway, Ivy Compton-Burnett studied classics. The more usual subjects were English or history. At Oxford, Vera Brittain started by doing English and then changed to history in order to try and make sense of recent events (the war). Holtby also studied modern history at Oxford, as did Rose Macaulay and Margaret Kennedy. But probably a large part of Olive's energies would be spent on things other than formal study. Winifred Holtby threw herself into every activity going at Oxford – singing, sport, debates, politics, committee work, acting. 'I spend my time . . . tearing about Oxford on a very rusty cycle, flying from lectures, tea parties, concerts, lacrosse matches, and all the thousand and one other things' (*TF*: 62; ellipsis mine).

All through her education, Olive would live under the threat that a family crisis might call her back home and put an end to her studies. Daughters were expected to lay aside their studies immediately in the event of a sick relative. Sons never were. In a *Time and Tide* article dated 1923, Vera Brittain comments caustically:

> The talents of a boy are always a source of pride to his parents . . . But in the average middle-class family the talents of a girl are seldom the source of anything but domestic controversy . . . Even if her claims are reluctantly acknowledged, and she is sent with her brother to training college or university, her handicaps are not yet eliminated. During the vacation he goes off cheerfully on a reading party . . . But the similar grind of his sister is no such excuse for relaxation. Her return for the vacation is regarded in most middle-class households as an opportunity for her mother to 'get a little rest now Mary is at home.' (*TG*: 122; ellipses mine)

Both Brittain and Holtby experienced these domestic demands in their own lives. Entering higher education would give Olive a breathing space from the constrictions of family life and an opportunity for self-development, but it did not mean she could entirely shake off the constraints of the 'feminine' role. And she would not necessarily be expected to do anything with her education afterwards: ' "The Cambridge and Oxford Colleges are excellent training schools for housewives," ' says Mrs Chapel in Rose Macaulay's novel, *Crewe Train* (Macaulay 1926/1985: 255).

For Olive, the First World War might well provide her first opportunity to break out of constricting feminine roles and enter hitherto undreamed-of occupations. After a year at Somerville, Holtby joined the Women's Auxiliary Army Corps and her experiences in France are recounted in Vera Brittain's *Testament of Friendship* (1940). Brittain herself, like Enid Bagnold, E. M. Delafield and so many other middle-class women, became a VAD nurse. Holtby declared:

> One of the few good features of the war of 1914 was that it gave an opportunity for women to prove their individual capacity. Running hospitals, conducting operations, holding high positions in the Civil Service, working as farmers, engineers and bus conductors, driving lorries, making shells, cleaning windows, and finally replacing soldiers at the base in Queen Mary's Army Auxiliary Corps, they threw down a challenge to those who had hitherto relegated them to kitchen, nursery or drawing-room. (*TG*: 94–5)

Whatever type of war work she did, Olive would find her horizons expanded and she would come into contact with a whole range of people she would not otherwise have met, an inestimable advantage for a writer. There were also psychological benefits in terms of enhanced self-esteem and self-confidence, as Ray Strachey outlines:

> Another change . . . was brought about by the war years, and that was the change in the outlook of women themselves. For the first time hundreds of thousands of them had experienced the joys of achievement; they had been of consequence and had done things they felt to be important; they had been encouraged to show enterprise and ambition, and they had been more or less adequately paid . . . They saw what the world was like for men; and neither an Act of Parliament nor season of reaction, nor any other thing could thereafter take that knowledge from them. (Strachey 1928: 349; ellipses mine)

Strachey is being a little over-optimistic here, as we shall see. Nevertheless, after the war more middle-class women did start to think of having long-term careers. They were often encouraged in this by their families who feared that lack of marriage partners or their own dwindling resources would make it necessary for their daughters to support themselves. This development was bound to exacerbate differences between middle-class daughters and their mothers who had never contemplated paid work outside the home. In addition, Olive would have become accustomed to greater freedom of movement during the war. Vera Brittain wrote to her fiancé: ' "I picture to myself Mother's absolute horror if she could have seen me at 9.15 the other night dashing about and dodging the traffic in the slums of Camberwell Green" ' (*TY*: 212). Olive would have gone about unchaperoned for the first time and seen sickness and death at close quarters. Whatever she did next, either resume her interrupted university career, like Brittain and Holtby, return home, or take up a profession, the war years would have permanently changed her outlook and increased her separation from her mother. 'The past had been blasted to hell . . . in 1917 . . . the old order was dead', wrote H. D. in *Bid Me to Live* (H. D. 1960/1984: 24; ellipses mine).

Those mothers who did try to preserve 'the old order' by, for example, keeping their daughters at home, began to be criticised after the war. There are searing accounts of the wasted lives of daughters at home in such works of fiction as *The Crowded Street* (Holtby), *The New House* (Lettice Cooper), *The Unlit Lamp* (Radclyffe Hall) and *Thank Heaven Fasting* (E. M. Delafield), to name but a few. In F. Tennyson Jesse's novel, *A Pin to See the Peepshow*, Dr Ackroyd tells his friend: ' "It's no good, Almond, you can't keep young Julia at home doing nothing, even if you could afford to. That's the way to make women husband-hunters and nothing else" ' (Jesse 1934/1979: 63). In Holtby's novel, *The Crowded Street*, Mrs Hammond is bitterly reproached by her daughter Connie: ' "[you] wouldn't let us work or go away, or have any other interests, because you were afraid of our spoiling a chance of a good marriage" ' (Holtby 1924/1981: 152). The tensions engendered by unmarried daughters living at home themselves became a breeding ground for a feminist critique. Novel after novel written by women in the inter-war period demonstrates sympathy for the dutiful daughter trapped at home and castigates the selfishness of parents who keep her there.

It is more than likely that Olive would do some kind of work after the war, though the massive expansion of job opportunities for women during the First World War did not last. Working women, no longer 'our gallant girls', became 'scroungers' who were robbing returning soldiers of their rightful jobs. In theory the Sex Disqualification (Removal) Act of 1919 gave Olive access to the professions. If her family could afford it, she could train for the Bar, or become a doctor, a teacher or a civil servant. In practice progress was slow. Most of these professions operated some form of a marriage bar and after the war they began to shut their doors to women on all sorts of spurious grounds. Teaching, for example, had a relatively high status and was a well paid job for women, but they received only four-fifths of male rates for the same job and, by 1926, three-quarters of local education authorities had brought in some form of marriage bar. The life of a teacher could vary enormously, depending on the establishment in which she found herself. The, on the whole, positive picture of school life in *South Riding*, can be contrasted with the picture in Orwell's novel, *A Clergyman's Daughter*, where Dorothy perceives 'that by one of two well-beaten roads every third-rate schoolmistress must travel: Miss Strong's road, via whiskey to the workhouse; or Miss Beaver's road, via strong tea to a decent death in the Home for Decayed Gentlewomen' (Orwell 1935/1990: 259).

Even to get as far as contemplating a career outside the home, Olive would have to face many hurdles: parental opposition, an insufficient education, a government intent on returning women to the home, as well as psychological pressure from advertisers bombarding her with images of cosy domesticity. In an article published in 1929, Holtby emphasised the widespread prejudice against women in management: 'it is nearly always the man who sits at the big desk with the telephone and the woman who sits at the little table with the typewriter' (*TG*: 61). And she pointed out the damaging psychological effect on women of being paid less than men for the same work: they lose interest in the work and respect for themselves. Vera Brittain made a similar point in an article published in 1928, where she argued that obstacles to women's progress in the professions were based on prejudices of the most primitive kind, one of which 'is the belief that "business" is the chief concern of a man's life but personal relationships the main interest of a woman's' (*TG*: 125-6).

If she had sufficient talent, Olive could earn her living by her pen as many middle-class women did during the inter-war period. She could write journalism, like Holtby, Brittain, Rebecca West, Storm Jameson and many others. Or she could join the growing number of popular novelists. In Rose Macaulay's novel, *Keeping Up Appearances* (1928), the heroine reflects that her success with her novel *Summer's Over* 'should afford them journeys abroad, feed and clothe their little ones, pay their income-tax, their gambling debts, their car and wireless licences' (*KUA*: 132). Clearly novel writing was one of the more lucrative professions for a woman.

Earning enough money to live comfortably would be imperative if Olive were to remain unmarried. The 1920s have been described as 'the era of the spinster' (Beauman 1983: 59). The shift in balance between the sexes due to wartime male losses created over one million 'surplus' women: ' "It's extraordinary," ' says a character in F. M. Mayor's novel, *The Rector's Daughter*, ' "to see those crowds of girls getting older, and all unmarried. I'd quite forgotten about them; I've been out of England so much, and it comes upon one as a shock" ' (Mayor 1924/1973: 20). These 'surplus' women were believed to constitute a serious threat to the social fabric: 'the spinster came to represent a nation in decline, the literal embodiment of all dominant culture's worst fears' (Hobby and White 1991: 96). This is exemplified in Annie's outpouring of loathing at the end of Dorothy L. Sayers' novel, *Gaudy Night*: ' "it's women like you who take the work away from the men and break their hearts and lives. No wonder you can't get men for yourselves and hate the women who can" ' (Sayers 1935/1991: 427).

Greater opportunities for education and work, wider availability of birth control and a little more sexual freedom made the single professional woman's lot slightly more tolerable than in earlier generations. Single women were now more likely to embark on an affair: one thinks of Rose Macaulay's long-running relationship with Gerald O'Donovan. In other ways the growing debate during the inter-war years about women's sexuality and women's right to sexual pleasure actually worsened the position of the unmarried woman. To repress one's sexual desires came to be regarded as unhealthy and Holtby, for one, felt under pressure to defend her unmarried state: 'Today, there is a far worse crime than promiscuity: it is chastity. On all sides the unmarried woman today is surrounded by doubts cast not only upon her attractiveness or her common sense, but upon her decency, her normality, even her sanity' (*TG*: 91–2).

Some women writers did their best to counteract the popular view of spinsters. Sylvia Townsend Warner's novel, *Lolly Willowes*, is a glorious subversion of the usual presentation of the single woman as leading a dull life. Dorothy Sayers likewise gives a positive portrayal of spinsterhood and the professional woman in *Gaudy Night* where she calls into question popular Freudian notions about the repressed spinster and where indeed the entire success of the plot depends on the reader being prejudiced against spinsters. Sayers was not the only inter-war writer of detective fiction to be interested in the figure of the spinster: Agatha Christie's Miss Marple enables her creator to harness the potential of the spinster as a force outside patriarchal society (see Shaw and Vanacker 1991: *passim*).

Despite these spirited defences of spinsterhood, if Olive were to remain a spinster she would be likely to be economically and emotionally vulnerable. Sylvia Townsend Warner's short story 'The Property of a Lady', published in 1935, describes the plight of Miss Cruttwell, 'a single woman of sixty living on a small pension' (Warner 1990: 311). Miss Cruttwell reflects 'how, all her life long, she had kept the lady-standard flying, had been scrupulously clean, scrupulously honest, scrupulously refined, and nothing had come of it save to be old and neglected and lonely' (*ibid.*). Olive was also likely, unless she had a very unusual mother, to have to live with the knowledge that she had somehow failed her mother by remaining unmarried: in *South Riding*, Mrs Beddoes regards Sybil, her unmarried daughter, as her chief failure. The dominant discourse relating to the spinster was difficult to resist during the inter-war years even for the most independent-minded women.

During the inter-war years, lesbianism became more visible. This was partly a result of the 1928 Radclyffe Hall trial when, as Virginia Woolf wrote: 'At this moment all our thoughts centre on Sapphism . . . all London they say is agog with this' (*Letters* vol.3 1977: 55; ellipsis mine). There began to emerge a discourse about lesbianism, but not one guaranteed to make the lesbian feel better about herself. In 1921, during the course of a House of Commons' debate on the Criminal Law Amendment Bill which would have made lesbianism a criminal act, MPs spoke of the lesbian as a lunatic who ought to be imprisoned or given the death penalty. The amendment failed to become law only because the government refused to accept any alteration to the bill (Pugh 1992: 79). The greatest disadvantage in being a lesbian in the inter-war years was not legal but psychological. Sexologists would have convinced Olive she was a doomed invert, Freud told her she was suffering from arrested development, popular fiction informed her she was a vampirish predator, clinically sick or just plain ridiculous. Even a woman as strong-minded as Vita Sackville-West was so influenced by the prevailing ideology as to refer to her lesbian side as her 'perverted nature' (Faderman 1985: 366). Unless she frequented circles like Natalie Barney's Parisian salon, secrecy would have been the keynote of Olive's life if she was a lesbian. Her own mother would probably not have understood her daughter's sexuality. In Rose Macaulay's novel, *Dangerous Ages* (1921), the only thing Mrs Hilary disapproves of about her daughter Pamela's relationship with Frances is that too much involvement with another woman will prevent her from getting married. For some women, like Woolf and Sackville-West, the secrecy was part of the attraction of having sexual relationships with women.

Marriage was still the expectation of most women in the inter-war years and it is what Olive would have been encouraged to think of by her mother, though few mothers would have been as extreme as Mrs Cocks in Margaret Kennedy's novel, *The Ladies of Lyndon* (1923), who believes in girls marrying at eighteen, before their characters are formed. Agatha Cocks passes straight from her mother's sway into that of her husband. Disaster is waiting to happen. As Winifred Holtby remarked: 'No woman leading an incomplete, stunted sort of life is going to make a really admirable wife' (*TG*: 55). In *Crewe Train*, Rose Macaulay satirises through the words of Denham's mother-in-law the 'stunted' life of the stay-at-home wife of the period:

> 9.30–9.45: see the servants; 9.45–10: do the flowers; 10–11: read the papers and write one's letters; 11–1: serious reading; 1–1.30: lunch . . . 1.30–2.30: lie down; 2.30–4: exercise or gardening, either alone or with

friends; 4–5: tea and see friends . . . And so on, do you see? It regularises
the day so, and prevents one drifting and idling the time away, as one's
often inclined to do. (Macaulay 1926/1985: 256; ellipses mine)

Inter-war novels even by conservative women tend to demolish the unrealistic
and sentimental picture of the housewife's life promoted by the media and
advertising and thus make possible a feminist critique. In *Forever England.
Femininity, Literature and Conservatism Between the Wars* (1991), Alison Light
categorises this kind of writing as 'conservative modernism'. An example of
this is Jan Struther's *Mrs Miniver* where the heroine reflects: 'Every morning
you awake to the kind of list which begins: Sink-plug. Ruffle-tape. X-hooks.
Glue . . . and ends: Ring plumber. Get sweep. Curse laundry. Your horizon
contracts, your mind's eye is focused upon a small circle of exasperating detail.
Sterility sets in; the hatches of your mind are battened down' (Struther 1939/
1989: 93; ellipsis mine). In E. M. Delafield's novel, *The Way Things Are*, Laura
Temple's unsatisfactory life is parcelled out between her children, her husband,
'the servants, the management of their home, and the Nursing Association, the
Women's Institute and the Girl Guides,' (Delafield 1927/1988: 5). Delafield
continually points out the deleterious effect of household preoccupations on
women's intelligence: 'Today, as they drove, she tried not to think about the
difficulty of finding a new house-parlourmaid, nor about Johnnie's temper, nor
about Edward's loose front tooth, but when she had conscientiously banished
these subjects, her mind seemed a blank' (*op. cit.* 38). In an article published in
1932, 'I Denounce Domesticity!', Brittain wrote: 'with few exceptions, the
gifts of every woman who marries . . . are dissipated and submerged owing to
the stultifying persistence of an unadapted, anachronistic home life' (*TG:* 140;
ellipsis mine). She argued for streamlining of housework, communal housing
arrangements and education of women in their responsibilities outside the
home.

Marriage was one area where Olive's attempt to live a life different from her
mother's might well come to grief. In fact, it is one area where Olive might
envy her mother for, as Jane Lewis has pointed out, in many ways the burden
on women during the inter-war years was greater than before the war:

> The encouragement given to middle-class wives during the inter-war
> years to devote more time to both housewifery and childcare marked a
> departure from the ambivalent nineteenth century attitudes regarding the
> degree of personal involvement in domestic tasks compatible with
> cultured, ladylike activity. (quoted in Beddoe 1989: 103)

The point is subtly made in Rosamond Lehmann's novel, *The Weather in the
Streets* (1936), where Mary, belonging to the younger generation, prides herself

on making all her children's clothes and is sentimental, not to say infantile, about children. The two older women, Lady Spencer and Aunt Blanche, show much less interest in housewifely accomplishments, Aunt Blanche declaring that she is a hopeless knitter and that she has always disliked babies.

Olive may be living in a house similar to the one in which her mother lived, but it would now be much more burdensome to run. During the inter-war years the shortage of domestic servants became a great problem for middle-class households. Laura Temple in *The Way Things Are* runs Applecourt, a fairly large nine-bedroomed house, with the help of a cook-general, a house-parlourmaid, a children's nurse and a gardener. The house in which she had been brought up 'entirely resembled Applecourt, except that it had been more comfortable, because everything had been much less expensive and difficult, in the time before the war' (Delafield 1927/1988: 4). Because working-class women after the war so much resented the restrictions of domestic service, there was a constant awkwardness between employer and employee that had not existed before the war. In *The New House*, Lettice Cooper contrasts Rhoda's shyness with the servants with her mother's confidence: 'Regarding them at the bottom of her heart as automata, she handled them with assurance and precision, while Rhoda was secretly afraid of asking too much, and got a far more unwilling and inefficient service' (Cooper 1936/1987: 101). Even a woman as self-assured as Mrs Miniver has sometimes to face 'the cold mulish glint in the cook's eye; the holiday nurse who had been with the best families' (Struther 1939/1989: 19).

If Olive moved to one of the new middle-class housing estates that sprang up during the inter-war years, life there would bring its own problems namely isolation, lack of amenities, unaesthetic surroundings. Elizabeth Bowen conveys the feeling of living on these new estates in her short story, 'Attractive Modern Homes', published in 1941: 'The semi-detached house was box-like, with thin walls: downstairs it had three rooms and a larder, upstairs, three rooms and a bath. The rooms still smelled of plaster, the bath of putty' (Bowen 1985: 521). Mrs Watson's isolation in this flimsy house where 'almost no one passed, and nobody looked in' (*op. cit.* 522) is well caught by Bowen. In despair, she says to her husband: ' "I don't know what a house like that is meant for," ' (*op. cit.* 526). Living on such estates reinforced the division between the public world of work and the life of the home. For women who had worked in offices or other professions where they had mixed with people all day, the abrupt switch to staying at home alone could be devastating. The heroine of Macaulay's novel, *Keeping Up Appearances*, reflects: 'Husbands go out to work, to companionship and sanity, leaving behind their women (so often) to do that work inside houses which becomes mechanical and is also lonely, leaving their minds free to turn to and fro on themselves' (*KUA*: 70).

Although she might lack the domestic help her mother had enjoyed, Olive had new inventions – vacuum cleaners, washing machines, electric cookers, refrigerators – to help make her house easier to run. In theory. In practice, women were now bombarded with so much good advice on how to run a home that ever higher and higher standards were set for them. Women's magazines which proliferated in the inter-war years (Beddoe records sixty new ones launched between 1920 and 1945) pursued a cult of domesticity, advising women on such vital matters as how to get sea stains out of brown boots. John Stevenson points out the paradox that 'at a time when women might theoretically aspire to a wider role in society as a result of smaller families and an increase in job opportunities, advertising consistently urged them to concentrate their free time and extra income within conventional stereotypes of a woman's place and role' (Stevenson 1990: 178). Given this cult of domesticity, the time taken up by household duties and the psychological pressure on married women not to work outside the home, Olive would have to be very determined indeed if she was to pursue any kind of a career after marriage and the pressure on her not to work after her marriage would be increased if she had children: in *The Way Things Are*, 'mothers of young children' keep saying to Laura 'that they supposed she didn't have much time for writing *now*, with two little boys to look after' (Delafield 1927/1988: 14).

During the inter-war years the position of mothers was largely determined by anxiety on the part of the authorities over the falling birthrate. Even before the First World War there had been government action to bolster the institution of motherhood, though most of the measures passed placed the emphasis on the child rather than the mother (see Pugh 1992: 15). During the inter-war years the focus shifted slightly from child to mother and a substantial amount of legislation was passed that directly affected the position of mothers. This included the 1918 Maternity and Child Welfare Act requiring local authorities to appoint committees for maternity and child welfare (Pugh 1992: 18); the 1920 Maintenance Orders (Facilities for Enforcement) Act and the 1922 Married Women (Maintenance) Act making it easier for married women to gain maintenance for themselves and their children; the 1922 Infanticide Act removing the charge of murder for a woman guilty of killing her child where she was shown to be suffering from the effects of her confinement; the 1922 Law of Property Act placing mothers on an equal footing with fathers as to inheritance of property from intestate children; the 1925 Guardianship of Infants Act giving mothers equal right to appoint guardians for their children; the 1925 Criminal Justice Act making the married woman legally responsible for her own crimes, thus recognising in law her separate existence; and the 1935 Law Reform Act giving married women the same rights over their property as single women and men. The law was beginning to allow married women and mothers some degree of control over their own lives. In theory, Olive's life as a mother should be a little easier than that of her own mother but, as we shall see, reality was not as rosy as this legislation would seem to suggest.

As a mother during the inter-war years, Olive would be expected to attain new scientific standards not only in housekeeping but in childcare as well. She would be subjected to pressures unknown to her own mother. Women's magazines of the period were packed with features on childcare, child health and children's clothing. Manuals on child-rearing written by psychologists and medical experts proliferated. Women were made to feel there was one right way of bringing up children. Deirdre Beddoe comments that this psychological pressure to be the perfect mother 'may well be connected with the emergence of the phenomenon of "surburban neurosis" or depression in women living on new estates' (Beddoe 1989: 104).

Rosamond Lehmann has described as well as anyone the problems of mothers with young children during these years. In Lehmann's novel, *A Note in Music*, Norah reflects that 'motherhood had proved in anticipation chiefly a physical process; in realization – not overwhelmingly glorious: an enormous worry and responsibility, an enormous hindrance to liberty' (Lehmann 1930/ 1982: 139). Even the well-balanced and well-off Kate in *The Weather in the Streets* exclaims:

> God, I wish they were all grown up! If I could have a wish that would be it. Grown up and – all right – independent – off my hands . . . It seems such *years* before one can hope to feel they're all safely through . . . Perhaps one never will . . . Sometimes when I get back from London or somewhere and smell eucalyptus coming from the bathroom *again* and know they'll *all* catch it and Christopher'll have a temperature and Priscilla a cough – I go quite . . . I feel what's the use, why not leave them out on the grass all night, or something (Lehmann 1936/1981: 257; ellipses mine)

In such passages, Lehmann seems deliberately to be demolishing the rosy view of motherhood presented in women's magazines and childcare books of the period.

E. M. Delafield is another writer who does a good job of highlighting the unrealistic advice handed out to mothers. The childcare manuals Laura Temple reads in *The Way Things Are* ('The little books about Education, about Diet, and about Sex-Enlightenment of Children by their Mothers') are quoted whenever Laura runs into difficulties with her children. They are never any help. 'Never meet opposition with opposition' is hardly applicable when Laura is faced with her son throwing himself on the floor in a tantrum. They recommend 'pleasant, gentle reasonableness', but, watching Nanny jerk her son to his feet 'by a form of ju-jitsu known only in nursery circles . . . Laura could not help reflecting how effective physical violence always seemed to be, although so much opposed by every enlightened modern authority' (Delafield 1927/1988: 51; ellipsis mine). Delafield's wit ensures that we are on Laura's side against the unrealistic advice of the 'experts'.

There was a new frankness abroad about the difficulties of motherhood. Even a man as innately conservative as Harold Nicolson noted in his diary for 1934 that:

> women who would have been quite happy and contented as married in 1910 are now feeling restless and nervous . . . Gwen, for instance, [his sister] thirty years ago would have felt herself fortunate at having a faithful husband and five adoring children. But now she feels that these obligations limit herself, that there is a more important function for her somewhere beyond the function of wife and mother. (Glendinning 1983: 270; ellipsis mine)

When he wrote to his wife, Vita, reproaching her for engaging a nanny to look after their two boys during the summer holidays, Vita wrote back to say that if he had to have charge of them himself 'you would be screaming at the end of the week . . . Why then is it different for me? Sex, I suppose. Well, I don't see that it makes any difference, so there' (*op. cit.* 199; ellipsis mine). There was a new frankness, also, about the misery of pregnancy. Rose Macaulay's description of Denham's morning sickness in *Crewe Train* – 'Denham felt, and often was, sick in the mornings' (Macaulay 1926/1985: 135 – may seem tame now, but it shocked many of her readers. In *The Weather in the Streets*, Rosamond Lehmann gives a more detailed description: 'Morning: wake heavy from heavy sleep, get up, one must be sick, go back to bed; nibble a biscuit, doze, half-stupefied till midday; force oneself then to dress, each item of the toilet laborious, distasteful, the body a hateful burden' (Lehmann 1936/1981: 263). Even Mrs Miniver speaks of 'the morning sickness and the quite astonishing pain' (Struther 1939/1989: 19). Despite Woolf's pessimism as to whether it could be done, these middle-class women were beginning to 'write the body'.

Olive would be likely to have a smaller family than her mother and she would be more likely to use birth control: the number of middle-class people using mechanical means of birth control (sheaths, douches, diaphragms) rose during the inter-war period. Olive might even read Marie Stopes's *Married Love* which, published in 1918, had sold nearly half a million copies by the mid 1920s (Laura Temple has a copy in her drawer). In 1921 Marie Stopes opened her first birth-control clinic in Holloway Road, North London and by the Second World War the Family Planning Association was operating more than sixty birth-control clinics in Britain (Stevenson 1990: 155).

If birth control failed, Olive might have recourse to abortion. Abortion was illegal during the whole of the inter-war period; nevertheless, an official surmise in 1939 of the number of abortions performed annually estimated the figure at between 110,000 and 150,000 (Beddoe 1989: 109). Olive might first try a hot bath and gin, or even some of the tablets advertised in newspapers: in *A Pin to See the Peepshow* when Julia becomes pregnant we are told, 'No Female Pill advertised failed to pass her lips, but beyond making her feel wretchedly ill, they achieved nothing' (Jesse 1934/1979: 273). When pills failed to produce the desired result Olive might have recourse to some doctor who, like the ghastly Tredeaven in *The Weather in the Streets*, performed abortions as a sideline. After some bargaining, Olivia pays eighty pounds to Tredeaven. Obviously only well-off women could afford this method; all the same the abortion is botched, endangering Olivia's life. In *A Pin to See the Peepshow*, Julia pays Mrs Humble ten pounds to have the abortion performed in a room above a newspaper shop though she is well aware of the risks: 'She had heard so much of girls who had died after an adventure such as she was planning. Why the *News of the World* was full of them every week' (Jesse 1934/1979: 283).

Ironically, if she did choose to give birth, Olive still risked death. At a time when mortality generally and infant mortality specifically were falling rapidly, maternal mortality actually rose from the end of the First World War till 1934, pointing up government hypocrisy in proclaiming the value of mothers to the nation. Vera Brittain wrote in 1930 of 'the savagery of this country's contemptuous indifference towards the needs of maternity' (*TG*: 133). In Rebecca West's novel, *The Thinking Reed* (1936), Isabelle is well aware after her miscarriage that 'had she been a sailor's wife, rough nursing and an over-worked doctor might by now have lowered her into the black earth' (West 1936/1992: 311). In Enid Bagnold's *The Squire* (1938), the midwife fantasises about running a clinic far away in the country where mothers could give birth in peace, under hygienic conditions.

One of the results of smaller families was that women began to take an interest in the sexual side of marriage. Encouraged by Marie Stopes's insistence that men should develop their sexual skills in order to enhance their wives' sexual pleasure, women during the inter-war period had new expectations about their right to sexual satisfaction and demonstrated a willingness to speak openly of these issues. In her article, 'The pursuit of married love: women's attitudes toward sexuality and marriage in Great Britain, 1918-1939' (1982), E. Holzman examines letters written by middle-class women to Marie Stopes asking for advice on how to improve their sex lives with their husbands. Holzman concludes that in matters of sexuality, this generation of women was transitional: they were prepared to work to improve their sexual enjoyment but they remained very much committed to marriages based on love and companionship even when the sexual side failed to come up to the standards set by Stopes.

Organisations such as the Women's Institute and the Women's Co-Operative Guild, though placing the emphasis on women as wives and mothers, tried to alleviate some of the problems of women at home by encouraging them to get involved in outside activities. But what were feminists doing to improve Olive's position as a mother during the inter-war years? During this period, a public debate arose between the Old, equal rights Feminists, such as Holtby and Brittain, and the New Feminists who believed that the feminist agenda must be modified to highlight issues specifically affecting women as women, such as family allowances, protective legislation, birth control and housing. In 1919, Eleanor Rathbone took over the presidency of the National Union of Societies for Equal Citizenship (NUSEC). Recognising the fact that the majority of women were likely to be primarily wives and mothers, rather than career women, and believing that feminism had to come to terms with this, Rathbone set out to emphasise the specific need of mothers. There were elements of conservatism in Rathbone's arguments which the Old Feminists disliked. Equal rights feminists like Holtby felt that mothers should be encouraged to come out of the home and disliked the New Feminist emphasis on the special needs of women, arguing that women's 'difference' had often been used against them. The debate came to a head in 1927 when NUSEC passed an amendment declaring that in future they would support protective legislation. This was an enfringement of the equal rights ideology. Eleven members of the executive council resigned from NUSEC and some of them subsequently joined the Six Point Group founded by Lady Rhondda in 1921 and which remained loyal to the equal rights agenda.

In general, then, feminists during the inter-war years concentrated on equal pay, family allowances and more flexible forms of organisation in the work-place and in the home. But it is doubtful whether the emphasis of the New Feminists on women as wives and mothers was helpful to Olive in the long run. Legislation concerning women tailed off sharply in the 1930s and Dyhouse remarks: 'It can be argued that divisions amongst feminists frustrated the achievement of any distinctively feminist economic theory of the family and women's work in the inter-war period' (Dyhouse 1989: 104). By the end of the inter-war period, feminism had scattered into a number of pressure groups concentrating on one or more issues and by the 1930s, many women had turned to other problems such as unemployment at home and the rise of fascism abroad. Let down by the state and, it has to be said, by feminists themselves, Olive might have found greatest comfort as a mother in the fictional portrayals of the trials of motherhood by such writers as Rosamond Lehmann, E. M. Delafield and others.

Almost every problem a married mother faced at this time was exacerbated in the case of the single mother including, even, the danger of dying in childbirth. In 1930, Vera Brittain wrote of 'the appalling mortality amongst unmarried mothers' (*TG* : 134). Most of society was still hostile to the idea of single motherhood: in *Mrs Dalloway* (1925), Clarissa Dalloway is quick to condemn her neighbour's wife who has had a baby outside marriage. When she discovers she is pregnant, Olivia Curtis in *The Weather in the Streets* toys with the idea of single parenthood, but this is presented as no more than a fantasy. Even well-educated, independent-minded women like Rebecca West and Dorothy L. Sayers faced difficulties. Concealing her pregnancy from everyone outside her immediate family, Sayers gave birth in 1924 to a son and straightaway handed him over to the care of a cousin, contributing nothing to his life henceforth, apart from money. When Rebecca West's son was born, he was trained to call her 'Auntie'.

If Olive became separated from her husband she might face an agonising choice between raising her child on next to no money or leaving the child in the care of someone else whilst she earned money. Such a choice faced Storm Jameson and is painfully recalled in her autobiography, *Journey from the North* (1969) where she leaves her son behind in Yorkshire in order to find work in London. 'I tried to think clearly. From a single moment of exultance in having landed the job I dropped into the blackest pit. To give up my child in return for four pounds a week in an advertising office was plain madness . . . Don't go, I told myself . . . I must, I answered' (*Journey from the North* vol.1 1969: 135; ellipses mine).

However, unless the marriage was absolutely irretrievable, Olive would have been unlikely to divorce her husband. Legislation of 1923 and 1937 put women on an equal footing with men as regards divorce, but figures for divorce did not rise significantly during the inter-war period. With the prevailing cult of domesticity the social pressure was on women not to divorce their husbands. In *The Weather in the Streets* middle-class Olivia, separated from her husband, feels embarrassed about her ambiguous social position. Internalising her society's conventions, she is the first to disapprove of her situation: 'My marriage has failed and my life is empty, futile' (Lehmann 1936/1981: 59). Apart from social pressures there would be the economic disincentive to divorce: Olivia, trained to do nothing in particular, ekes out a hand-to-mouth existence in London.

What if Olive were to be widowed? The Widows' Pensions Act of 1925 removed the support of widows from the Poor Law and granted them a pension similar in standing to the old age pension, thus going some way towards recognising their status as separate human beings. To some extent this validation of the widow is reflected in women's fiction of the time. Vita Sackville-West's novel, *All Passion Spent* (1931), is a wonderful evocation of the opening out of a woman's life after the death of her husband. In *The Weather in the Streets*, Mrs Curtis, though not technically a widow, is freed by her husband's illness from her responsibilities as a married woman and reverts, much to her daughters' astonishment, to the tomboy behaviour of her youth. In a sense, these novels on widowhood are saying the same thing as the novels about motherhood: women must have interests outside the family if they are to recognise their full potential as human beings and, despite the cult of domesticity, women often achieve peace of mind when their domestic responsibilities cease. No wonder novel-reading was such a popular activity for middle-class women during this period.

In 1935, Holtby wrote: 'I have seen a revolution in social and moral values which has transformed the world I live in. It is a direct result of that challenge to opinion which we call the Women's Movement' (*TG*: 90). As we have seen, some things did get better for women after the First World War: there was more freedom of movement for them and more of an expectation that they would earn their own living, at least for a short time before marriage. However, the situation of women in the home and of mothers did not greatly improve during the period, and in some ways (shortage of domestic help, psychological pressure to raise standards, increase in maternal mortality) even fell back from what it had been before the war. As one surveys the position of women in the inter-war years, one cannot help feeling with Holtby that the New Feminists' stress on women as wives and mothers, though it did produce some benefits, was not helpful to mothers in the long run. By falling in with the prevailing cult of domesticity, New Feminism had a conservative effect, reinforcing women's position in the home. There was very little discussion during this period, even by feminists, of the possibility that men might take a greater share in domestic responsibility. Feminists tended to put their faith rather in communalised and professionalised services.

Nevertheless, though the duties of the woman at home remained difficult, lonely and time-consuming there was, as we have seen, a tendency in this period to recognise her right in law to a separate existence, as wife, mother or widow. There must be some connection between this legislation recognising a married woman's right to a separate existence and the increase in the fictional treatment of housewives and mothers. The First World War caused a rupture in women's history. No longer tied to repeating her mother's life, the daughter could now see her mother as a separate human being with her own story. In *The Lost Tradition. Mothers and Daughters in Literature* Susan Peck MacDonald argues that in nineteenth-century fiction mothers tend to be dead or absent or helpless, thus allowing space for the daughter to develop her own story (Davidson and Broner 1980: 68-9). In the inter-war period, as we shall see, the mother often becomes the focus of the daughter's story.

In the context of this emerging discourse on motherhood, it is important to bear in mind that it was during the first half of the twentieth century that anthropologists like Jane Harrison, Helen Diner and Robert Briffault (*The Mothers*, 1927) and myth-dealers like Robert Graves (whose *White Goddess* was published in 1948) were pursuing matriarchal myths. Once anthropologists started to look seriously at non-western societies, it began to be possible to envisage that the patriarchal, patrilineal family of western culture was not inevitable. Drawing on the work of J. J. Bachofen, R. Briffault and others, Helen Diner argues for the existence of a prehistoric civilisation centred around the female as mother, head of the family and great goddess, giver of life and embodiment of the natural order; while in *Mythology* (1924) and her earlier work, *Prolegomena to the Study of Greek Religion* (1903), Jane Harrison gives a fascinating account, in mythological terms, of the suppression of the mother and the splitting off of the daughter from the mother that occurs in a patriarchy.

This pursuit of matriarchal myths during the inter-war years parallels the renewed emphasis, in the spheres of legislation, social policy and fiction, on the figure of the mother. And it leads us to our next chapter where we shall see that female psychoanalysts of the inter-war period were revising Freud's phallo-centric theories in favour of a mother-centred psychoanalysis.

2

Psychoanalytical Theories of Motherhood

Psychoanalytical theory, like motherhood, is an unstable discourse which has been subject to many rereadings and rewritings. Classic Freudian theory evolved in a particular historical context and some feminists have been wary of it for precisely this reason: Luce Irigaray gives a powerful critique of psychoanalysis as historically and culturally conditioned in her article published in 1977 'The Poverty of Psychoanalysis' (Whitford 1991a: 79–104). But psychoanalysis is still a useful tool to describe processes for which adequate alternative explanations are lacking. This is especially so for the inter-war period when women were labouring under the difficulties of precisely the type of nuclear family analysed by Freud.

In the last decade of his life, Freud came round to the view that he had neglected the pre-oedipal stage in mother–daughter relations. In his 1933 lecture on 'Femininity' he says: 'the phase of the affectionate pre-Oedipus attachment is the decisive one for a woman's future: during it preparations are made for the acquisition of the characteristics with which she will later fulfil her role in the sexual function and perform her invaluable social tasks' (*SE* XXII: 134). Thus Freud recognised, late in his career, that the early mother–daughter relationship is crucial in the development of female identity, but he does not paint a very optimistic picture of that relationship. For Freud, the girl's entry into femininity is characterised by hostility to the mother for failing to make her a boy ('Some Character-Types Met With in Psycho-Analytic Work,' *SE* XIV). His account of the development of the human psyche rests on the premise that the infant begins life in a state of connectedness with the external environment, represented by the mother. Associated with this feeling of connectedness, women come to be regarded as a regressive influence, opposed to civilisation because they are unable to complete development as separate individuals. As long as the classic Freudian paradigm dominates, the mother will continue to be seen as an obstacle to individual growth, the point of danger, whilst the father will be the place of rescue, of separation and rationality.

In this context it is interesting to consider Freud's analysis of a female writer of the inter-war period, namely H. D. She was psychoanalysed by Freud during the 1930s and she gives an account of this analysis in *Writing on the Wall* (1944) and *Advent* (1948). Freud believed H. D. had come to him to find her mother, an artist, who had died in 1927. In transference she cast him in the role of mother and Freud felt uncomfortable with this (H. D. 1985: 147). He tried to get H. D. to move beyond the mother to acceptance of the father, arguing that her mother-fixation was at the root of her lesbianism and her hallucinations. In this way, H. D.'s analysis with Freud becomes a paradigm of patriarchal psychoanalysis in the inter-war period with the father attempting to break the daughter's attachment to the mother and to the mother's language. H. D. continued to insist on her maternal inheritance. In a dream movingly recounted in *Advent*, H. D. tries to reach her mother but her way is blocked by two male representatives of the patriarchy:

> I tried desperately to get back to my flat in Sloane Street, London. The flat is at the top of the house. As I enter the downstairs hall, a man and then a rough boy barred my way to the staircase and seemed to threaten me. I did not dare challenge them . . . As I stood threatened and terrified I call, loudly, 'Mother'. I am out on the pavement now. I look up at the window of my flat . . . A figure is standing there, holding a lighted candle. It is my mother. I was overpowered with happiness and all trace of terror vanished. (H. D. 1985: 174–5; ellipses mine)

As we shall see, this situation – the daughter trying to recover the mother, only to find herself blocked by the patriarchy – will recur in inter-war women's fiction, notably in the work of Virginia Woolf.

Despite Freud's unwillingness to validate the mother–daughter relationship, his analysis of H. D. had a happy outcome. The following years saw an extraordinary flowering of H. D.'s art which she herself attributed to the beneficial quality of Freud's analysis which had given her, she said, a sense of homecoming and allowed her to recognise the female source of her creativity. Affirming her ties with her mother, she declared: 'The mother is the Muse, the Creator and in my case especially, as my mother's name was Helen' (H. D. 1985: 41).

Similarly, though Antonia White's quartet of novels fictionalising her life would seem at first sight to illustrate Freud's hostile account of the mother–

daughter relationship, it is only when the heroine, Clara, recognises her bond with her mother that she finds a secure identity. In *Frost in May* (1933), Clara's scholarly father shapes his daughter's life. He sends her to a convent where her life is strictly ordered in a way which fits in with his very masculine thinking. In this world, Clara's mother is marginalised, her spontaneity an embarrassment to a matraphobic daughter only interested in gaining her father's approval. After enduring the breakdown described in *Beyond the Glass* (1954) Clara is able to free herself from her father's self-centred and damaging influence and establish her own identity. In the unfinished fragment, *Clara IV*, White describes Clara as disapproved of by her father but having a better relationship with her mother. The split is symbolised in Clara's face: her feminine front view and a 'faintly masculine profile' that 'never seemed really to belong to her' (White 1983: 68). White's quartet moves beyond Freud in showing the harm done to both mother and daughter by the father's attempt to appropriate the daughter and exclude the mother.

Unlike many professions psychoanalysis, perhaps surprisingly given its often misogynist views of women as passive and penis envying, was one in which women made considerable impact during the inter-war period. By 1940, 40 per cent of the analysts in Britain were women (Appignanesi and Forrester 1993: 6). It is on the work of the four 'founding mothers' of psychoanalysis – Helene Deutsch (1884–1982), Karen Horney (1885–1952), Anna Freud (1895–1982) and Melanie Klein (1882–1960) – which I particularly wish to concentrate. In the inter-war period these female psychoanalysts were transforming Freud's patriarchal and phallocentric theories and preparing the way for today's mother-centred psychoanalysis.

In 1925, Helene Deutsch published *The Psychoanalysis of Women's Sexual Functions* in which she uses her own mothering experience to go beyond Freud in emphasising the maternal as well as the patriarchal sources of women's sexuality (Sayers 1991: 38). Volume 2 of the *The Psychology of Women*, published in 1945, focuses on motherhood as women's culminating task. One of Deutsch's most valuable insights and one which has only recently been taken up by theorists is that mothering need not be limited to reproduction. Her aim, she says, is 'to attempt an understanding of the nature of motherliness, not only in the direct exercise of the reproductive function, but also as a principle radiating into all the fields of life, a principle innate in woman' (Deutsch 1945: 477-8). Women, she argues, as Kristeva and Irigaray were later to argue, 'can . . . make enormous contributions in the social, artistic, and scientific fields by drawing indirectly upon the active aspirations of mother- hood and the emotional warmth of motherliness' (*op. cit.* 487; ellipsis mine). This is an insight which is echoed in some inter-war women's writing, notably that of Winifred Holtby.

In Holtby's novel, *South Riding* (1936), Mrs Beddows, the first woman alderman in the county, is mother to her community and encourages Sarah Burton to perform a similar role. And at the end of Holtby's earlier novel, *The Crowded Street* (1924), Muriel Hammond escapes her dominating and selfish mother to live an independent life in London where her mothering skills, so conspicuously absent in her own mother, will be put to use in the public sphere. Holtby suggests in these novels that there is a cost: public mothering can involve as much self-suppression and self-sacrifice as private mothering. Neither Sarah nor Mrs Beddows nor Muriel have particularly happy personal lives. This raises the question as to whether it is of more benefit to women in the long run to limit mothering to a description of what happens between a woman and her child rather than attempting to apply it to other spheres where, if women take on a mothering role, they are liable to find imposed on them attitudes of self-sacrifice, attentiveness to the needs of others, etc.–in short, self-denial and masochism.

Deutsch also emphasises, against the tendency of the media in the inter-war period, that mothering is not essentialist but can mean different things to different women: 'Even psychically healthy women do not all experience motherliness in the same manner . . . The woman's relation to her husband and family, her economic situation, and the position of the child in her existence, give a personal color to each woman's motherliness' (Deutsch 1945: 54–5; ellipsis mine). This non-essentialist view of motherhood is valuable: even modern theorists of motherhood, such as Chodorow and Ruddick, have been accused of essentialising motherhood.

Perhaps because of her own experience of trying to combine motherhood with the demands of a busy professional life, Deutsch is alert to the difficulties of mothering. She speaks of two types of mothers:

> One type is the woman who awakens to a new life through her child without having the feeling of a loss . . . The other type is the woman who from the first feels a kind of depersonalization in her relation to her child. Usually such a woman has spent her affectivity on other values (eroticism, art, or masculine aspirations) or this affectivity was too poor or ambivalent originally and cannot stand a new emotional burden. The first type expands her ego through her child, the second feels restricted and impoverished. (*op. cit.* 55; ellipsis mine)

Again Deutsch's emphasis on the difficulties of mothering has parallels in inter-war women's fiction. In the previous chapter we noted the number of women novelists such as Rosamond Lehmann and E. M. Delafield who highlight the difficulties and constraints experienced by mothers of young children. Indeed, it is one of the aims of this study to illustrate the way in which female novelists and female psychoanalysts of the inter-war period seem often to be working along the same lines.

During the inter-war period also, Karen Horney argued, against Freud, that 'women's psychology is determined by innate identification with the mother, not by disappointed identification with the father' (Sayers 1991: 92); and she drew attention to men's envy of women's mothering. Horney's critique of Freud was spelled out in a series of papers published between 1924 and the early 1930s. One of the most inspiring elements in her writings is her insistence in, for example, 'The Flight from Womanhood' (1926) that the psychology of women has hitherto been considered only from the point of view of men. For Horney, the pressing question is to determine how far 'the evolution of women, as depicted to us today by analysis [has] been measured by masculine standards and how far therefore this picture fails to present quite accurately the real nature of women' (Horney 1967: 57). Nancy Chodorow locates the origins of psychoanalytic feminism in these early essays by Karen Horney (Chodorow 1989: 3).

Another leading woman analyst, Anna Freud, arrived in England in 1938. Her wartime experience of children's suffering at maternal separation influenced her stress on the importance of the mother in the child's early life: in a talk given in 1941, 'The Need of a Small Child to be Mothered', she emphasised that a child's first relation to its mother provides a pattern for its future relationships. Anna Freud's first book, *Introduction to the Technique of Child Analysis*, had appeared in 1927. In this she takes issue with Klein's argument that the therapist should take over all the parental functions in the transference. Freud, always keen to stress the importance of the mother in the child's emotional life, argues that space should be left for the child's parents. Unlike Klein who maintained that the child's super-ego developed very early, in tandem with the Oedipus complex, Anna Freud put forward the view that a child's super-ego is in a state of formation until the Oedipal conflict is resolved and is therefore still under parental and environmental influence. For Freud, the mother of early childhood is 'a real "environmental" mother, not a fantasy object whose name was breast' (Appignanesi and Forrester 1993: 300). In the British Psycho-Analytical Society the Anna Freud–Melanie Klein controversy continued through the inter-war period, with male psychoanalysts complaining that the Society was becoming 'woman ridden'. Finally, in 1946, an uneasy compromise was reached between the two sides, resulting in the establishment of two parallel training programmes (*op. cit.* 301).

Melanie Klein's influence on British analysts began to be felt from 1925 onwards, the year when Alix Strachey arranged for her to lecture at the Institute of Psychoanalysis in London. Object-relations theory is generally held to derive from Klein whose work with children opened up the possibility, as

Freud's stress on the Oedipal complex could not, of understanding women's pre-oedipal relationship with the mother. Klein found that the child first internalises and identifies not with the father, as Freud had claimed, but with the mother: 'My use of the term "object relations" is based on my contention that the infant has from the beginning of post-natal life a relation to the mother (although focusing primarily on her breast) which is imbued with the fundamental elements of an object relation, i.e. love, hatred, phantasies, anxieties and defences' ('The Origins of Transference' 1951 in Mitchell 1991: 203). Unlike Freud, Klein posits, in her paper 'Early Stages of the Oedipus Conflict' (published in 1928), a primary femininity phase for both sexes. The mother is central to the Oedipal drama, even in the formation of the super-ego which derives, in Klein, not from the father but from oral incorporation of the good/bad breast: 'the introjection of the breast is the beginning of the super-ego formation which extends over years' (Mitchell 1991: 203).

In the first few months of life, Klein suggests, the infant deals with internal anxieties by splitting itself and the object on which it vents its rage (the breast that goes away and frustrates it) into a good part and a bad part. 'The infant directs his feelings of gratification and love towards the "good" breast, and his destructive impulses and feelings of persecution towards what he feels to be frustrating, i.e. the "bad" breast' ('The Origins of Transference' Mitchell 1991: 202). At this stage the good and bad breasts are kept apart from one another. The infant gains its security from turning the good object into an ideal one as a protection against the dangerous and persecuting object. These processes are prevalent during the first three or four months of life and Klein terms them the paranoid-schizoid position. The ego's growing capacity for integration leads increasingly during these first few months to states in which love and hatred are synthesised. This brings the infant into the depressive position, for Klein the central position in a child's development. The infant's aggressive impulses and desires towards the bad breast are now felt to be a danger to the good breast as well. Increasingly the infant perceives and introjects the mother as a person and its depressive anxiety is intensified as it feels it is destroying a whole object by its aggression. This anxiety reaches its height, according to Klein, by about the middle of the first year. The infant continues to rage against the mother for the frustration she causes but, instead of fearing retaliation, it now feels guilt and anxiety for the damage it has done in its sadistic fantasies.

In working through the depressive position, the infant seeks to repair the earlier fantasised destruction of the actual and internalised mother. The ego becomes more unified and there is a growing perception of reality and adaptation to it. 'All the enjoyments which the baby lives through in relation to his mother are so many proofs to him that the loved object *inside as well as*

outside is not injured, is not turned into a vengeful person. The increase of love
and trust, and the diminishing of fears through happy experiences, help the
baby step by step to overcome his depression and feeling of loss' ('Mourning
and its Relation to Manic-Depressive States,' 1940 in Mitchell 1991: 155–6).
In the absence of adequate mothering, however, the infant may have difficulty
negotiating the depressive position, and its future mental health may be put at
risk. In any case, it was Klein's belief that the depressive position is never really
worked through. Loss in later life can reawaken our fear of losing the good
internal object.

Klein's analysis of the depressive position, reached when the child begins to
incorporate the good and bad mother in the same person and therefore begins
to see the mother as separate from itself, is of direct interest in understanding
the daughter's pre-oedipal relationship with her mother. Her view of art as
flowing, not from a Freudian sublimation of instinct but from a wish to repair
relations with others, in the first place with the mother, as outlined, for
instance, in her paper 'Infantile Anxiety Situations Reflected in a Work of Art
and in the Creative Impulse' (published in 1929), provides a helpful approach
to women's fiction of the inter-war period.

These four women (Deutsch, Horney, Freud and Klein) made an enormous
contribution to psychoanalysis. Their work, emphasising as it does the central
role of the mother, fits in with what we have already seen in Chapter 1, namely
the increasing focus on the mother in the inter-war period. Nevertheless,
though alternative readings to Freud's account of women's development
became increasingly common during the inter-war period, for the general
public psychoanalysis was associated not with these female psychoanalysts but
with the founding father, Freud. 'The late war-intellectuals gabbled of Oedipus
across tea-cups or Soho café tables,' says H. D. in *Bid Me to Live* (written in
1927). In Lettice Cooper's novel, *The New House*, one of the characters reflects:
'They talked a good deal of psychological talk about unconscious minds and
repressions; they fashionably called things Freudian. That kind of talk,
nowadays, was part of the furniture of an intelligent drawing-room. You
put everybody in their place by saying, She had a complex, of course; or, It was
his inhibitions,' (Cooper 1936/1987: 163).

The first translation of Freud came out in 1909 with new works appearing
almost annually thereafter. Popular works explaining Freud's theories to the
general public also began to appear. At second-hand, the general public knew
about repression, sublimation, dreams, the Oedipus complex, childhood
trauma. Even middlebrow writers could introduce psychoanalytical terms
into their novels in the confidence they would be understood. E. M. Delafield
in *The Way Things Are*, mentions repressions, sublimation and inferiority
complexes. At one point, Christine says to her sister:

'any decent analyst would tell you that you're doing yourself a great deal of harm by this constant pretence. It's bound to create the most frightful repressions. What sort of dreams do you have?' But Laura, even though she did live in the country, knew all about Herr Freud and his theories, and declined to commit herself in any way upon the subject of dreams. (Delafield 1927/1988: 109–10)

Laura has in fact 'studied a little psychology, obtained the loan of a volume of Havelock Ellis, and felt so little exhilarated by the life-stories there set out that she had a brief reaction in favour of Thomas à Kempis' (*op. cit.* 78).

Laura's distaste for psychoanalysis was shared by other women, whether out of a lingering sense of prudishness or because, like Winifred Holtby, they anticipated yet another burden on women. H. D. expresses this sense of the burden of psychoanalysis on women's lives in *Bid Me to Live*:

Why this vaunted business of experience, of sex-emotion and under-standing that they made so much of? It might be all right for men, but for women, any woman, there was a biological catch and taken at any angle, danger. You dried up and were an old maid, danger. You drifted into the affable *hausfrau*, danger. You let her rip and had operations in Paris (poor Bella), danger. (HD. 1960/1984: 136)

Nevertheless, during the inter-war period, contemporary interest in the uncon-scious not only contributed to the development of the stream of consciousness style of writing, as in Dorothy Richardson's *roman fleuve*, *Pilgrimage*, but also, in some cases, determined the themes of novels – in Rebecca West's *The Return of the Soldier* (1918), for example, or the works of May Sinclair.

May Sinclair's novel, *Mary Olivier: A Life* (1919), is an in-depth analysis of a mother-daughter relationship. Mary Olivier has been brought up in a household where Victorian gender divisions are rigidly enforced. Mary's greatest enemy in her efforts at self-fulfilment is her mother who thwarts her attempts at personal growth at every turn. Her mother's love is conditional on Mary conforming to rigid notions of femininity and Mary's tragedy is that she is unable to break the tie with her mother. The love between mother and daughter binds them in an unhealthy mutual dependency. Only at one point does the mother drop her guard, when she admits that her disapproval of her daughter's intellectual quest has not been based on moral principles: ' "I didn't like your being clever. It was the boys I wanted to do things. Not you . . . I was jealous of you, Mary. And I was afraid for my life you'd find it out," ' (*MO*: 325; ellipsis mine). This is a crucial scene showing how, in a patriarchy, women's self-development is all too easily hampered by other women: Mrs Olivier has been able to use the full weight of patriarchal society to justify her opposition to her daughter. It is also one of the few scenes in the novel where the mother speaks in her own voice rather than echoing the voice of the patriarchy. From here the relationship might have had a chance to develop into one between equals. But it doesn't. Instead the mother, left wandering in her mind after a stroke, becomes the daughter's child. And now that the mother is dependent, the daughter loves her more. At the same time, Mary realises she has never understood her mother: 'If only I had known what she was really like. Even now I don't know. I never shall' (*MO*: 376). The daughter recognises that she has never succeeded in viewing her mother from out-side, in seeing her as subject rather than object for her own needs. If the mother–daughter relationship has been an unhealthy one, this has been as much the daughter's fault as the mother's.

Much of Sinclair's novel is distinctly Freudian. Although Sinclair anticipates later feminist psychoanalytic writing on the symbiotic closeness of the mother–daughter relationship, there is no valuing of the mother's world in the novel. The mother is presented as a regressive influence, a hindrance to her daughter's fulfilment. This is so in other inter-war novels by women, notably Lettice Cooper's *The New House* where Rhoda's mother is shown to be an obstacle to her daughter's freedom. If Rhoda is ever to go out into the world it is her father's example she must follow: 'her father's willingness to embrace life was buried in her, deep under her mother's withdrawal from it' (Cooper 1936/ 1987: 314). So long as the daughter's liberty is bought at the price of denigrating the mother, there will never be any real progress in the mother–daughter relationship; women will be colluding in the patriarchy's wish to weaken women's power by separating daughter from mother.

In the inter-war period in France, Jacques Lacan was beginning his radical rereadings of Freud. In 1936 he presented his paper, 'The Mirror Stage', to the International Psychoanalytic Congress in Marienbad. To summarise briefly, according to Lacan in the pre-oedipal stage all children form half of an idyllic dyad with the mother and the new-born infant is not conscious of its separate existence. The first stage in individuation is the 'mirror-stage' which occurs between the age of six and eighteen months. The child's reflection in a mirror grants an image to the child of a whole and separate body which appears to be itself but this image is a fiction: it anticipates mastery of the body that the infant has not yet objectively achieved. The 'mirror-stage' inaugurates the 'Ima-ginary', so-called because the subject lives in an illusion of unity and harmony. For Lacan, the beginning of the formation of the ego is at this mirror stage and thus the ego is formed on the basis of an imaginary relationship of the subject with its whole body. The human subject will continue throughout life to look for this imaginary wholeness and unity.

In the post-war period, combining Freudian psychoanalysis with theories of structural linguistics and structural anthropology, Lacan moved psychoanalysis towards a concentration on language and developed his theory according to which the child only becomes a human subject when it moves out of the imaginary into the symbolic order, the system of language and culture, also called the law of the father. In Lacan's system, the child's original, dyadic relationship with the mother is interrupted by the figure of the father who splits up the dyad and forbids the child further access to the mother and the mother's body. The father thus appears to the child as a spoiler of pleasure. However, as Angela Leighton has pointed out, 'it is only by this break with the mother that the child can enter the other order of language and civilisation. The mother must be repressed or deserted in order that speech, writing and culture can be acquired' (Leighton 1989: 16).

Lacan used Freud's description of the Fort/Da game to illustrate the process by which language arises as a compensation for the loss of the mother. Freud had described how an eighteen-month old child, left alone in its cot, repeatedly lowered a cotton-reel on the end of a string out of sight and hauled it up again. When it was gone, he said 'Fort' (gone); when it came back he said 'Da' (here). For Lacan, this episode shows how a child, distressed by the mother's absence, seeks to gain control over the situation by using the cotton-reel as a symbol of the mother and supplying language to compensate for her loss. The child's recognition of the mother's absence breaks the imaginary unity of the mother–child dyad and initiates entry into the symbolic order. The loss or lack suffered is the loss of the maternal body and from now on the desire for the mother, or the imaginary unity with her, must be repressed. Lacan calls this the primary repression and 'it is this primary repression that opens up the unconscious. In the imaginary there is no unconscious since there is no lack' (Moi 1990: 99).

The advantage for feminists of Lacan's theory is that it avoids biological determinism: 'it is the strength of the concept of the symbolic that it systematically repudiates any account of sexuality which assumes the pre-given nature of sexual difference' (Mitchell and Rose 1982: 45). In the Lacanian scheme of things there is no subject prior to the acquisition of language. Lacan's theory also has advantages for mothers in that it shows that there will always be a dissatisfaction with the mother which has nothing to do with the historical mother's deficiencies. For, in Lacanian theory, 'this very mother, who makes such efforts to care for her infant, who seems to give as much as she can, is also a subject, itself based on a lack of being' (Benvenuto and Kennedy 1986: 174). So even if the caretaker is not the mother but the father or a nurse, there will be the same feeling of loss and dissatisfaction with the mother figure. For Lacan, this feeling of loss is the price of individuation which is essential to human growth and autonomy: 'To remain in the Imaginary is equivalent to becoming psychotic and incapable of living in human society' (Moi 1990: 100).

Nevertheless in Patsy Stoneman's words: 'Women still emerge from

Lacanian theory as doomed by the Oedipal structure, by language, the law, the name of the father, to less than masculine autonomy' (Stoneman 1993: 6). This is because, in Lacan's theory, girls make the entry into the symbolic differently from boys. Because she cannot identify sexually with the father, the girl's primal repression of the mother is incomplete. She thus retains some hidden access to the realm of the mother. As a result, her position in culture is less stable than that of a boy. Lacan's theory accounts for the sense of marginality women often feel to the language and culture with which they are surrounded. It accounts, for example, for Woolf's feeling that language is a masculine construct which has to be reshaped for women's use.

Lacan's description of the feminine bodily ecstasy which lies beyond the phallus and is not spoken within discourse may seem to confine women to their usual marginal position within the culture, but in fact some feminist writers, notably the French feminists, have chosen to celebrate this pre-oedipal bond. For others, like Jacqueline Rose, this celebration of the pre-oedipal bond is based on a misreading of Lacan. According to Rose, Lacan argues that: 'Woman is excluded *by* the nature of words, meaning that the definition poses her as exclusion' (Mitchell and Rose 1982: 49). She adds: 'Note that this is not the same thing as saying that woman is excluded *from* the nature of words, a misreading which leads to the recasting of the whole problem in terms of woman's place outside language, the idea that women might have of themselves an entirely different speech' (*ibid.*). In Lacan's terms, this latter view is an impossibility since, for him, men and women are only ever in language; a language outside language is a theoretical impossibility. Nevertheless even if the French feminist interpretation is based on a misreading of Lacan, it has been a fruitful misreading in terms of what it has to say about mother–daughter relations and is therefore worth examining in this context.

Luce Irigaray has emphasised the lack of linguistic, social, cultural, iconic and religious representations of the mother–daughter relationship in our culture as opposed, for instance, to the mother–son relationship. She reinterprets classical myths to reveal that in them daughters (Antigone, for example) have a choice between identifying with the patriarchy's laws and obliterating the mother, or identifying with the mother at the cost of exclusion and self-destruction. She concludes that the patriarchy 'forbids the daughter to respect the blood ties with her mother' (*Sexes et parentés* quoted in Whitford 1991b: 119) and insists that women must work to inscribe maternal genealogy into the symbolic.

In the lyrical monologue, 'And the One doesn't stir without the Other' (1981), Irigaray presents a negative mother–daughter relationship. The daughter is over-mothered. Her mother's nurturing leaves her with a feeling of paralysis: 'You take care of me, you keep watch over me . . . You fear that something will happen to me . . . But what could happen that would be worse than the fact of my lying supine day and night? Already half-grown and still in the cradle' (Irigaray 1981: 60; ellipses mine). Stifled, the daughter turns to the father but he knows only how to socialise his daughter, transforming her into 'a schooled robot,' 'a nearly perfect girl,' (*ibid.*), waiting for a man to come along. We are left to conclude that in a patriarchy it is only mothers who can truly liberate their daughters, a point anticipated in several novels of the inter-war period, for example, Antonia White's *Frost in May*, where the daughter turns away from her seemingly passive and powerless mother only to find that her father's aim is to mould his daughter to fit in with patriarchal stereotypes.

Robbed of the daughter's presence, the mother who has poured her entire identity into mothering, finds she has lost that identity: 'You look at yourself in the mirror. And already you see your own mother there. And soon your daughter, a mother. Between the two, what are you? What space is yours alone?' (*op. cit.* 63). In this essay, the mother and daughter remain locked in negativity. The daughter will repeat the mother's fate: 'I, too, a captive when a man holds me in his gaze; I, too, am abducted from myself. Immobilized in the reflection he expects of me. Reduced to the face he fashions for me . . . Trapped in a single function – mothering' (*op. cit.* 66; ellipsis mine). Irigaray's short poetic monologue is an almost perfect account of mother–daughter relations in the patriarchy and one which we will find reflected again and again in the novels of the inter-war period. There is, however, a move forward at the end of the essay when the daughter implores her mother not to become swamped by the maternal function: 'what I wanted from you, Mother, was this: that in giving me life, you still remain alive' (*op. cit* 67).

Irigaray urges the necessity of developing an intersubjective relationship between mother and daughter. In classic psychoanalysis, the mother is reduced to an object status and for the daughter to enter the patriarchal order, she must give her mother up but, says Irigaray, 'The woman cannot reduce her mother to an object without reducing herself to an object at the same time, because they are of the same sex' (*Sexes et parentés* quoted in Whitford 1991b: 44). The only hope for healthy feminine identity (and healthy mother–daughter relationships) is for the daughter to recognise the mother as subject, for then: 'A woman would be directly in intersubjective relation with her mother. Her economy is that of the *between-subjects*, and not that of the subject–object relation' (*Sexes et parentés* quoted Whitford 1991b: 45). The mother must be separated from the woman so that the daughter can come to identify with a woman who has a socially valorised identity, rather than with a phallic or a castrated mother.

As we shall see, some novels in the inter-war period work round to this idea that a healthy mother–daughter relationship depends on each recognising the separate identity of the other. To give an example: in Lettice Cooper's novel,

The New House, Rhoda Powell leads the life of a daughter at home, exhausted by her mother's emotional demands and mentally drained by a series of never-ending trivial household tasks. However, her mother is not entirely to blame for the unhealthy dependency between mother and daughter: there is a part of Rhoda that clings to her mother because she is afraid of the risks involved in leaving home: 'there was something in herself holding on to her mother, aiding and abetting her mother's continual desire not to let her go' (Cooper 1936/1987: 31). She is aware that she is unable to be objective about her mother:

> Her mother was a little, pretty, elderly lady whose face was lifted by animation out of its peevish lines, not formidable. We make people formidable to ourselves, it is part of that novelist's tale. We make them into policemen and park-keepers for fear we should pick pockets or walk on the grass. If only I could keep on seeing Mother as I do now, a little, pretty, elderly lady, not formidable! (*op. cit.* 154)

Through Rhoda, Lettice Cooper anticipates theorists like Irigaray when she posits seeing the mother as subject as a way out of the impasse of the mother–daughter relationship.

In an interview, 'Women-mothers, the silent substratum of the social order,' Irigaray sums up her ideas:

> So what is a mother? Someone who makes the stereotypical gestures she is told to make, who has no personal language and who has no identity. But how, as daughters, can we have a personal relationship with or construct a personal identity in relation to someone who is no more than a function? In a sense we need to say goodbye to maternal omnipotence (the last refuge) and establish a woman-to-woman relationship of reciprocity with our mothers, in which they might possibly also feel themselves to be our daughters. In a word, liberate ourselves along with our mothers. That is an indispensable precondition for our emancipation from the authority of fathers. In our societies, the mother/daughter, daughter/mother relationship constitutes a highly explosive nucleus. Thinking it, and changing it, is equivalent to shaking the foundations of the patriarchal order. (Whitford 1991a: 50)

In Rosamond Lehmann's novel, *Invitation to the Waltz*, the mother, Mrs Curtis, though initially all-powerful in the domestic sphere, gives up some of her maternal omnipotence towards the end when she allows her elder daughter to override her authority. In turn, her daughters begin to step out of their relationship as daughters and see their mother as a person in her own right. They wonder about her life before she became a mother: 'Perhaps she looked back and thought with a sense of loss: how happy I was then; comparing all she had now – husband, home, children – unfavourably with having nothing. And they experienced a faint uneasiness' (Lehmann 1932/1981: 35). In Lehmann's later novel, *The Weather in the Streets*, after her husband has become incapacitated, Mrs Curtis begins to express a previously suppressed part of her personality. Her daughter Olivia remarks:

> She's changed, I think – or gone back to something. Now she's alone so much she seems to turn things over in her mind. She makes pronouncements which fairly make one sit up; about education being no use and one can overdo self-control, and there's a lot in this new psychology, and trying to direct other people's lives is unpardonable . . . All the old manner but such different matter I feel quite shocked. (Lehmann 1936/ 1981: 358; ellipsis mine)

In the absence of her husband, Mrs. Curtis ceases to feel that she need uphold patriarchy's values. Nothing shows more clearly how the seemingly all-powerful mother is herself oppressed in a patriarchy and how liberation of the mother can, as Irigaray suggests, lead to radical social questioning, though in this case, ironically, the daughters are left 'shocked' and 'uneasy' by the mother's rebellion.

As a footnote to this aspect of the discussion of motherhood in Irigaray, I would like to bring in her notion of the placental economy which she develops during the course of an interview in 1987 with Hélène Rouch, a biology teacher. Rouch's study of the relations between mother and the child in the uterus led her to conclude that 'these relations, which the patriarchal imagination often presents (for example, in psychoanalysis) as in a state of fusion, are in fact strangely organised and respectful of the life of both' (Irigaray 1993: 38). In Rouch's study, the placenta provides the mediating space between mother and foetus which are thus *never fused*. As Rouch points out, this at least raises questions about psychoanalysis's view of the initial fusion between mother and child which has to be broken in order for the child to achieve a separate identity by a third term, the father or the law, or the name of the father:

> Surely all that's needed is to reiterate and mark, on another level, a differentiation that already exists during pregnancy thanks to the placenta and at the moment of birth, as a result of the exit from the uterine cavity? It seems to me that the differentiation between the mother's self and the other of the child, and vice versa, is in place well before it's given meaning in and by language, and the forms it takes don't necessarily accord with those our cultural imaginary relays. (*op. cit.* 42)

Though literal separation (by a placenta) is not necessarily synonymous with psychological separation, this early physical separation of mother and child appears to cast doubt on Lacan's (and Freud's) theories of pre-oedipal fusion and links up with Daniel Stern's observations of early mother–child interaction. I will come back to this point later.

Another aspect of Irigaray's work relevant to the theme of motherhood and women's writing is her call to women to bring the body of the mother into language: 'we must also find, find anew, invent the words, the sentences that speak the most archaic and most contemporary relationship with the body of the mother' (Whitford 1991a: 43). In the Lacanian scheme of things, as we have seen, recovering the mother's language is an impossibility and indeed there are contradictions in Irigaray's statements as to what would constitute this woman's language, derived from the mother's body: 'What a feminine syntax might be is not simple nor easy to state, because in that "syntax" there would no longer be either subject or object, "oneness" would no longer be privileged, there would no longer be proper meanings, proper nouns, "proper" attributes' (*This Sex Which is not One* quoted in Whitford 1991b: 46). This would seem to contradict earlier passages in which Irigaray stressed the need to respect the mother's separate identity.

Irigaray's celebration of love between women, her emphasis on recognising the mother as a subject and her call for daughters to stand with, not against, the mother, are all very positive and counteract earlier feminists' neglect or downgrading of the mother. As in the case of Helene Deutsch, Irigaray encourages her readers to enlarge their vision of the maternal: 'we are always mothers once we are women. We bring something other than children into the world, we engender something other than children: love, desire, language, art, the social, the political, the religious, for example' (Whitford 1991a: 43).

Like Irigaray and Deutsch, Hélène Cixous widens the scope of mothering beyond the biological role:

> The mother, too, is a metaphor. It is necessary and sufficient that the best of herself be given to woman by another woman for her to be able to love herself and return in love the body that was "born" to her . . . In women there is always more or less of the mother who makes everything all right, who nourishes, and who stands up against separation. ('The Laugh of the Medusa' in Marks and de Courtivron 1981: 252; ellipsis mine)

Like Irigaray, Cixous uses Derridean deconstructionism to expose the dualities on which western culture and western philosophy are based and which function to the disadvantage of women, particularly mothers:

> *Where is she?*
> Activity/passivity,
> Sun/Moon,
> Culture/Nature,

Day/Night,
Father/Mother,
Head/heart,
Intelligible/sensitive,
Logos/Pathos.
('Sorties' in Marks and de Courtivron 1981: 90)

These binary oppositions marginalise mothers, placing them on the side of passivity: 'In the extreme the world of "being" can function to the exclusion of the mother. No need for mother – provided that there is something of the maternal: and it is the father then who acts as – is – the mother. Either the woman is passive; or she doesn't exist,' (*op. cit.* 92).

Cixous's own vision of the mother is more positive than these patriarchal binary oppositions. The mother, she argues, stands for the pre-symbolic world of songs and rhythms which has been lost on entry into the symbolic order but which the girl child can still distantly hear. Women have a privileged relationship to this voice because of their imperfect repression of the mother: 'a woman is never far from "mother" (I mean outside her role functions: the "mother" as nonname and as source of goods). There is always within her at least a little of that good mother's milk. She writes in white ink' ('The Laugh of the Medusa,' in Marks and de Courtivron 1981: 251). The mother is not, as in Freud and Lacan, a forbidden place that prevents speech or against which the daughter has to struggle to emerge as subject; for Cixous, the mother *is* the daughter's source of speaking, she liberates the daughter into her language – open-ended, anti-rational, fluid, as befits the fluidity of the body's sexual energies. In 'Difficult Joys,' Cixous says, '*Personally, when I write fiction, I write with my body. My body is active, there is no interruption between the work that my body is actually performing and what is going to happen on the page,*' (Wilcox *et al.* 1990: 27). Toril Moi comments: 'Cixous's mother-figure is clearly what Melanie Klein would call the Good Mother: the omnipotent and generous dispenser of love, nourishment and plenitude. The writing woman is thus immensely powerful: hers is a *puissance féminine* derived directly from the mother,' (Moi 1990: 115). We shall see Virginia Woolf in various stages of her writing career trying to tap into this power.

However, we are still left with the problem of how this *écriture féminine* is to manifest itself in the material reality of a patriarchal society. If daughters find their female voice by doing what in Lacanian terms is impossible – returning to the lost body of the mother and speaking from it – does that not leave the daughters marginalised, oppressed, silenced like their own mothers? Where does the mother speak in a patriarchal culture? As Cixous herself puts it in 'Difficult Joys': 'Can a mother write as a mother? Do we have mothers writing?

Why doesn't a mother write as a mother? The sacrifice of the mother – the silence of the mother' (Wilcox *et al.* 1990: 24). In the end, despite some inspirational writing, Cixous does not provide a practical resolution to the problem of the mother's powerlessness.

For a way out of some of the impasses arrived at in the work of Irigaray and Cixous (essentialism, marginalisation and silencing of the mother), we may turn to the work of Julia Kristeva. Kristeva's post-Lacanian theory of human individuation involves a first stage which she calls the *chora*, a Platonic term which she appropriates to represent the womb space of the mother. In this stage the human baby is no more than a space of sensory-motor impulses which cannot yet be said to be a subject or personality. From this stage comes the *semiotic*, in Kristeva's terms, an anterior language of the body which is the pre-condition for language. The semiotic is characterised by the production of sounds, rhythms and gestures which are not yet meaningful. On top of this stage is imposed the symbolic order, the order of the father, which functions in a similar way to the law of the father in Lacan. According to Kristeva, the semiotic continues to be glimpsed in dreams, madness and wherever the surface of rational discourse is broken: 'the call of the mother . . . troubles the word: it generates hallucinations, voices, "madness" ' ('About Chinese Women,' Moi 1986: 156-7; ellipsis mine).

Here, the biological link with the female is broken for in Kristeva, unlike Irigaray, the pre-oedipal mother embraces both masculinity and femininity. Therefore any strengthening of the semiotic will lead to a weakening of traditional gender divisions rather than to an emphasis on femininity. Kristeva confronts the problem of where women are to speak in a patriarchy by arguing that women must take up a place between the symbolic and the semiotic. If women refuse the power of the symbolic: 'we will forever remain in a sulk in the face of history, politics and social affairs' ('About Chinese Women,' Moi 1986: 156), in other words we will remain marginalised and ineffective. If, however, women refuse to heed the call of the maternal chora, we will find ourselves forced to adopt a pseudo-masculine role. We will become 'guardians of the status quo, the most zealous protectors of the established order' ('Women's Time,' Moi 1986: 201). Women, says Kristeva, must refuse both of these extremes and practise 'an impossible dialectic,' moving unceasingly between silence and sense, between semiotic and symbolic: 'How can we do this? By listening; by recognizing the unspoken in all discourse, however Revolutionary, by emphasizing at each point whatever remains unsatisfied, repressed, new, eccentric, incomprehensible, that which disturbs the mutual understanding of the established powers' ('About Chinese Women,' Moi 1986: 156). Clearly this is a strategy that can be used by both men and women. The feminine for Kristeva becomes identified with whatever is marginalised and repressed by the language of the patriarchy and 'woman' as such does not exist: 'In "woman" I see something that cannot be represented, something that is not said, something above and beyond nomenclatures and ideologies' ('La femme, ce n'est jamais ça,' in Marks and de Courtivron 1981: 137). This assertion is troubling, to say the least, for writers who wish to affirm their identity as women. Indeed, Kristeva rejects any idea of an *écriture féminine*: 'Nothing in women's past or present publications seems to allow us to affirm that there is a feminine writing,' she stated in an interview in 1977 (Moi 1990: 163). Kristeva's vision includes gains (a way out of essentialism) and losses (of Cixous's inspirational view of the mother's language).

Kristeva also has things to say specifically about the representation of motherhood in western culture and she criticises the inadequacy of Freud's discourse on motherhood where the mother is viewed simply as an object for the child's needs. The solution for Kristeva lies firstly in close examination of 'the incredible construct of the Maternal that the West elaborated by means of the Virgin,' (Moi 1986: 179). In 'About Chinese Women,' Kristeva analyses the victory of patriarchal monotheism (Judaism) over earlier, matriarchal civilisations and points out that Christianity added to the Judaic tradition an insistence on female virginity and martyrdom: 'Universalist as it is, Christianity does associate women with the symbolic community, but only provided they keep their *virginity*. Failing that, they can atone for their carnal *jouissance* with their martyrdom' (*op. cit.* 145-6). What must be repressed is any sign of maternal *jouissance*. Yet, Kristeva argues in 'Stabat Mater', even for Christianity this has been impossible. Mary's 'milk and tears' are 'the metaphors of non-speech, of a "semiotics" that linguistic communication does not account for' (Moi 1986: 174). Despite vigorous efforts to suppress it, the mother's *jouissance* does emerge in the figure of Mary, Kristeva concludes. It might be added, though, that the reference to Mary's 'tears' suggests an element of masochism.

Kristeva argues that in order to recuperate the mother as subject one needs to listen carefully to what mothers say. In 'Stabat Mater' (1974), she suggests that feminist attacks on traditional representations of motherhood as constraining and oppressive for women, leave out of account women's continued desire to have children. Prompted by her own experience of motherhood, Kristeva points to the need for a new understanding of the mother's body and a new discourse on maternity. In an article published at the same time as 'Stabat Mater', she writes: 'While a certain feminism continues to mistake its own sulking isolation for political protest or even dissidence, real female innovation (in whatever social field) will only come about when maternity, female creation and the link between them are better understood' ('A New Type of Intellectual: The Dissident,' Moi 1986: 298). Like Irigaray she finds links between the artist and the mother:

It can be said that artistic creation always feeds on an identification, or rivalry, with what is presumed to be the mother's *jouissance* . . . maternity as such can favour a certain kind of female creation . . . at least in so far as it lifts fixations, and circulates passion between life and death, self and other, culture and nature, singularity and ethics, narcissism and self-denial. (*op. cit.* 297–8; ellipses mine)

Again the special link between mother and daughter maintained by Irigaray and Cixous is lost: in Kristeva's theory male artists are as capable as females of experiencing this maternal *jouissance* – see her essay 'Motherhood According to Bellini' (1980). In fact her theory becomes problematic here for, as at least one critic has pointed out, Kristeva comes perilously close to suggesting that while men have access to the semiotic through language, women's access is through the biological experience of giving birth (Kaplan 1992: 40). An inter-war novel, *The Squire* by Enid Bagnold, is a perfect illustration of Kristeva's description of pregnancy as a time when the semiotic disrupts the symbolic. The novel presents women's time. The husband is away; 'the squire,' expecting her fifth child, feels herself to be outside chronological time, 'half-dazed, half-mystic, she had felt the walls of her life stretch and grow thin . . . released from life, released from time, released from death' (Bagnold 1938/1987: 153; ellipsis mine).

Pregnancy, in Kristeva's view, can provide the basis for a new ethics, based not on singularity but on community: 'the child's arrival . . . extracts woman out of her oneness and gives her the possibility . . . of reaching out to the other, the ethical' ('Stabat Mater' Moi 1986: 182; ellipses mine). With this idea that motherhood can lead to a new ethic of attentiveness to the needs of others, Kristeva comes close to Sara Ruddick's notion of maternal thinking (see below). Kristeva elaborates on this new ethic in a moving passage in 'Women's Time':

> The arrival of the child . . . leads the mother into the labyrinths of an experience that, without the child, she would only rarely encounter: love for another. Not for herself, nor for an identical being, and still less for another person with whom 'I' fuse (love or sexual passion). But the slow, difficult and delightful apprenticeship in attentiveness, gentleness, for-getting oneself. (*op. cit.* 206; ellipsis mine)

Note that, like Hélène Rouch, Kristeva here explicitly rejects any notion of *fusing* of identity between mother and child, though she does emphasise self-forgetfulness on the mother's part. Similarly, in *The Squire*, the mother merges her own needs with those of her children to the extent that she has hardly any sense of life outside them: ' "You are myself, Lucy, you children are my family, my future, my skin. If I were starving and fed you it would be I who received the food!" ' (Bagnold 1938/1987: 268).

There is a beautiful account of the beginning of an apprenticeship in maternal love in Rosamond Lehmann's memoir *The Swan in the Evening* (published in 1967, but describing her daughter's birth in 1934). Mother and new-born daughter lie together in silence in the hospital room:

> She and I were alone. I heard her before I saw her. She was making strong, broken noises of protest, sorrow, from some unidentifiable region near my bed. 'Yes, yes, I know,' I said. 'Never mind, I know.' Immediately she was silent, listening. In this soundless nought, recognition started to vibrate, like a fine filament, between us; quickened, tautened. I swung in living darkness, emptiness; in the beginning of the deepest listening of my life. (Lehmann 1967, unpaginated)

Here we notice two things – the immediate bond between mother and child ('Yes, yes, I know,') and the intersubjectivity of the relationship (the daughter's listening reciprocated by the mother's listening) with no suggestion, as in Kristeva and *The Squire*, of self-forgetfulness on the part of the mother.

An examination of the theories of Irigaray, Cixous and Kristeva suggests that, despite some visionary writing, these theorists have not really solved the conflict between the mother as object and mother as subject and, in Kristeva's case, the particular bond between mother and daughter which is so crucial in Irigaray and Cixous and so inspirational for the woman writer, has been lost. I would now like to examine briefly what recent developments in object-relations theory have to tell us about motherhood.

Following on from Melanie Klein, theorists of the American object-relations school argue that the self is constructed in social relationships rather than through instinctual drives. They place emphasis on the first three years of a child's life in forming identity. Since this is a time when the primary caretaker is usually the mother, like Klein, American object-relations theorists stress the primacy of the mother–child bond as opposed to Freud's emphasis on the Oedipal conflict with the father. In their view, children establish their identity earlier than Freud said – between the age of eighteen months and three years – as a result of the two sexes being handled differently.

Why are the sexes handled differently? In *The Reproduction of Mothering. Psychoanalysis and the Sociology of Gender* (1978), Nancy Chodorow argues that the monopoly of childcare by women leads to a dangerous polarisation of gender positions whereby women are encouraged to display skills of empathy and nurturing and men are socialised to be aggressive, non-empathetic and emotionally repressed. This being so, women crave more intimacy in their relationships than men can provide and they seek to recreate with their babies the symbiotic bonds they first enjoyed with their own mothers. Rather than being a phallic substitute, as in Freud, the baby becomes a way of recreating the daughter's closeness with her mother. But mothers also have to prepare their children for life outside in the patriarchy. According to Chodorow, mothers perpetuate the cycle whereby women are skilled in empathy and men are not, by treating their sons as separate and independent whilst merging their own identity with that of their daughters; so that girls emerge from being mothered with a capacity for empathy built into their definition of self in a way that boys do not. In other words, women are psychologically prepared for mothering by being mothered by women; they grow up with relational capacites and needs which commit them to mothering. In Chodorow's view, asymmetries in the relational experiences of girls and boys growing up account for crucial differences in feminine and masculine personality: girls come to define and experience themselves as continuous with others; boys come to define themselves as more separate and distinct. Chodorow's solution to breaking this cycle is to advocate shared parenting by women and men.

Radclyffe Hall's novel, *The Unlit Lamp*, is a good illustration of Chodorow's theory that mothers turn to their children to fulfil emotional needs left unmet by men. The Ogden household is rigidly patriarchal: Colonel James Ogden is a bully whose wife has become worn out serving him. Mrs. Ogden looks to her daughter Joan to supply the nurturing she lacks in her relationship with her husband. She tells Joan: ' "You see, you've always seemed to make up for it all, what I missed in James I more than found in you" ' (Hall 1924/1981: 128). Mrs Ogden's neediness makes her prey on Joan, binding her daughter to her with emotional blackmail. Prevented from studying medicine, Joan leads the diminished life of a daughter at home. This type of life, as we saw in the previous chapter, had come under attack even before the First World War. Lady Loo says in Hall's novel: ' "Well, times are changing and mothers will have to change too, I suppose" ' (*op. cit.* 118). But the situation, as *The Unlit Lamp* shows, is more complex than this: mothers can only change if men also change and learn to provide women with the emotional nurturance they need – and this, as Chodorow and others have argued, involves widespread changes in our attitude to childrearing.

Jungian studies of the mother as mythical archetype, an inward image at work in the human psyche, and finding expression in individual and collective life in myths, symbols and dreams, provide another approach to motherhood. However, as Demaris Wehr has pointed out, there are problems for feminists in the Jungian analysis: 'Jung's account of the mother's significance [when describing the force of the anima in the male psyche] is conspicuously one-sided, lacking in empathy for the person who is feared. The woman/mother is made an object, an other' (Wehr 1988: 109). While it is true that women are experienced by infants as having absolute power, mothers themselves are more likely to think of themselves as powerless, their 'power' being reduced to the duty to service their child's needs. Nevertheless, the Jungian approach can be useful for extracting submerged mythic motifs in women's writing. Rosamond Lehmann's novel, *The Ballad and the Source* (1944) is a retelling of the Demeter-Persephone myth with, woven in, the archetype of the terrible, devouring mother. Robbed of her daughter, Ianthe, Mrs Jardine vows to wreak vengeance on patriarchal society for the wrong it has done her, but only succeeds in harming the people close to her. Her Medusa-like gaze turns lovers, husband and daughter to stone. Yet the novel also shows that Ianthe has been damaged by being deprived of her mother. Brought up by her father, Ianthe has been taught to repress her body and everything connected with her female side. In the end such suppression leads to Ianthe's breakdown. Lehmann's novel invites a conclusion similar to that of Antonia White's quartet: though patriarchal society may do everything in its power to separate daughter from mother, without her mother a daughter has difficulty establishing her identity as a woman.

The writings of the French feminists on mothering and those of the American object-relations school coincide in their emphasis on women's fluid identity. Jung likewise stresses the continuity of identity between mother and daughter: 'Every mother contains her daughter within herself, and every daughter her mother . . . This participation and intermingling gives rise to that peculiar uncertainty as regards *time*: a woman lives earlier as a mother, later as a daughter. The conscious experience of these ties produces the feeling that her life is spread out over generations' (Jung and Kerenyi 1963: 162; ellipsis mine). This fluidity of identity between mothers and daughters finds expression in Enid Bagnold's novel *The Squire*: ' "Lucy," whispered the squire, and had an odd sense that Lucy was herself, that she herself was her own mother, that these three women were one' (Bagnold 1938/1987: 264). And Storm Jameson's autobiography poignantly illustrates the closeness of the bond between mother and daughter: 'It seemed that a nerve led direct from my young mind to hers: I knew instantly what she wanted me to say, what it would please her to hear, what she wanted' (*Journey from the North* vol.1: 32). On her mother's death, Jameson wrote: 'the story is not at an end. Her life did not end then; it goes on echoing through mine, and will echo there until it and I are both silenced' (*op. cit.* 355).

Women's fluid identity should not be idealised: too much empathy between mothers and daughters can result in mothers being incapable of seeing their daughters as separate from themselves. As Jean Grimshaw argues in *Feminist Philosophers* (1986), a real ability to care for others includes the ability to detach oneself from them. Moreover, is not this emphasis on women's fluid sense of self simply a red herring? Does it not proceed from an analysis of women's psychology within a particular kind of society that has taught them to suppress their needs, rather than constituting a theory valid for all time? The element missing from most psychoanalytical theories of mother–daughter relations is a sense of the mother as a subject in her own right, independent of her child's needs. There are, however, some writers who have looked at mothering from the mother's point of view.

Sara Ruddick's work on maternal thinking (*Maternal Thinking. Towards a Politics of Peace*, 1990) places the mother at the centre as subject. Ruddick argues that out of women's experience of mothering there has arisen a distinctive female approach to ethical problems with an emphasis on responsibility, care for others, openness, attentive love, resilience, all qualities which, she suggests, are undervalued or ignored in male dominated, capitalist societies where the emphasis is on individualism and achievement. However, as Jean Grimshaw points out in *Feminist Philosophers*, the mother–child relationship cannot be a successful paradigm for other sorts of relationships since in the mother–child relationship the responsibility is not mutual. Women who practise maternal thinking in the public arena, at least as it exists in Western capitalist societies, are too often likely to find that attentiveness, resilience, responsiveness etc., result in chronic self-denial. The concept of maternal thinking, while useful in stressing the uniqueness of the mothering task and the qualities it fosters, does little to address the needs of the mothers themselves and indeed it can be too easily used against their interests.

Vita Sackville-West's novel, *All Passion Spent* (1931), is a good illustration of this. Lady Slane's way of thinking – creative, intuitive, responsive to the individual – is so completely at odds with the masculine world in which she lives that her children think her simple. They view her merely as an object, an appendage to their father. Lady Slane's life has been damaged and thwarted by the patriarchal world, but not irrevocably: at the end of the novel, she achieves a real maternal act when she urges her great granddaughter, Deborah, to pursue the artistic vocation she herself has been unable to fulfil. But, though Sackville-West might seem in *All Passion Spent* to anticipate contemporary feminist theorists such as Ruddick in celebrating maternal thinking, her praise of Lady Slane is not undiluted. Maternal thinking can have a beauty of its own but the cost to the individual woman is too high, as Lady Slane knows:

> Was there, after all, some foundation for the prevalent belief that woman should minister to man? . . . Was there something beautiful, something active, something creative, even, in her apparent submission to Henry? . . . Was not this also an achievement of the sort peculiarly suited to women? of the sort, indeed, which women alone could compass; a privilege, a prerogative, not to be despised? All the woman in her answered, yes! All the artist in her countered, no! (Sackville-West 1931/1983: 176; ellipses mine)

The argument against privileging maternal thinking in one sex could not be more forcibly put.

Another, perhaps more hopeful approach to viewing the mother as a subject in her own right, results not from the work of psychoanalysts, but from the observations of clinical psychologists. In *The Interpersonal World of the Infant* (1985), Daniel Stern argues for the baby's capacity for intersubjective emotional relating from nine months. His study stresses mothering as a partnership between mother and child, unique to the individuals comprising it and shaped by their interactions. This has several important implications for our concept of motherhood. Firstly, Stern sees mothering not as a fixed construct but as a task that is always unique to the individuals concerned: a mother is only a mother when interacting with her child. Secondly, he shows that the infant sees the mother as separate and the mother sees the infant as separate and this interpersonal connecting allows for later adult mutuality. Thirdly, Stern points to the fact that the infant is born already programmed for individuation (and if we take into account Rouch's placental theory, the child is a separate entity even in the womb). This frees us from the classic Freudian paradigm whereby the child is initially fused with the mother and only achieves individuation by overthrowing the mother with the help of the father.

In *The Bonds of Love,* Jessica Benjamin uses the clinical observations of developmental psychologists like Piaget and Stern, to investigate the notion of intersubjectivity:

> The need for *mutual* recognition, the necessity of recognizing as well as being recognized by the other – this is what so many theories of the self have missed. The idea of mutual recognition is crucial to the intersubjective view; it implies that we actually have a need to recognize the other as a separate person who is like us yet distinct. This means that the child has a need to see the mother, too, as an independent subject, not simply as the 'external world' or an adjunct of his ego. (Benjamin 1990: 23)

Benjamin insists that the disposition to separation and individuation is present in the mother–child dyad and that mutual recognition, including the child's ability to recognise the mother as a person in her own right, is as significant a developmental goal as separation. Obviously this has profound implications for the classic phallic theory of the mother as simply an object for her baby's needs and indeed more generally for society's approval of the self-sacrificing mother who obliterates herself for the sake of her child. Such a mother, Benjamin suggests, cannot give her infant the sense of identity her child needs.

To the theories of Benjamin and Stern, may be added the personal observation of one mother who struggled throughout her sons' childhoods to hold on to her sense of herself as a separate being. In her powerful and painfully honest account of her own experience of motherhood, Adrienne Rich writes: 'I don't know how we made it from their embattled childhood and my embattled motherhood into a mutual recognition of ourselves and each other. Probably that mutual recognition, overlaid by social and traditional circumstance, *was always there*, from the first gaze between mother and infant at the breast' (Rich 1977: 32; my emphasis).

It is these kinds of studies (Stern, Benjamin) which seem to me to offer the best hope for seeing mother as a subject in her own right and the mother–child relationship as one between two mutually loving but autonomous beings. The issue is not one of rejection of or separation from the mother but of a positive, supportive, interactive connection between two individuals, *both* of whom grow and change. This kind of supportive and changing relationship is depicted in Edith Olivier's inter-war novel, *The Love Child* (1927). Olivier's account is written, unusually for the period, from the point of view of the mother and the daughter in the novel is a fantasy child conjured up by Agatha Bodenham out of her loneliness and self-suppression. Agatha feels that Clarissa is 'the only being who had ever awoken her own personality, and made it responsive,' (Olivier 1927/1981: 16). Mother and daughter live out a symbiotic relationship in an imaginary world controlled by Agatha. However the demands of the patriarchy, in the shape of the law and of religion, soon threaten the pre-oedipal world in which Agatha tries to contain Clarissa. By various ruses Agatha manages to circumvent both police and clergy. The patriarchy has tried to separate daughter from mother by bringing the daughter into its sphere of authority and has failed. Agatha constructs their relationship outside its authority.

The next threat to the mother–daughter relationship comes when Clarissa is seventeen and expresses a desire to drive, dance and play tennis. Agatha has no choice, the mother–daughter relationship must be renegotiated if it is to survive. Clarissa pulls her mother out into the world and, rather unusually for the time, we see the daughter's power to transform the life of her mother as Agatha learns to appreciate poetry and music. Even out in the world, mother and daughter might have been able to retain their closeness were it not for David who is in love with Clarissa. The novel becomes a battle of wills between Agatha and David. Clarissa feels torn between them: ' "I can't belong to two people," ' she tells David, ' "I am Agatha's," ' (*op. cit.* 190). David replies: ' "I will be all that she has been, and far, far more," ' (*op. cit.* 191). He kisses her and, since this is fantasy, Clarissa vanishes like a shooting star. What is Olivier saying here? That the mother–daughter bond may be claustrophobic but at least it allows the daughter freedom; whereas heterosexual love spells, as in so many myths, death for the individual woman? Agatha tells David: ' "I gave her life to her, and you have taken it away," ' (*op. cit.* 204). *The Love*

Child is an extraordinarily powerful and unusual tale, showing why women need daughters, how their mothering of daughters is often a re-mothering of themselves, and why the mother–daughter relationship is inevitably precarious in a patriarchal society.

The multiplicity of psychoanalytical theories of motherhood invites an eclectic approach to women's fiction of the inter-war period. While some of the novels mentioned above echo psychoanalytical thought in the inter-war period, some move beyond it and anticipate later developments. It would therefore seem unduly limiting to constrain our textual analysis in the following chapters to any one theory; different theories become appropriate to different texts and authors.

Our survey of theories of motherhood prompts several questions which may be borne in mind when we come to examine our six inter-war women writers. Do these writers feel that the act of writing depends in some way on the mother's absence or death, as in Lacan, or do they like Cixous see the mother as the source of their writing voice? Do they feel marginal or empowered as women writers? Do they have a notion of writing as a way of repairing relations with the mother (Klein)? Do they view the mother as a regressive influence, as in Freud, or do they attempt to look back through their mothers, as Irigaray urges? Do they take an essentialist view of motherhood or do they see the mothering task as varying according to the situation of the woman involved in it? Do they try to extend the notion of motherhood to other spheres and is this a success? Are they, like some of the novelists already mentioned, aware of the difficulties of the mothering task? Indeed do they seek to give the mother a voice or are these just daughters' stories and, if so, do these daughters recognise the mother's separate identity or is the mother presented simply as an object for her daughter's needs? Is there any anticipation of Irigaray's theory that strengthening the mother–daughter relationship may be a way of undermining the patriarchy?

Being women themselves, we might hope these writers may be more able than male writers of the time to look beyond their culture's fetishisation of the mother. Already, in some of the inter-war novels mentioned in this chapter, we have observed that the moment of liberation for the daughter comes when she is able to see her mother as subject, as another suffering, vulnerable, occasionally joyful, woman.

3

Rose Macaulay: Flight from the Mother

In several papers published during the inter-war period, Karen Horney analyses the psychology of women growing up in a society which favours the male. In her paper, 'Inhibited Femininity. Psychoanalytical Contribution to the Problem of Frigidity' (1926–7), she states: 'Our culture, as is well known, is a male culture, and therefore by and large not favourable to the unfolding of woman and her individuality' (Horney 1967: 82). A woman growing up in such a society, Horney suggests, will have 'no faith in women's capacity for achievement and is rather inclined to identify with the masculine disregard for women' (*op. cit.* 75). In an earlier paper, 'The Flight from Womanhood. The Masculinity-Complex in Women as Viewed by Men and by Women' (1926), she expands on her view that Western civilisation is masculine and that necessarily women will be encouraged to identify with male values at the expense of female: 'a girl is exposed from birth onward to the suggestion – inevitable, whether conveyed brutally or delicately – of her inferiority, an experience that constantly stimulates her masculinity complex' (*op. cit.* 69). In this chapter, I would like to explore Horney's descriptions of the woman in flight from her own womanhood in the context of Rose Macaulay's inter-war fiction.

Rose Macaulay's first novel appeared in 1906 but it was not until her eighth, *Non-Combatants and Others*, published in 1916, that she featured a female protagonist. The shock of the First World War, the pain she felt because she was not a man and could not fight, forced Macaulay for the first time to face the reality of her womanhood and place a woman at the centre of a novel. A comparison may be drawn here with Virginia Woolf who at times of war, 'this preposterous masculine fiction,' found herself becoming 'steadily more feminist' (*Letters vol.2* 1976: 71, 76). *Non-Combatants and Others* is predominantly a mother–daughter story for there are three sets of mothers and daughters in the novel, each embodying a different attitude to the war.

The heroine, Alix Sandomir, is an artist. She shares her creator's weak nerves, weak stomach and boyish figure. She is also lame, a physical symbol of her psychical maiming by the war. Her initial reaction to the war is, as Macaulay's had been, one of envy that her gender prevents her from joining the fighting. She tells her brother Nicholas: ' "I want to go and help to end it . . . Oh, it's rotten not being able to; simply rotten . . . Why *shouldn't* girls?" ' (*NC*: 141; ellipses mine). Alix's decision to ignore the war is partly forced upon her by her society's gender divisions. She tells Nicholas: ' "I can't bear the sight of khaki; and I don't know whether it's most because the war's so beastly or because I want to be in it . . . It's both" ' (*ibid.*; ellipsis mine). She is in that impossible in-between position in which many women find themselves in times of war, both wanting and not wanting to defend their country (on this point, see Gill Plain, *Women's Fiction of the Second World War*, 1996: *passim*).

At Wood End where Alix is living when the book opens, mothers and daughters are cheerfully, even exaggeratedly, engaged in the war effort. Alix's aunt is secretary of the local Belgian committee, her daughter Margot is a member of the Women's Volunteer Reserve, Betty is driving an ambulance car in Flanders and Dorothy, like so many middle-class women of the period, is a VAD. The jarring note amidst all this activity is provided by John Orme who has returned from the front horribly scarred. It is John raving in his sleep which finally drives Alix away from Wood End. The war is coming too close for her liking.

Alix goes to stay with more distant relatives, the Framptons. If mother and daughters at Wood End agree on the importance of the war effort, in the Frampton household the war is treated as a backdrop to more urgent everyday concerns. In a conversation at breakfast between Kate and her mother, the report of a Zeppelin raid on the East coast is sandwiched between Kate's fussing over the inadequacies of their 'girl' and the inferior quality of the bacon supplied by their butcher. Macaulay shows her gift for precise social observation: shortage of good food and difficulties with domestics were precisely the sort of selfish concerns on the part of non-combatants about which Vera Brittain complained on her return to civilian life (*TY*: 429). The continual juxtaposition of the serious and the trivial shows up the Frampton women's lack of judgement and muddled thinking.

It is the death of her brother Paul and, even more, the revelation of the way in which he died (not a hero's death, but suicide) which brings home to Alix how untenable life with the Framptons is. Rejecting the examples of the mothers and daughters she has been presented with, Alix begins to explore a third attitude towards the war: ' "Not throwing oneself into it and doing jobs for it, in the way that suits lots of people; I simply can't do that. And not going on as usual and pretending it's not there, because that doesn't work. Something *against* the war, I want to be doing, I think. Something to fight it and prevent it coming again" ' (*NC*: 141). This is where Alix's mother comes in.

A socialist and a feminist, Daphne Sandomir believes in educating people to work for international co-operation and permanent peace. Energetic, competent and unsentimental, Daphne urges Alix to join the SPPP (the Society for Promoting Permanent Peace, an invention of Macaulay's) but leaves her free to make her own decision. The relationship between Daphne and her daughter is adult, even ideal, with each respecting the other's differences. When Daphne does intervene in Alix's life, it is to rescue her daughter from the psychological damage done to her by a patriarchal society's militarism and gently guide her towards personal growth. Embedded in *Non-Combatants and Others* is the Demeter-Persephone myth which Macaulay will use again in *The World My Wilderness*.

Daphne is a mother who, despite her pacifism, refuses to privilege motherhood. In 'Woman in War' (1911), Olive Schreiner argued that mothers have a special responsibility and a special power to oppose war. Similar arguments appear in Charlotte Perkins Gilman's *Herland* (1915). The idea that motherhood is opposed to militarism has been taken up, as we saw in Chapter 2, by later feminist theorists. In *Maternal Thinking*, Sara Ruddick says of the mother: 'By virtue of her mothering she is meant to be an initiator of peace and a witness against war. She represents a practice whose aims and strategies contradict those of war' (Ruddick 1990: 221). Daphne resists such arguments from biology:

> She could talk of the part to be played by women in the construction of permanent peace without calling them the guardians of the race or the custodians of life. She didn't draw distinctions, beyond the necessary ones, between women and men; she took women as human beings, not as life-producing organisms; she took men as human beings, not as destroying-machines. (*NC*: 170)

Daphne may exemplify maternal thinking at its best in her detached concern for Alix and her wider concern for world peace, but she never claims that such care is the prerogative of mothers.

The war contributes to the growing misunderstanding between Alix and her friend, Basil Doye, who returns from the front as from a different country. Basil's reaction to the horror of war is to revert to stereotypes about women. The romance plot in *Non-Combatants and Others* is downplayed in favour of the story of the heroine's quest to come to terms with the war and in that quest it is

Alix's mother, not her lover, who is the crucial influence. Macaulay joins other women writers of the period in 'writing beyond the ending'. In theory this should be empowering, but the mother–daughter relationship in this novel does not quite ring true.

Daphne Sandomir is an idealised, larger than life mother, combining motherhood with a busy professional life in a way that, as we saw in Chapter 1, was very difficult to do in this period except for a tiny minority of women. She is a type that recurs in Macaulay's inter-war fiction (see, for example, Evelyn Gresham in *Crewe Train* or Mrs Folyot in *Keeping Up Appearances*). In her paper, 'A Contribution to the Psychogenesis of Manic-Depressive States' (1935), Melanie Klein makes some pertinent comments on the idealisation of mothers:

> In some patients who had turned away from their mother in dislike or hate [as we shall see Macaulay did at this period], I have found that there existed in their minds nevertheless a beautiful picture of the mother . . . The real object was felt to be unattractive – really an injured, incurable and therefore dreaded person. The beautiful picture had been disassociated from the real object but had never been given up. (Mitchell 1991: 125; ellipsis mine)

In *Non-Combatants and Others*, Macaulay writes entirely from the daughter's point of view and the mother–daughter relationship resembles that between two mutually respectful colleagues. The emotions are omitted. The numerous problems Macaulay thereby glossed over become apparent when we examine her next presentation of mother–daughter relationships – in *Dangerous Ages*, published in 1921.

Dangerous Ages portrays four generations of women. There is Grandmamma aged eighty-four, tranquilly enjoying her books, her card games and her naps. Of all the women in *Dangerous Ages* Grandmamma has best come to terms with life. Her brand of rather cynical detachment mirrors Simone de Beauvoir's description of the elderly woman: 'The old woman commonly becomes serene towards the very end of her life . . . Old women take pride in their independence; they begin at last to view the world through their own eyes; they note that they have been duped and deceived all their lives; sane and mistrustful, they often develop a pungent cynicism' (Beauvoir 1972: 607; ellipsis mine).

Grandmamma's daughter, Mrs Hilary, is less intelligent and more vulnerable than her mother. A widow of sixty-three, Mrs Hilary has devoted her life to her children and now that they are grown up she is left without a purpose in life. Her over-investment in her children has made her emotional, self-pitying and childish. In her portrayal of Mrs Hilary, Macaulay foreshadows an important strand in feminist thinking which argues that relegating women to childrearing and domestic work infantilises them (see, for example, Betty Friedan's *The Feminine Mystique*, published in 1965).

Adrienne Rich has said: 'The nurture of daughters in a patriarchy calls for a strong sense of self-nurture in the mother' (Rich 1977: 245). Feeling worthless herself, Mrs Hilary can transmit to her daughters no positive image of womanhood. She does not love all her children equally but favours those whose lives conform most closely to society's gender stereotypes. Her elder son, Jim, a doctor, ranks highest in her affections since he is doing 'a man's job' and her daughter Neville comes next for she has married and had two children. The difference between them is that while society's gender divisions enable Jim to lead a fulfilling and productive life, Neville feels trapped and wasted. Mrs Hilary's behaviour, like that of Mrs Ramsay in *To the Lighthouse*, reinforces society's sexist stereotypes and makes it inevitable that her daughters will rebel against her.

There is little sympathy for the mother in the portrait of Mrs Hilary. Macaulay lacks the compassion of other women writers of the period for the mother figure and the insight of writers like Woolf into the way in which mothers become entangled in the patriarchal discourse. But the portrait of Mrs. Hilary is perhaps more revealing than her creator intended. What emerges from the description of Mrs Hilary's untidiness and thinness indicates self-neglect and low self-esteem. She is a woman who is emotionally demanding, certainly, but also deeply depressed. In the over-familiarity of family life her problem goes undiagnosed and uncured. This is not the only instance we will find in Macaulay's writing where reading against the grain reveals more sympathy with women than the text overtly expresses.

The portrayal of the next generation of women in *Dangerous Ages* centres on Mrs. Hilary's three daughters, Neville, Pamela and Nan. Neville has succeeded in escaping her mother's influence in so far as she is a good mother to her children, allowing them freedom and independence: 'To interfere would have been part of the middle-aged, old-fashioned mother, and for that part Neville had no liking' (*DA*: 130). She performs a nurturing role towards her own mother, bolstering up Mrs Hilary's flagging self-esteem, and she mothers her younger sister Nan. The price of all this mothering for Neville has been the deterioration of her intellectual powers and the ruin of a promising career, as she discovers when she tries to defy her age and resume her interrupted medical studies. Her brother Jim explains: ' "She can't get back the clear, gripping brain she had before she had children. She's given some of it to them. That's nature's way, unfortunately" ' (*DA*: 115). There is no recognition in the novel that Neville's years as a mother might have developed in her distinctive strengths and perceptions which could be usefully employed outside the home.

It is as if mothers were somehow doomed to siphon off their intelligence to their children.

Mrs Hilary's daughter Pamela is freest from her mother's influence. Pamela is a social worker living in London and sharing a flat with Frances. The question of Pamela's sexuality is left open. It is characteristic of Macaulay to be reticent about sexual matters but she must surely have known that in depicting two women living together she was inviting her readers to conclude they were lesbians; 1921 was after all the year in which lesbianism was hotly debated as the House of Commons considered whether to make lesbianism a criminal act. By this date, as we have seen in Chapter 1, it was difficult for women to live together without being suspected of lesbianism. Pamela is the most balanced of Mrs Hilary's daughters. Her choice of lesbianism, whether sexual or women-orientated in Adrienne Rich's sense of a lesbian continuum, has left her free to pursue a professional career, combining it with a satisfying relationship in a way that Neville and Nan cannot.

Mrs Hilary's youngest daughter Nan, unmarried and a novelist, has a complicated relationship with her mother. She is the least favourite of all Mrs Hilary's children. In a moment of insight Mrs. Hilary suggests that this is because Nan is the one who most resembles herself. Devaluing herself in comparison with her husband, Mrs. Hilary devalues the child who most resembles her. Nan, for her part, is irritated by Mrs Hilary's emotional demands, by her prejudices and opinionated outbursts. Yet of all the daughters it is Nan who has been least successful in breaking away from her mother. She suffers from acute matraphobia:

> 'I'm like mother.' That was Nan's nightmare thought. Not intellectually, for Nan's brain was sharp and subtle and strong and fine, and Mrs Hilary's an amorphous, undeveloped muddle. But where, if not from Mrs Hilary, did Nan get her black fits of melancholy, her erratic and irresponsible gaieties, her passionate angers, her sharp jealousies and egotisms? The clever young woman saw herself in the stupid elderly one; saw herself slipping down the years to that. That was why, where Neville and Pamela and their brothers pitied, Nan, understanding her mother's bad moods better than they, was vicious with hate and scorn. For she knew these things through and through. (*DA*: 81)

Because of her fear of resembling her needy, dependent mother, Nan curbs all expression of her emotions until it is too late. Adrienne Rich's words are illuminating here: 'Our personalities seem dangerously to blur and overlap with our mothers'; and, in a desperate attempt to know where mother ends and daughter begins, we perform radical surgery' (Rich 1977: 236). Perplexed and hurt by what he sees as her rejection of him, Barry turns to Gerda.

Dangerous Ages shows how a daughter's relationship with her mother is crucial in determining her adult relationships with men, an ironic confirmation of Freud's theories (see above, p.22) by a writer hostile to Freud.

This point is made even more clearly when Nan enters into a relationship with a married man, Stephen Lumley. The responsibility for this relationship is laid directly at Mrs Hilary's door: her attempted interference between Nan and Stephen is the final determining factor in Nan's decision to commit herself sexually to him. Even more than this, it is her mother's character which is blamed for driving Nan into Stephen's arms: 'In the very thought of Stephen, with his cynical humour, his clear, keen mind, his lazy power of brain, Nan had found relief all that day, reacting desperately from a mind fuddled with sentiment and emotion' (*DA*: 252). The daughter chooses a man who will help protect her against her mother and the mother in herself.

Yet Nan has difficulty in separating herself from her mother, a problem, as we saw in Chapter 2, to some extent shared by all women who are mothered by women. Unnurtured by her mother Nan remains a needy, hungry little girl inside. Her outburst of tears with her mother in Rome is a sudden reversion to childish dependency:

> They held each other close. It was a queer moment, though not an unprecedented one in the stormy history of their relations together. A queer, strange, comforting, healing moment . . . it could not last. The crying child wants its mother; the mother wants to comfort the crying child. A good bridge, but one inadequate for the strain of daily traffic. The child, having dried its tears, watches the bridge break again, and thinks it a pity but inevitable. The mother, less philosophic, may cry in her turn, thinking perhaps that the bridge may be built this time in that way; but, the child having the colder heart, it seldom is. (*DA*: 253–4; ellipsis mine)

In this crucial passage the onus for the breakdown of the mother–daughter relationship is laid at the daughter's door. 'There remain the moments,' adds the narrator, 'impotent but indestructible' (*DA*: 254). It is the nearest Macaulay comes in this book to expressing sympathy with the mother's point of view.

Dangerous Ages is a novel which deals realistically with women's lives in a patriarchal society where childrearing is left to the women. It shows how such childrearing can deform a woman's character (Mrs Hilary) or ruin a woman's professional life (Neville). It is, essentially, a pessimistic book. Although Neville at the end seems to be moving towards some sort of career in social work, we cannot help feeling that this is second best for her and that her real vocation was to be a doctor. Even Gerda's happiness leaves questions in the reader's mind. At present she is able to combine marriage and work but what if there are children? Will she still be able to carry on working or will she repeat her mother's pattern of a broken career?

At the same time, the portrait of these women is curiously detached. There is no celebration in the novel of the distinctive and positive qualities of women's lives and there is little criticism of the male characters who, although feminist and liberal in theory, in practice tend to behave less than perfectly. Rodney has pursued his career at the expense of his wife's; Jim discourages Neville from pursuing her professional ambitions; Barry insists on marriage against Gerda's wishes. The most overtly sexist character in the book is a woman, Mrs Hilary, but there is no analysis of the way patriarchal discourses have operated to produce her sexism. *Dangerous Ages*, though it analyses the situation of women, is not a kind book to women. The depiction of Neville's situation leads to the depressing conclusion that childrearing softens the brain without hope of recuperation. Women are presented as having two choices: either to identify with the mother and become marginalised (Neville) or to repress the mother and identify with the father (Nan). But this latter choice involves repressing the body as well, so Nan loses the man she desires.

In *Non-Combatants and Others* the mother–daughter relationship is evaded; in *Dangerous Ages* it is faced only to be presented in a deeply pessimistic way. This pessimism ties in with Macaulay's views on women's lives in general. In many of her inter-war novels and articles Macaulay protests sharply against a society which denies women equality on the basis of their gender. In *Potterism. A Tragi-Farcical Tract* (1920), Jane Potter reflects that: 'Women were handicapped; they had to fight much harder to achieve equal results. People didn't give them jobs in the same way' (*P*: 5). In *Keeping Up Appearances* (1928), Daphne pinpoints the psychological disadvantages to women of being treated as a group apart: ' "I get a horrid fear sometimes that, if men go on and on saying these things about us, we shall *become* like that, hypnotised, you know, by labels. We shall become like the woman of man's theorising. Ghastly. She is such a gruesome creature" ' (*KUA*: 171; ellipsis mine). We might compare Karen Horney's statement in her paper, 'The Flight from Womanhood' that: 'women have adapted themselves to the wishes of men and felt as if their adaptation were their true nature' (Horney 1967: 56–7).

But if Macaulay objected to discriminating against women on account of their gender she objected to privileging them on that account too: ' "But the silliest part of it," added Audrey, "is when some man says, 'Granted that women are mental and moral imbeciles, haven't they a magnificently adequate defence and justification? They are the life-creators, the mothers of the race. Isn't that enough?' " ' (*Crewe Train*, 1926/1985: 168 and compare *Told by an Idiot*, 1923/1983: 250). And we have seen that *Non-Combatants and Others* refuses to endorse the view that women are naturally less violent than men because of their ability to become mothers.

On the face of it Macaulay, like Brittain and Holtby, seems to have been an Old Feminist arguing in favour of equal opportunities for women and objecting to the New Feminist emphasis on women's special role as mothers. The truth is slightly more complicated than this, for the fact is that Macaulay did believe there were irreducible differences between the sexes and, moreover, differences that were not culturally constructed but rooted in biology. In an essay, 'What I Believe' published in 1931 she wrote: 'women are physically less and frailer in every capacity, and it is not likely that the brain should be excepted' (*Nation* 16 December 1931: 666). In a crisis, particularly one requiring physical courage, women, she believed, were liable to be let down by their weak nerves and weaker constitution than men. This was a generalisation *ad feminam* for though Macaulay was physically active all her life, climbing trees and swimming daily in the Serpentine until well into her seventies, there were occasions, as when she failed to sit her finals at Oxford or during her brief stint as a VAD in the First World War, when her nerves let her down.

Statements about women's frailty permeate Macaulay's novels. In *Keeping Up Appearances*, Daphne says: ' "Men – taking the average, I mean – are enormously abler, for instance. Really enormously, both in body and mind. Stronger all round, in nerves and muscle and brain, more creative and inventive, and with more sense" ' (*KUA*: 172). Other of Macaulay's characters – Mrs Folyot in *Keeping Up Appearances* (*KUA*: 367), Stanley Garden in *Told by an Idiot* (Macaulay 1923/1983: 129) – repeat Daphne's observation about women's weak constitution. The argument remains rooted in biology; it is never taken further and suggested, for example, that the reason for women's nerves being in worse shape than men's might be because of their peculiar and repressive social conditioning. For Macaulay, though in a different way from her contemporaries, a woman's anatomy was her destiny. A woman's body was something to be kept sternly in check for it was liable to hinder her efforts at equality with men. This is particularly the case with motherhood.

In her immensely popular series of novels published during the 1920s and early 1930s, motherhood is presented as a problem and a stumbling block to the woman who wants equality. Jane Potter knows she could write a better book than her brother, 'only there was this baby, which made her feel ill before it came, and would need care and attention afterwards. It wasn't fair. If Johnny married and had a baby it wouldn't get in his way' (*P*: 216). Being a mother in a society which devalues mothers is a problem for the woman determined, as Jane is, to hang on to her career: 'Jane gave the party to show people that Charles didn't monopolise her, that she was well and active again, and ready for work and life. If she wasn't careful, she might come to be regarded as the mere mother, and dropped out' (*P*: 223). Motherhood is never compatible with freedom in Macaulay's novels. When Denham realises she is pregnant again she knows that 'the struggle to live in her own way was over . . . Because she loved Arnold . . . she would bear his child, tend and rear it, become a wife and a mother instead of a free person' (*Crewe Train*, 1926/1985: 250; ellipses mine).

Kristeva has said: 'We cannot gain access to the temporal scene, that is, to the political and historical affairs of our society, except by identifying with the values considered to be masculine' (Moi 1986: 155). Reading these inter-war novels, we have the feeling that what Macaulay wants is for all women to be men, with men's intelligence and men's courage minus the womanly 'nerves' and minus the womb. Her tomboyish heroines may seem to reject their society's gender stereotypes, but in fact they are gendered, they are adolescent boys like Imogen Garden in *Told by an Idiot* (1923) who at eighteen 'was still, in all her imaginings, her continuous, unwritten stories about herself, a young man' (Macaulay 1923/1983: 220) or they are 'amusing bachelors' like Rome Garden in the same novel (*op. cit.* 66). Again, Karen Horney's comments in her paper, 'Inhibited Femininity,' are pertinent: 'an unconscious attitude of envy renders the woman blind to her own virtues. Even motherhood appears only as a burden to her. Everything is measured against the masculine' (Horney 1967: 75). However, towards the end of her life, Macaulay wrote a novel in which motherhood is presented in a different light. For this reason, even though it falls slightly outside our period, it is worth examining *The World My Wilderness*.

As the First World War prompted her to find for the first time her woman's voice, so the disasters of the Second World War occasioned in part a change of vision for Macaulay. *The World My Wilderness*, published in 1950, has generally been read as a lament on the collapse of Western civilisation caused by the war and as a, partly autobiographical, account of a spiritual quest. There is much to support this view. Macaulay uses the bombed ruins around St Paul's in the City of London as a metaphor for the rootlessness and decline in morality following the Second World War. Seventeen-year-old Barbary who makes her home in these ruins becomes the symbol of a lost generation bewildered by its experiences during the war. Haunted by guilt over the death of her step-father, Barbary searches for a forgiveness which she feels can be found only within the church from which she believes herself to be excluded. Barbary's elder brother, Richie, is Macaulay's chief spokesman for the lament on the passing of a civilisation: 'No civilisation had lasted more than a thousand years; this present one, called western culture, had had its day' (*WW*: 152). And it is with Richie that the book ends.

However, another reading of the novel is possible, one which Macaulay may not have intended, but which is present throughout as a sub-text. In this reading, Western culture was already corrupt before the war, and Barbary's redemption will come, not from the church, which is no use to her, but from her mother, Helen.

There are flaws in the representatives of Western civilisation in *The World My Wilderness*. Richie's reaction against a rising generation of philistines is largely the result of class snobbery. It is a society which is highly patriarchal. Sir Gulliver's chauvinist attitudes lead him to shuffle off responsibility for Barbary first on to Helen and then on to Pamela. At the end of the book his feelings towards her are revealed to have been based on the notion of ownership: when he learns Barbary is not 'his', he has no further interest in her. This 'civilisation' requires a certain type of woman – the sort Richie feels he would like for a wife, 'graceful, adaptable, conventional, ladylike . . . a gentle, merry slip of a girl, he pictured her . . . the prettiest deb of her year . . . Not one of those mocking, free-spoken Bohemian intellectuals of Bloomsbury, Newnham, or the Quartier Latin' (*WW*: 199; ellipses mine). It produces women like Pamela, conventional to the point of obtuseness.

Into this class based, patriarchal, insular, frequently unjust society bursts Helen, a woman who defies or, more accurately, ignores its conventions in a spirit of anarchy that at times makes her resemble her daughter, Barbary. Helen possesses the figure of a Greek goddess: 'She was a large woman, long-legged, with the low, full breasts, the firm, robust waist and dignified hips of the Milo Venus' (*WW*: 17). This type of womanly figure is generally associated in Macaulay's novels with idleness, selfishness and amorality (see, for instance, Rosalind in *Dangerous Ages*). Helen possesses all of these traits, but she possesses others as well. She is independent and self-confident, she is skilled in the 'masculine' pursuits of classical languages, chess and scholarship. The opening scene of *The World My Wilderness* reverses the usual convention whereby the nude in a painting is a young woman and the painter is a man: here, the artist is Helen and the nude with the superb flesh tones is her father-in-law. Like many of Macaulay's heroines, Helen transcends stereotypes but this time, crucially, not because she is a tomboyish androgyne, but as a woman and, more particularly, as a mother.

Helen is a woman who makes up her own rules, rejecting the ideals of patriotism and family which are the bedrock of the patriarchal society in which she lives: ' "As to one's country, why should one feel any more interest in its welfare than in that of other countries? And as to the family, I have never understood . . . why it should be an ideal . . . it is a convenience, often a necessity, sometimes a pleasure, sometimes the reverse; but who first exalted it as admirable, an almost religious ideal?" ' (*WW*: 142; ellipses mine). Helen's attitude comes close here to the question asked by Woolf in her essay *Three Guineas*: 'But the educated man's sister – what does "patriotism" mean to her?

Has she the same reasons for being proud of England?' (Woolf 1992: 162). Helen is the woman as outsider. Celebrating woman's exclusion from the structures of power, Kristeva writes that woman 'is an eternal dissident in relation to social and political consensus, in exile from power, and therefore always singular, fragmentary, demonic, a witch' (Moi 1987: 113), a description which fits the way some of the characters in the book view Helen. Sir Gulliver observes 'Helen's tremendous spell – perhaps no one ever quite escaped from it. Richie had not; he had not' (*WW*: 40).

For most of the novel Helen lives on the borders of the symbolic order, able to compete on equal terms with men but never entirely accepted by them. She practises what Kristeva in 'About Chinese Women' calls 'an impossible dialectic'. Moving between the symbolic and the semiotic, refusing to identify entirely with either may, as Kristeva point out, have its pitfalls:

> If patriarchy sees women as occupying a marginal position within the symbolic order, then it can construe them as the *limit* or borderline of that order. From a phallocentric point of view, women will then come to represent the necessary frontier between man and chaos; but because of their very marginality they will also always seem to recede into and merge with the chaos of the outside . . . It is this position that has enabled male culture sometimes to vilify women as representing darkness and chaos . . . the borderline is seen as part of the chaotic wilderness outside. (Moi 1990: 167; ellipses mine)

The phallocentric view of Helen as representing 'darkness and chaos' is frequently articulated by the representatives of Western civilisation in the book, particularly in relation to her role as a mother.

Helen's experiences as a mother have developed in her a different approach to ethical questions from that approved by the patriarchal society in which she lives. Freud argued that women's approach to ethical problems is typically different from that of men and he concluded that therefore it is inferior: 'I cannot evade the notion . . . that for women the level of what is ethically normal is different from what it is in men . . . they show less sense of justice than men' (*Some Psychical Consequences of the Anatomical Distinction Between the Sexes* quoted in Grimshaw 1986: 187; ellipses mine). This statement has caused much anger. However, recent feminist theory has argued that women do have a different ethical sense from men, but one that is not inferior and which is related to the different psychic development and experience of women, in particular to their experience of mothering and of being mothered by women: 'it is women's mothering which has been one of the main sources of their distinctive priorities and approach to ethical problems' (Grimshaw 1986: 227).

As we saw in Chapter 2, the concept of 'maternal thinking' has been

developed by philosophers like Sara Ruddick who has argued that motherhood encourages such qualities as flexibility, resilience, attention to gesture,
expression and behaviour, and placing a high value on relationships. All these
qualities are exemplified by Helen in her relationship with her children. She is
flexible enough to understand both Barbary's anarchic instincts and Richie's
retreat into the comforts of civilised life. Her approach to childrearing is
undogmatic. When Sir Gulliver disciplines Barbary by sending her to bed early
for a week, her mother lightens this rather severe punishment by playing
amusing games with her. Women, it has been argued by Ruddick and others,
notably Carol Gilligan in *In a Different Voice* (1982), are more likely to see moral
problems in terms of human relationships, rather than abstract rules. At the end
of the novel, Helen agrees that Sir Gulliver has a legal right to keep Barbary but
points out that by forbidding her to join her mother in France, he will be
breaking Barbary's heart.

   Helen has a principle – the maintenance of relationships. It is largely
unstated but clearly present throughout the book. Out of love for Maurice, she has tolerated his collaboration during the war. Her passing off of
Barbary as Sir Gulliver's child is on one level dishonest, but it reveals her desire
to preserve her relationship with her husband and give Barbary a father.
Because her priority is the maintenance of human ties, Helen attempts to
seduce Sir Gulliver in an effort to win Barbary from him without breaking off
her relationship with him. He resists through a typically 'masculine' effort of
the will and she is forced then to win back her daughter in a way which
irrevocably damages her relationship with Sir Gulliver. That she regrets the
ending of this relationship is made clear. She would have preferred to have
persuaded him by love but that, she recognises, would have injured Sir
Gulliver's sense of self. Like Richie's, Sir Gulliver's sense of identity seems
a fragile thing, easily undermined. Helen's very flexibility gives her a stronger
self-identity than either of these two men. Her chief virtue – the preservation
of relationships – is pursued throughout the novel and provides a source, as we
shall see, from which redemption may come.

   However, in the society in which Helen lives, preserving relationships is not
recognised as a valid moral principle and even she fails to recognise it as such.
Helen repeatedly describes herself as idle, selfish and self-indulgent. She tells
Richie: ' "I've no conscience of any kind, my dear. It seems to have been left
out of me," ' (*WW*: 91). Her situation has been described by Jean Grimshaw:

   I suspect that it is sometimes the case, not that women do not act on
   principles, but that the principles on which they act are not recognised
   (especially by men) as valid or important ones. Thus, to act so as to
   maintain relationships, despite belief that certain behaviour is wrong, may

be seen as a weakness, as a *failure* of principle. It may, however, more adequately be represented as simply a difference of priorities. (Grimshaw 1986: 210)

The representatives of patriarchy in the novel fail to recognise Helen's priorities. Sir Gulliver condemns her tolerance of Maurice's collaboration as barbaric. The break-up of their marriage is seen as entirely her fault, an interpretation Helen accepts, though Sir Gulliver, with his rigid code of honour, his icy temper and his dry, legalistic approach to life, cannot have been an easy man to live with. He clearly sees Helen, in the words of Kristeva quoted above (p.59), as representing the threat of 'darkness and chaos' in his strictly ordered patriarchal life.

Richie too blames Helen. She does not fit into his view of what a woman should be. He feels that 'he and his fellows could not have struggled through so frightful, so hideously uncongenial a war, only to be rewarded with barbarism, with one's mother going out for her own dinner parties' (*WW*: 199). In Richie's scheme of things, women are supposed to be the primary carers. Grimshaw points out that women 'are especially vulnerable to charges of not-caring, since they are so often seen as defined by their caring role and capacities' (Grimshaw 1986: 217). Helen is, as we have seen, a good carer. She paints her children's rooms, tells them stories and entertains them. Despite the temporary fracture in her relationship with Barbary she enjoys being a mother. It is simply that her priorities are different from those of her son. Pamela, the patriarchal woman, also labels Helen selfish. Her understandable jealousy and fear of Helen degenerates on occasion into a proprietorial attitude towards Sir Gulliver and even towards Sir Gulliver's money: 'Who *pays* Mrs Cox I should like to know? flashed through Pamela's mind' (*WW*: 219). When they condemn Helen's selfishness, these representatives of 'civilised' society – Sir Gulliver, Richie and Pamela – reveal more about themselves than they realise.

Helen's maternal thinking does not (unlike Mrs Hilary's in *Dangerous Ages*) arise out of her own needs but out of careful attention to those of her daughter. It is for her mother's presence that Barbary yearns and so, at the end of the novel, Helen says: ' "I shall take care of her. Whatever other relationships I may have, she will come first . . . She'll be mine for always" ' (*WW*: 247; ellipsis mine). In future, as Helen makes clear here and in other passages, the mother–daughter relationship will override all others, even those with men: 'it's Lucien who must go, not my child, not Barby. She's always been first; she always will be, whatever she does' (*WW*: 211). 'Maternal thinking' (attention to the needs of others) represents hope for post-war society in counterbalance to Richie's pessimism. If, by having Barbary to live with her again, Helen can forgive even the murder of a much-loved husband, it must be possible for others to forgive too. Rather than prolonging grievances like those hunting down collaborators in France, Helen's love heals Barbary through forgiveness and reconciliation.

At the end of the novel, Helen is on the side of her daughter's selfhood, rescuing her from the father who has tried to make her fit into his society. Embedded in the text is the myth of Demeter, the goddess who raised her daughter Persephone from the underworld. In her discussion of the Demeter-Persephone myth, Adrienne Rich comments: 'Each daughter, even in the millenia before Christ, must have longed for a mother whose love for her and whose power were so great as to undo rape and bring her back from death' (Rich 1977: 240). This is, in effect, what Helen does for Barbary, rescuing her daughter from the patriarchal household of her father whose way of life nearly caused her death, and by her forgiveness healing the trauma caused by her torture and rape by German soldiers.

It may be reading against the grain to interpret Helen's actions as guided by principles of 'maternal thinking,' a concept Rose Macaulay, with her dislike of privileging mothers, would have in all probability rejected. It is likely that, as Jane Emery suggests in her biography (Emery 1991: 28–9), Macaulay intended Helen to be seen as some sort of pagan goddess, hedonistic and amoral, 'a force of nature,' Richie calls her (*WW*: 151). She is compared to Milo's Venus and the Lady of Elche. The pictures Helen paints on the walls of the Villa Fraises have mythical subjects and the bedtime stories she tells Barbary are from Greek mythology. Collioure is presented as a sensual paradise presided over by a hedonistic goddess. In Chapter 1 we saw that during the inter-war period scholars like Jane Harrison, whom Macaulay once met (Emery 1991: 136), were investigating early matriarchal cultures. In *Mythology* (1924), Harrison describes the matriarchy presided over by the Mother-God as communal, cooperative and life-giving, fostering women's independence and creativity and egalitarian relationships with men (for more on Harrison, see Chapter 7). So in Collioure Helen lives an independent life, free to express her creativity and to meet men on her own terms.

In creating this goddess-like creature Macaulay, perhaps inadvertently, tapped into some larger questions about motherhood. The fact that when reviewers criticised the book, Helen was the character they picked on to censure, suggests there was something about her portrait which made them uneasy. For Helen is disruptive of the patriarchal order. Not only her actions, but even her body makes the inhabitants of this patriarchy feel uncomfortable. Its 'generous, ample curves' are disapproved of by the 'thin and patriotic' Madame Michel (*WW*: 9). It casts a spell over Sir Gulliver: 'His eyes could not leave her face, her body, the curve of the hand that rested on her knee' (*WW*: 239). It provokes Pamela's jealousy: 'Her beauty shone richly magnificent . . .

it burnt into Pamela's nerves and senses, a flame that seared' (*WW*: 235; ellipsis mine). Helen's body dominates every scene where she appears. It is finally revealed as having transgressed, in the circumstances of Barbary's conception, the fundamental patriarchal law of legitimacy. *The World My Wilderness* is built around Helen's body, for the plot is ultimately resolved with reference to it – the revelation about Barbary's conception. For the first time Macaulay is writing the female body rather than censoring it.

When we turn to Helen's daughter, Barbary, we find that her story is Lacanian. It opens as the original, dyadic, satisfying relationship with the mother is broken off. She is sent to stay with her father who attempts to force her to enter the symbolic order (to 'civilise' her). At the same time, in the absence of her mother, Barbary seeks salvation in religion. Both these attempts to enter the symbolic order fail: 'his clever, cultured, law-bound civilisation was too remote' (*WW*: 84). So does her attempt to make a home amongst civilisation's ruins, for the ghosts of the City of London are all patriarchal ones – merchants and lawyers and clergymen. She almost dies there. Barbary's story is a potent illustration of the dangers to daughters of living in a patriarchy without the mother's protection.

Barbary belongs outside civilisation: 'Barbary was going back where she belonged, to the waste margins of civilisation' (*WW*: 110). For the crime of murder, she has been thrown out of the maternal Eden for a time but in the end she is brought back by her mother. Henceforth, Barbary will be protected by the maternal body from the world of the Law/the lawyer's world of her father. For Barbary, if the cost of entering civilisation is to break with her mother, the cost is too high. In the end, she and her mother will live outside the patriarchal order altogether: 'Helen supposed that neither of them would ever be in this room, this house, again' (*WW*: 251).

By the end of the novel, Helen has given up practising Kristeva's 'impossible dialectic.' She and Barbary will live henceforth in the female wilderness outside the patriarchy. Helen has absorbed enough of the values of the patriarchy to believe that the world into which she is taking Barbary is less noble than that of the Father: 'I am taking my child away from the higher to the lower' (*WW*: 250–1). Yet, if the world to which Helen will take Barbary is a wilderness, it is also a world of love: 'She must have sunshine, geniality, laughter, love' (*WW*: 251). It is a world where female sexuality finds free expression, as is evident in the subtext of the nature imagery at Collioure. It is a world of female bonding. This is lightly dwelt on, but Helen's description of her female friendships (*WW*: 98) gives a glimpse into the submerged world of female solidarity in a patriarchy. At the end, Helen shows solidarity even with Pamela whom she seeks to reassure. Such female bonding is an important part of being a woman in a patriarchy where, Chodorow and others have pointed out, an exclusive relationship with a man does not provide sufficient emotional satisfaction for a woman: 'Woman identification is a source of energy, a potential springhead of female power' (Rich 1987: 63). Helen's bonds with women reinforce her confidence in her identity as a woman.

Collioure is a place where the mother–daughter relationship can flourish. By presenting Collioure as a natural paradise, Macaulay hints at a mythical golden age in the mother–daughter relationship, anticipating Irigaray's description:

> There was a time when mother and daughter were the figure of a natural and social model. This couple was the guardian of the fertility of nature in general and of the relationships to the divine . . . The mother–daughter couple ensured the safeguard of human nourishment and the site of the oracular word . . . at that time the daughter respected her mother and her genealogy. (*Sexes et Parentés* quoted in Whitford 1991b: 177; ellipses mine)

This world remains on the margins of the symbolic order: the mother–daughter bond is powerless to subvert the patriarchal order in Irigaray's sense. A parallel may be drawn with Virginia's Woolf's failed attempt in this period to retrieve the mother's world (see Chapter 7). Nevertheless, by presenting the maternal world of Collioure as a more attractive place than the rigidly ordered household of Sir Gulliver, Macaulay does at least provide an alternative to the world of the patriarchy.

The World My Wilderness, with its revalorisation of motherhood and the female body, is startlingly different from Macaulay's previous work. This time the admired mother is not, like Daphne Sandomir, one of Macaulay's 'mental neutrals' (the phrase is Macaulay's own, from *Mystery at Geneva*, 1922: 150). She is a recognisably womanly woman. There are many passages which express Barbary's haunting need of her mother: 'Barbary had been a wild baby, a nervy, excited child, her mother her tower of refuge' (*WW*: 19); 'she was for ever her mother's' (*WW*: 84). Sir Gulliver tells Helen: ' "The child's whole heart is fixed on you, as it always has been" ' (*WW*: 242). In this late novel, fear and hatred of the mother in Macaulay's work have dissolved. The mother has become, as in Woolf, a rescuer and a nourisher, a place of refuge for a daughter battered by life in the patriarchy. The reasons behind this change of emphasis become clearer when we look at Macaulay's life.

For much of her life Rose Macaulay was in flight from the mother, both from her own mother's influence and from the woman inside herself. Grace Macaulay had desperately wanted her second child to be a son. Whether out of a desire to please her mother or because boys were allowed more freedom and adventures or, more likely, through a combination of motives, Macaulay spent the early part of her childhood living out a fantasy that she was a boy and would join the Navy when she grew up. Again, Horney's analysis of what she terms 'the masculinity complex' in women is illuminating: 'The dreams and symptoms of many women clearly demonstrate that basically they have not come to terms with their femininity. On the contrary, in their unconscious fantasy lives they have maintained the fiction of having actually been created as males' (Horney 1967: 76).

Though this fantasy had eventually to be given up, in adulthood Macaulay managed to escape many of the burdens borne by the average woman of her time by dint of earning her own living and not marrying. The life to which she aspired, and to some extent attained, was the kind of life to which she thought everyone entitled, namely one freed from the prison of gender. In her society, males were more likely to achieve this freedom than females. The very shape of her body echoed Macaulay's refusal of womanhood: she was painfully thin all her life and contemporaries frequently commented on her tomboyish figure. Androgyny for Macaulay was a means of escaping life as a woman and killing off, she hoped, the sexuality that was so troubling to her.

Certainly if her own mother was anything to go by, a woman's life would seem best avoided. From being a lively, well-educated young woman with a sure sense of her vocation as a teacher, Grace Conybeare declined after her marriage into an exhausted, domineering mother overburdened by the cares of her large family. Grace became a warning to her daughter of the dangers of women abandoning intellectual pursuits for domesticity. Macaulay's solution to living in a rigidly gendered society was to identify with her scholarly father's sceptical, reasoned approach to life as opposed to what she saw as her mother's excessive emotionalism and inconsistency.

Fleeing from mother to father is not without risks: as we have seen, in Irigaray's monologue, 'And the One doesn't stir without the Other' (1981), the daughter turns to her father only to find that he wants to socialise her to conform to his society's view of femininity. Upon her return to England at the age of thirteen, Macaulay was told very firmly by her father that she must give up talk of joining the Navy and behave like a young woman. This sudden revelation of the gendered society into which she had been born, together with her growing sexual awareness, seems to have triggered off some kind of crisis during Macaulay's teenage years. Like twelve-year-old Cary in *Keeping Up Appearances*, she felt revulsed by sex and, longing to reject the realities of her female body, immersed herself, like Maggie Tulliver, in Thomas à Kempis. Grace had tried to protect her daughters from sexual awareness for as long as possible, censoring passages in their reading by pasting pages together and inculcating them with the notion that sexuality equalled sin, a notion that Macaulay was never entirely to shed: the centrality of sexuality in Freud's thesis was one of Macaulay's main bones of contention against him (Emery 1991: 189).

It was Macaulay's father, too, who forbade her (aged twenty-eight) to go on a caravan holiday with Rupert Brooke. Once again her father was showing her that she could not claim the freedom of a man but, though Macaulay felt some resentment at this exertion of paternal authority (Emery 1991: 127), she never expresses against her father the hostility she felt towards her mother. As Dorothy Dinnerstein explains in *The Rocking of the Cradle*: 'To mother-raised humans, male authority is bound to look like a reasonable refuge from female authority' (Dinnerstein 1978: 175). In *Told by an Idiot*, Stanley Garden reflects: 'Men are marvellously restful. Eternal symbols of parenthood and the stability of life, to which women come back, as to strong towers of refuge, after their excursions and alarms' (Macaulay 1923/1983: 129).

What her upbringing gave Macaulay was a classic case of matraphobia. Adrienne Rich has defined matraphobia as a fear of the mother's power and a fear of becoming like her: 'Where a mother is hated to the point of matraphobia there may also be a deep underlying pull towards her, a dread that if one relaxes one's guard one will identify with her completely' (Rich 1977: 235). Macaulay fled her mother's domination, identified with her father and the wider world of scholarship to which he introduced her, but remained inwardly fearful that in the end it would be her emotional, irrational, thwarted mother she would turn out to resemble. *Dangerous Ages* was written at the height of her matraphobia while Macaulay was still living at home with her mother and saw no possibility of escape. Mrs. Hilary is generally taken to be a portrait of Grace Macaulay. Stephen Lumley is, partly, a portrait of Gerald O'Donovan, the married man with whom Macaulay had a lifelong relationship. As we have seen, in the novel Nan blames her mother for her affair with Lumley. Was Macaulay, sexually uncommitted as yet to O'Donovan (Emery 1991: 183), getting ready to blame her mother for their relationship? Is this novel a veiled threat to her mother along the lines of 'look what will happen if you go on behaving like this'? *Dangerous Ages* is a book written to punish her mother, an expression of rage on the part of a daughter who fears she will never break free.

By the time *The World My Wilderness* was published, Grace Macaulay had been dead for twenty-five years. Her daughter had firmly established herself in the professional world, she had no need to fear she was going to turn out like her mother, stranded without intellectual resources in later years. But Grace's death left Macaulay with a lingering sense of guilt. Her sister, Jean, said: 'I believe Rose was rather conscience-stricken about Mother's death' (Emery 1991: 205). When E. M. Forster's mother died in her eighties, Macaulay wrote to him: 'One thing, one touch of bitterness that her going can't have for you is what one so often feels – to wish that one had been different and nicer oneself, which does so embarb the pain of loss . . . My own mother (whom I loved) died in her 60s and I could envy you,' (Letter dated 1945, quoted in Emery 1991: 205; ellipsis mine). The awkwardness of the syntax here and the distancing effect of the 'one' indicates some sort of struggle still going on in Macaulay's mind. At the same time she is now able to state clearly that she had loved her mother.

Though seemingly content for most of the time with the pseudo-male role she had carved out for herself in the patriarchy, periods of war seem to have thrown Macaulay into turmoil and led her to rediscover the female principle. The First World War revealed the precarious nature of her foothold in the symbolic: she might identify with the male role but she was not allowed to fight for her country like a man. By the time of the Second World War she had realised that the symbolic order was itself flawed and dangerous to women. Emery sees the drowning of Ellen, the strange, mermaid-like creature in *And No Man's Wit* (1940), as symbolising Macaulay's fear that 'her most feminine self could not survive in the masculine landscape of war and politics,' (Emery 1991: 261). *The World My Wilderness* is, like *Non-Combatants and Others*, an attempt to heal herself at a time of personal crisis with a consoling image of a mother who nurtures her daughter.

Soon after writing *The World My Wilderness*, Macaulay was received back into the Anglican church, the church of her mother (her father had been agnostic). Scattered throughout Macaulay's letters to Father Johnson, the priest instrumental in bringing her back into the church, are references to Grace. A picture emerges of a self-confident, thoughtful, amusing woman who exercised an enormous influence on her daughter's life. Grace's opinions are cited with approval and the dark side of the mother–daughter relationship has entirely disappeared: 'My mother did amuse every one, as did my grandmother before her, and that is a great gift' (Macaulay 1961/1968: 278). Remembering her early Scripture lessons with her mother, she writes: 'I think my mother was a very wonderful person, with an extraordinary magnetising gift, and she kindled a kind of fire when she spoke of religion and being good. I have never since met anyone with so much gift for it' (Macaulay 1962: 138). In returning to the Anglican church there is definitely a sense in which Macaulay was being reconciled with her mother. This impulse towards reconciliation lies behind *The World My Wilderness*. In this novel, one of her finest, Macaulay discovered that, rather than being a hindrance, the mother's voice can be a source of inspiration for the woman writer.

4

Elizabeth Bowen: The Mother Betrayed

' "I hate women," ' says Lois in Elizabeth Bowen's second novel, *The Last September*, ' "But I can't think how to begin to be anything else" ' (Bowen 1929/1987: 99). Lois's dilemma is shared by many of Bowen's younger heroines: they are anxious to gain grown-up status, but not as women. ' "I don't know what I was meant to be," ' says Portia in *The Death of the Heart* (*DH*: 79). Lois and Portia are typical of the daughter figures in Bowen's novels. Like Rose Macaulay's tomboy heroines, they reject the patriarchy's text for their lives; unlike Macaulay's heroines who frequently possess an internal image of themselves as boys or young men, Bowen's young women look to older, more powerful women in an effort to establish their identity. Some of these mother figures are content with their lives as women: ' "I do like being a woman" ' says Mrs Kerr in *The Hotel* (*H*: 11). But some are in silent revolt against the narratives in which they have been imprisoned. Laurel's mother in *Friends and Relations* thinks, in relation to her daughter: 'I wish there were something else she could be, not a woman . . . *I can't bear life for her!*' (Bowen 1931/1946: 150–1; ellipsis mine). There is an ambivalence in Bowen's novels, on the part of both mothers and daughters, towards being a woman at all.

This ambivalence is hardly surprising in a patriarchal society where, as Karen Horney has pointed out (see Chapter 3), women and the bonds between them are constantly devalued. In *The Hotel* (1927) Sydney tells Mrs Kerr: ' "you and I are supposed to assume, or to seem everywhere to assume, that that man down in the garden could be more to either of us than the other" ' (*H*: 60). Unlike Macaulay who tries to evade her society's gender divisions by downplaying the differences between the genders, Bowen does not under-estimate the impact of those divisions on women's lives. Many of her heroines express the sense of being insecurely inscribed in the symbolic and a dissatisfaction with the roles prescribed for them as women.

In Bowen's earliest novel, *The Hotel*, Sydney seeks from Mrs Kerr a clue to a way of living a woman's life while avoiding the stereotypes of wife and mother. Sidney wants her identity to be mirrored back in Mrs Kerr's gaze; only then will she exist as a person: 'It became no longer a question of – What did Mrs Kerr think of her? – but rather – Did Mrs Kerr ever think of her? The possibility of not being kept in mind seemed to Sydney at that moment a kind of extinction' (*H*: 14). Ironically, it is because Mrs Kerr escapes the stereotype of conventional motherhood that she is unable to provide the validating motherly gaze Sydney needs.

Mrs Kerr is the first in a long line of powerful older women in Bowen's work. Such motherly sentiments as she expresses are a pose. She uses her son, Ronald, as a weapon against Sydney's demands for intimacy and deliberately humiliates Sydney by flaunting her motherhood. Though she cannot put this into words, Sydney suspects some 'falsity; an imposture' (*H*: 63) in Mrs Kerr's new-found feeling towards Ronald and in fact Mrs Kerr's motherhood *is* a fake: she responds to her son's obvious desire for a home by saying, ' "How long is it, I wonder, since you and I have kept house? Perhaps I have deprived you of something? – I cannot feel that I have" '(*H*: 95). She soon tires of his company: 'She tugged gently at a fold of her tea-gown on which he happened to be sitting and swept him away from her with a gesture' (*H*: 166).

Mrs Kerr rejects the role of the all-sacrificing, self-abnegating mother. Yet what other part is left to her in this society? She is a widow, but apparently an unmourning one, for her behaviour is confused with that of a divorcee (*H*: 54). She makes the experienced matrons in the drawing-room uneasy: ' "One is never comfortable in talking to her" ' (*H*: 52). She is a deviant in their world, refusing to conform to their stereotypes of widow and mother: ' "I say, if Milton doesn't come soon we shall run it fine," called Ronald in an unnatural, loud voice. Another woman would have jumped at this excuse to hurry back into the Hotel agitatedly calling . . . But Mrs Kerr stood there, and women's hearts hardened' (*H*: 171–2; ellipsis mine).

In her book, *Heroines and Hysterics*, Mary Lefkowitz outlines the life patterns available to women in the myths that still act on us today. She points out that in classical mythology, marriage and childbirth invariably lead to the death of the individual woman. These myths tell us that, celibacy apart, the only way for a woman to preserve her identity 'is to destroy the husband or children who have taken it away' (Lefkowitz 1981: 43). Mrs Kerr never mentions her husband and by the end of the novel she has effectively ended Ronald's hopes of maternal affection. Producing this sort of woman-as-destroyer is the danger society runs when it attempts to limit women to the roles of wife and mother.

In *The Hotel*, Elizabeth Bowen places the reader in an interesting dilemma: if we dismiss Mrs Kerr as a cruel and uncaring woman, aren't we also denying the mother's right to selfhood? Bowen points up the inadequacies of patriarchal stereotypes about motherhood. Ignoring these stereotypes, Mrs Kerr negotiates a place for herself in the symbolic on her own terms. Perhaps it is for this reason that, unlike so many of Bowen's characters, she can say: 'I'm not a Feminist, but I do like being a woman' (*H*: 11).

Rejection by Mrs Kerr leaves Sydney in a state of extreme shock, even paralysis. Seeking refuge in convention, she turns to Milton and accepts his previously rejected proposal of marriage. As we have seen, marriage in classical myth spells the death of the female as individual. This is the case here for it is automatically assumed that Sydney will give up her medical studies: ' "She was going, you know, to have been a doctor," ' says Eileen Lawrence (*H*: 126). Engaged, Sydney comes to feel that she has no personality of her own. She has been written into the patriarchal text: 'She stood between Tessa and Mrs Kerr as inanimate and objective as a young girl in a story told by a man' (*H*: 156). A near-fatal road accident makes Sydney realise that she must escape the confines of this text. Breaking off her engagement with Milton, she will not, however, return to Mrs Kerr whose cruelty she now recognises. In *The Hotel*, Sydney rejects the patriarchal text for women's lives but gets no help from her chosen mother figure as to how to live in the patriarchy without conforming to its text. Her story is left open-ended.

For mothers who do not succeed, as Mrs Kerr does, in moving beyond the stereotypes to establish their own identity, there is a danger they will be written out of the patriarchal text altogether. In *The Last September*, Lois's mother, dead years ago, is reduced in the text to a few scratchings on a window pane and a drawing on a wall. On the pane she has scribbled her maiden name, Laura Naylor; on the wall she 'had written L.N.; L.N., and left an insulting drawing of somebody, probably Hugo. She had scrawled with passion' (Bowen 1929/1987: 132). Both drawing and scratchings express the mother's rage and her attempt to assert her individuality. In Bowen's last novel, *Eva Trout* (1966), the eponymous heroine has been motherless from the age of two months. Iseult asks Eva's guardian, Constantine Ormeau: ' "Eva, of course, can't remember her?" "Alas. Motherless from the cradle." "So I had thought. Yet – this you may not know, Mr. Ormeau? – she maintains she remembers hearing her mother shriek." "Quite impossible." ' (Bowen 1966/1987: 39–40). Reduced to a shriek or faint scratchings on a window, these mothers bear out Irigaray's statement that our culture 'is based upon the murder of the mother' ('Women-Mothers, the Silent Substratum of the Social Order,' Whitford 1991a : 47).

Thwarted and silenced, not surprisingly Bowen's mothers turn in on themselves: ' "I saw then that all her life her power had never properly used itself," ' Naomi Fisher says of her mother in *The House in Paris* (*HP*: 183). The description, in this novel, of Mme Fisher lying on her sickbed provides a terrible picture of the mother's trapped energies: 'She lay, still only a little beyond surprise at this end to her, webbed down, frustrated, or, still more, like someone cast, still alive, as an effigy for their own tomb' (*HP*: 47-8). Behind Mme Fisher's slow decline lies a history of thwarted power.

In her house in Paris, Mme Fisher has played the role of surrogate-mother to the 'daughters' in her charge, policing them and preparing them for their role in the patriarchy. Her power is all the more terrifying for being unobservable: 'She asked no questions, but knew: she knew where you went, why, with whom and whether it happened twice. Though Paris was large, you were never out of her ken' (*HP*: 103). She is a woman who, in Phyllis Lassner's words: 'uses motherhood for power she cannot find anywhere else' (Lassner 1990: 83). As a mother of daughters, however, Mme Fisher's influence in the patriarchy is limited and in her relationship with Max Ebhart she spies a greater opportunity for power, bearing out Freud's theory that mothers transfer to sons the ambition they are compelled to suppress in themselves.

Mme Fisher wishes to mould Max, a rootless Jew, in order to give him access to the power she herself has been denied in a patriarchal society. For a time she is successful. Max tells Karen: ' "As she saw me, I became" ' (*HP*: 138). She controls not only Max's career but also his sexuality: ' "Any loves I enjoyed stayed inside her scope" ' (*HP*: 139). To test her authority, she brings Karen and Max together and then destroys Max's belief in his love for Karen by casting doubt on his motives. Mme Fisher thus becomes for Max the devouring mother, swallowing up his attempts at independence by her terrible understanding of him. Naomi says: ' "I saw then that Max did not belong to himself. He could do nothing that she had not expected; my mother was at the root of him" '(*HP*: 182). The only way for Max to escape Mme Fisher's knowledge of him is to kill himself.

In her effect upon Max, Mme Fisher resembles Jung's archetype of the terrible devouring mother (as opposed to the nurturing, life-giving Great Goddess in Jane Harrison's works). According to Jung and his disciple, Neumann, the Great Mother, the loving and the terrible mother originally worshipped as a goddess, became submerged with the development of the patriarchy so that today she survives only as part of the collective unconscious. The loving mother became split from the terrible mother and it is the latter who has come to represent 'within male mythology and psychology, the grasping (female) unconscious whose power to fascinate, and ultimately castrate, must be permanently destroyed by the (male) hero' (Elias-Button in Davidson and Broner 1980: 202). In his study, *The Great Mother*, Neumann points out that the irruption of the archetype of the devouring Mother into the male psyche can induce suicidal leanings (Neumann 1963: 149).

In Bowen's novel, however, the exercise of maternal power when pushed to the extreme is deadly to the mother as well as to the child. Naomi says that when her mother's influence ' "had used itself she was like the dead, like someone killed in a victory" ' (*HP*: 183). Recent feminist writing has emphasised the potentially creative powers of the Medusa-mother (see, for example, Elias-Button 1980) but Mme Fisher never succeeds in harnessing her anger to anything positive. Even when physically paralysed, her destructive will lives on: in her brief conversation with Leopold, she plants enough ideas in his mind to wreak havoc for years to come in his relationship with his mother. This last exercise of authority in all probability kills her.

Naomi Fisher is the typical daughter of a powerful mother – masochistic, clumsy, inefficient. Jung's description of the daughter who identifies completely with her mother fits Naomi uncannily: 'She is content to cling to her mother in selfless devotion while at the same time unconsciously striving, almost against her will, to tyrannize over her, naturally under the mask of complete loyalty and devotion,' ('Psychological Aspects of the Mother Archetype' 1938 in Jung 1986: 117). So Mme Fisher, when reprimanded by Naomi, tells Henrietta: ' "You see? . . . I am under control" ' (*HP*: 49; ellipsis mine).

Jung continues: 'These bloodless maidens are by no means immune to marriage. On the contrary, despite their shadowiness and passivity, they command a high price on the marriage market . . . they are so empty that a man is free to impute to them anything he fancies' (Jung 1986: 117; ellipsis mine). Max, who needs the peaceful refuge Naomi can provide, thinks of her as 'furniture or the dark' (*HP*: 146). Not until much later does he realise that he has been mistaken in Naomi's character: ' "she is more than stone; she desires to be desired" ' (*HP*: 163). Like her mother, Naomi attempts to shape Max's future and, later, that of his son. She forces Karen and Max to meet in order to test their feeling for each other. She takes control of Leopold's destiny by placing him with the Grant Moodys. Yet, in the end, all her actions are ineffective. She is powerless to keep anyone safe. Even Henrietta runs rings round her. Her endless knitting, symbol of the fate-governing role of women (see Neumann 1963: 227–33), keeps slipping out of her control: 'one of Miss Fisher's needles clattered on to the parquet and she dived after it: something had been too much' (*HP*: 49).

Mme Fisher is not the only mother in *The House in Paris* who is destroyed in the process of exercising maternal power. Though on a more realistic, less Gothic level than Mme Fisher, Mrs Michaelis ruthlessly polices her daughter's life. If the atmosphere in Mme Fisher's house in Paris is full of suppressed rage, life in Mrs Michaelis's house is carefully edited. Karen's mother has successfully suppressed her own emotions ('Mrs Michaelis had not wept for years, and never in the drawing-room,' *HP*: 126) and she expects her daughter to do the same. When passion threatens to disrupt her household, Mrs Michaelis moves swiftly to contain it, fighting to preserve her home and her values by adopting a policy of silence which completely disempowers her daughter: 'Karen saw what was ruthless inside her mother. Unconscious things – the doors, the curtains, guests, Mr Michaelis – lent themselves to this savage battle for peace. Sun on the hall floor, steps upstairs in the house had this same deadly intention not to know' (*HP*: 173). Karen reflects: 'She has made me lie for a week. She will hold me inside the lie till she makes me lose the power I felt I had' (*HP*: 174). There is no sympathy here for a mother under pressure from a patriarchal society. Mrs Michaelis is presented as having so completely identified with her society's values that she will fight to preserve them, even at the price of her daughter's happiness. Karen thinks: 'Love is obtuse and reckless; it interferes. But when mother does not speak it is not pity or kindness; it is worldliness beginning so deep down that it seems to be the heart' (*HP*: 174).

In an effort to wrest some of the power from her mother and affirm to herself the reality and importance of her night with Max, Karen breaks the silence between them. Mrs Michaelis immediately counters by downplaying the importance of Karen's affair with Max (she was missing Ray, it's just another of the wild ideas she has had ever since she was a child, she is young, in a year's time she will have forgotten all about this). She paints Max's motives in the worst possible light (he took advantage of her innocence, he is after her money, he is a Jew on the make). Mrs. Michaelis continually denies her daughter a point of view. Karen's attempts to establish an identity in opposition to her come to nothing. With the news of Max's death, Mrs Michaelis moves in to re-establish harmony in the home: 'in these weeks since the telegram she had, as a mother, risen to her full height, wrapping up in gentleness and in a comprehension that sometimes came too close' (*HP*: 178-9). This last phrase shows how near Mrs Michaelis comes to being, like Mme Fisher, an all-devouring mother, killing by understanding.

Mrs Michaelis's reaction to Karen's pregnancy is very like that of the mothers described by Helene Deutsch in her chapter on 'Unmarried Mothers' in *The Psychology of Women,* mothers 'whose middle class morality suffers a heavy blow from their daughters' illegitimate motherhood, and whose main concern is to preserve the family's social prestige' (Deutsch 1945: 359). Mrs Michaelis dies shortly after Karen's marriage to Ray. In one sense she has triumphed – she has 'passed off' Karen's indiscretion and seen her daughter's social position safely secured – but it is a victory won at the price of her health and, in the end, her life. The struggle to socialise her daughter destroys the relationship between them: Karen cannot bear to be with her mother after Leopold's birth. The description of Mrs Michaelis dying 'more or less peacefully' (*HP*: 219) sounds terribly ironic.

In Bowen's novel, the exercise of maternal power kills mothers as well as their offspring. The fate of both Mme Fisher and Mrs Michaelis shows that while the image of the terrible devouring mother may be, as Jung and Neumann argue, all-powerful in the collective unconscious, in the context of life in the patriarchy her power is limited and often destructive to herself. There is a discrepancy between the powerful mother of the psyche and the actual historical position of mothers. More clearly than Macaulay, Bowen shows the way in which mothers are trapped in the patriarchal text.

There are other devouring mothers in Bowen's novels, from the interfering Lady Naylor in *The Last September* (1929) to the darkly farcical Mrs Kelway ('Muttikins') in *The Heat of the Day* (1949). Always their power is limited. Lady Naylor's discouragement of Gerald as a suitor for Lois, though devastating at the time, is rendered pointless since shortly afterwards he is killed in the Troubles. In *To the North* (1932), Lady Waters's meddling bungles everything and leads directly to two deaths. In *The Heat of the Day*, Mrs Kelway's power, though coruscating in the home, does not extend past her front door: 'It was the indoors she selected, she consecrated . . . this was a bewitched wood. If her power came to an end at the white gate, so did the world' (Bowen 1949/1987: 110; ellipsis mine).

Some of these dominant mothers (Mrs Kerr, Mme Fisher) rebel against the patriarchal text for their lives; others (Mrs Michaelis, Mrs Kelway), eagerly embrace that text. But there are also in Bowen's novels mothers who are rebellious but not devouring; women whose refusal to mother, rather than being a protest against society's roles for women, comes from some deep-seated psychological resistance within themselves. Such a woman is Karen Michaelis who features in *The House in Paris* as both daughter and mother. In this context, the novel becomes a frightening account of the psychology of women, particularly in relation to motherhood, a theme on which, at times, Bowen anticipates the work of Helene Deutsch. As we saw in Chapter 2, in contrast to the rosy picture of motherhood presented by the media in the inter-war period, Deutsch points out the reluctance of some women to mother.

The tripartite structure of *The House in Paris* enables Bowen to pose the question: what is a mother? In Part One the yearning of a child for his mother is shown. Lacking his mother's validating glance, Leopold searches for an identity. Henrietta, the little English girl, becomes 'his first looking-glass' (*HP*: 34–5). In Leopold's fantasy, a mother is someone who identifies with her child's wishes in every way. He tells Henrietta: ' "She's the same as me" ' (*HP*: 59). The narrative in Part One breaks off at the point where it is borne in on

Leopold that this is not what a mother is. Karen has refused to play her part in his fantasy. He is forced to recognise her subjectivity: 'She was not, then, the creature of thought. Her will, her act, her thought spoke in the telegram . . . So she lived outside himself; she was alive truly' (*HP*: 194; ellipsis mine). Part Two of *The House in Paris* sends us back into the past for the mother's story.

The account of Karen's relationship with her mother reveals the extent to which a daughter's sense of identity may be formed by her mother and her own capacity for mothering helped or hindered by that relationship. Mrs Michaelis wishes to write her daughter into the romance plot and Karen herself feels a strong pull to make her life resemble her mother's. Though aware that the world has shrunk and her future closed off after her engagement to Ray, nevertheless 'Karen was glad to fall back on her mother's view of things' (*HP*: 69). It is only in Ireland, visiting Aunt Violet, that Karen realises how indelibly she is becoming written into the conventional woman's text. Her aunt's questions unsettle her: 'having been so much a woman all through her own life, had she hoped her niece might be something more? Her open-minded questions touched a spring in Karen that young people dread: all your youth you want to have your greatness taken for granted; when you find it taken for granted, you are unnerved' (*HP*: 85).

Karen both wants and does not want to be 'something more' than a woman. Frightened of Max as a young girl (or of her feelings for him), Karen allows herself to fall in love with him only when she sees how well he can fit into her world. As a young girl, with what Bowen calls a young girl's 'natural love of the cad' (*HP*: 108), Karen had exaggerated whatever was anti-social in Max. Meeting him again, as Naomi's fiancé, 'her Michaelis view of life quickly fitted him in' (*HP*: 108). Even in passion, Karen remains her mother's daughter, seeking safety. Max tells her: ' "You were not made to leap in the dark either" ' (*HP*: 112).

Leopold comes into being as an act of rebellion on Karen's part. Spending a night with Max has been too easy. She has got away with rebellion without anyone knowing: 'I am let back, safe, too safe; no one will ever know . . . What they never know will soon never have been . . . I shall die like Aunt Violet wondering what else there was; from this there is no escape for me after all' (*HP*: 152; ellipses mine). She thinks (wrongly, as it turns out), that 'to be with Ray will be like being with mother' (*HP*: 153). A child, however, would provide permanent proof of her rebellion: 'He would be the mark our hands did not leave on the grass . . . They would not know where to turn to save me for themselves . . . The street would stay torn up' (*HP*: 153–4; ellipses mine).

Motherhood becomes linked in Karen's mind with rebellion against her mother's world. In volume 2 of *The Psychology of Women*, Deutsch, analysing the psychology of the 'unmarried mother,' found that 'a hateful protest against the mother often contains revenge tendencies, and when a young girl becomes . . . an unmarried mother, she often . . . fulfills a fantasy' (Deutsch 1945: 349; ellipses mine). When Karen later takes fright at her power to rebel and regresses to imitating her mother, she has also to reject Leopold who has been part of her rebellion. Again Deutsch is illuminating: 'Social fears often prevent a woman from experiencing the fulfilment of her greatest longing as a real joy and the most motherly young women are often ready to renounce their illegitimate children . . . under pressure of the instinct of self-preservation' (Deutsch 1945: 48; ellipsis mine). In this context, it seems to me that Phyllis Lassner (1990: 73–96) is mistaken when she describes Karen's refusal to mother as a protest against motherhood *per se*. Karen rejects Leopold because she fears him. In her mind, he stands for the passionate side of her nature on which she turns her back when she finally marries Ray. One could compare the earlier Bowen novel, *Friends and Relations*, where the child Hermione, 'a preposterous child for Janet' (Bowen 1931/1946: 53), expresses all the passion Janet, her mother, has repressed.

Motherhood for Karen is not a trap, but a challenge. Accepting, not rejecting, Leopold would have been her rebellion. But Karen is too much her mother's daughter. She cannot carry through her revolt. In her marriage to Ray she becomes passive, deferring to her husband's wishes, 'wanting most of all to live like her mother' (*HP*: 218). As Deutsch explains:

> Very often such women transfer the centre of gravity of the conflict to outward reality and attempt to resolve it by renouncing the child. Here the inner world is disavowed, the woman is guided by the outside world, and she imagines that by adjusting herself to its demands she can achieve the *status quo ante*. This disavowal of the inner world is not always permanently successful . . . she is exposed to the danger of a subsequent reaction. (Deutsch 1945: 378; ellipsis mine)

Of one unmarried woman who gave up her child, Deutsch notes: 'her behaviour revealed that despite her renunciation, she had not achieved her goal of liberating herself from her sense of guilt. She lived in perpetual fear that someone might discover that she was an unmarried mother . . . She behaved like a hunted criminal' (Deutsch 1945: 353; ellipsis mine). Karen too behaves as if she were a 'criminal', punishing herself for having had an illegitimate child by a masochistic submission to Ray.

Karen's emotional paralysis and hysteria at the thought of Leopold arise because she refuses to leave her mother behind. She imitates her mother's tactics, employing against Leopold the same strategy of silence her own mother had employed against herself: 'The husk of silence round him was complete' (*HP*: 219). Unable to disentangle herself from her mother, Karen becomes blocked in her own mothering and is incapable of expressing her need for Leopold except through hysteria. Deutsch's comment on the neurotic mother is relevant to Karen's feelings about Leopold: 'The child loses his original meaning and is subjected to emotional impulses that were not meant to concern him . . . as a part of his own mother, who directs toward her child her masochistic fury against herself, he is hated or rejected,' (Deutsch 1945: 329; ellipsis mine). So Karen tells Ray: ' "He is more than a little boy. He is Leopold. You don't know what he is" ' (*HP*: 215). In the portrait of Karen Michaelis, Bowen presents a frightening picture of a woman ashamed to express her own needs and afraid of her power to rebel.

Emotionally blocked, Karen is unable to rise to the challenge posed by Leopold. A resolution is brought about by a man, Ray, who is capable, because he *is* a man, of putting some distance between the child and himself. As Nancy Chodorow has said: 'fathers know their children more as separate people than mothers do' (Chodorow 1978: 180). In turn, the child knows his father 'under the sway of the reality principle,' (*op.cit.* 179–80). Leopold, who has such difficulty separating his real mother from his fantasies about her, is quickly made aware of Ray as a personality outside his own: 'He was made conscious of someone's being consciously other than Leopold' (*HP*: 222 3). It seems problematic to regard *The House in Paris* as an explicitly feminist text, as Lassner does, when the solution is achieved by a man and paternal love is presented as more rational and effective than maternal love. In Bowen's novel it is women, both mothers and daughters, who have difficulty establishing intersubjective relationships.

As we have seen, many of Helene Deutsch's comments on unmarried mothers can be applied to Karen Michaelis, showing once again the way in which female novelists and female psychoanalysts in the inter-war period were observing similar situations and drawing similar conclusions. Bowen always resisted the label feminist for herself because she felt it denied the importance of the non-professional woman and the sphere of personal relations which was what fascinated her as a novelist (Glendinning 1977: 59). Her interest in women in the home and her presidency of the Women's Institute at Headington, align Bowen with the period's New Feminists and their emphasis on wives and mothers. Arguably, Bowen belongs to that tradition of conservative women writers identified by Alison Light in her book *Forever England* (1991) who were attempting to refashion domestic life. In *The House in Paris*, Bowen may not provide a feminist resolution, but she certainly highlights the dangers of confining women to the domestic sphere and the problems women experience in mothering. She undermines the notion, so prevalent in newspapers and advertising of the period, that all women are naturally fitted to mother. In Bowen's short story, 'The Little Girl's Room', Clara Ellis exclaims:

' "Women – how they ever bring up their own children!" Mrs Letherton-Channing pulled off one or two dead roses. "Look how they fail," she said placidly' (Bowen 1985: 430).

The theme of women's resistance to motherhood is continued in Bowen's next novel, *The Death of the Heart* (1938). Anna Quayne has built her life around fear of failure. Actual failures, in her career, in a love affair, have only strengthened her resolve not to commit herself. She had expected to have children but two miscarriages make her retreat from any further exposure to false hopes. As Deutsch says: 'Many women express their fear of motherhood by becoming functionally incapable of it' (Deutsch 1945: 292). In the unnurturing environment Anna has created at Windsor Terrace life is 'edited' (*DH*: 171) of family feeling and indeed of any kind of emotion. The arrival of Thomas's half-sister Portia in search of a home and a family exposes the flaws in Anna's manner of living. Anna has carefully constructed a text for her life and she does not want Portia interfering with it. Anna's way of life is worldly and it requires a complex, sophisticated mind to read it with any sympathy; Portia's innocent, blindly literal reading simply points up Anna's inadequacies; she cannot rise to the text of family life Portia has prepared for her. 'Well, she'll never find any answer here, thought Anna . . . It's no use her looking everywhere like that. Who are we to have her questions brought here?' (*DH*: 246; ellipsis mine). Among the reasons why some women find it difficult to mother, Helene Deutsch notes 'a feeling of insufficiency with regard to the great emotional demands of motherhood' (Deutsch 1945: 47). Anna's fear of failure prevents her from even trying to rise to Portia's demands.

In her portrayal of women who refuse to mother, Bowen interestingly runs counter to current psychological thinking on women. Both the object-relations theory favoured by American feminists such as Chodorow and French feminism represented by, for example, Irigaray and Kristeva present women as having fluid ego boundaries and seeking relationships with others. In Bowen, it is women – Mrs Kerr, Anna Quayne – who flee connection and seek to maintain boundaries between themselves and others. Yet, despite these elder women's lack of encouragement, younger women look to them for a clue as to how to achieve grown-up status: in *The Death of the Heart*, as in *The Hotel,* Bowen shows a daughter figure actively seeking out a 'mother' because the latter seems to hold a key as to how to negotiate life in the patriarchy. In the earlier novel, Sydney's story was left open-ended; *The Death of the Heart* suggests a possible resolution to the daughter's story.

In *The Death of the Heart*, sixteen-year-old Portia has to learn to read the complex text of life at Windsor Terrace where 'people said what they did not mean, and did not say what they meant' (*DH*: 59). Nothing in Portia's previous life has prepared her for this kind of text. The intense, symbiotic relationship she had with her mother, Irene, has left her, for the purposes of understanding upper middle-class life, illiterate: 'Untaught, they had walked arm-in-arm along city pavements, and at nights had pulled their beds closer together or slept in the same bed – overcoming, as far as might be, the separation of birth. Seldom had they faced up to society – when they did, Irene did the wrong thing, then cried' (*DH*: 56). The fashionable girls' school to which Anna sends Portia highlights the latter's ignorance of how to behave in society: 'Irene herself – knowing that nine out of ten things you do direct from the heart are the wrong thing, and that she was not capable of doing anything better – would not have dared to cross the threshold' (*DH*: 56).

Portia, however, has to cross the threshold. In Lacanian terms, she has to leave behind the symbiotic relationship with the mother and join the world of the father, the world of language and civilisation. It is indeed a letter from the father, bequeathing Portia to Thomas and Anna, that first threatens the dyadic unity of mother and child which is then finally broken up by Irene's death. At Windsor Terrace, Portia substitutes for the absent mother, language (her diary).

It has been suggested by one feminist critic (Chessman 1983: 69–85) that Portia yearns to get back to the symbiotic relationship with her mother. This does not seem quite to be the case. By taking up her pen, Portia signifies her acceptance of the phallus (in Lacanian terms, the law of the father). She knows she has no choice but to acquire language and enter the symbolic order: she is 'aware of the world in which she *had to live*'(*DH*: 29; my emphasis). Discussing Lacan, Toril Moi has said: 'The subject may or may not like this order of things, but it has no choice: to remain in the Imaginary is equivalent to becoming psychotic and incapable of living in human society' (Moi 1985/1990: 100). Repressing her desire for the pre-oedipal mother, Portia enters the symbolic order (writes her diary) in order to understand the patriarchal 'mother,' Anna. That Anna is a patriarchal woman is established in the first scene in the novel where she obligingly writes herself down in order to conform to St Quentin's (malicious) view of women: 'she had this little way of travestying herself and her self-pities, till the view she took of herself, when she was with him, seemed to concert exactly with the view he took of her sex' (*DH*: 8).

Though Portia embarks on her diary in an attempt to understand the patriarchal mother, the memory of her silent communication with the pre-oedipal mother, Irene, remains with her and inspires her need for a truer language than that used by Anna and her friends (on this point I am in agreement with Chessman 1983: 80). In an interesting passage St Quentin shows his awareness of, in Kristeva's terms, the semiotic that presses upon symbolic language and is glimpsed in dreams, madness, fissures in discourse and of Portia's closeness to it: ' "I swear that each of us keeps, battened down inside himself, a sort of lunatic giant – impossible socially, but full-scale – and that it's the knockings and batterings we sometimes hear in each other that keeps our intercourse from utter banality. Portia hears these the whole time; in fact she hears nothing else" ' (*DH*: 310).

Searching for this simpler language, Portia finds herself up against the myriad subterfuges of language in the patriarchal world of Windsor Terrace. Failing to understand Anna's subtleties, she reports her conversations literally and in so doing, lays bare all Anna's little selfishnesses and cruelties. The daughter, living up to her Shakespearian name, judges the patriarchal mother and exposes her limitations. There follows, though Portia is only half-conscious of this, a power struggle between 'mother' and 'daughter', each trying to wrest the text of their relationship from the other.

Anna, the patriarchal woman, dismisses Portia's diary as 'deeply hysterical' (*DH*: 10), a favourite male response to women's writing. ' "It was not like *writing* at all" ' she says (*DH*: 11).The text in which she seeks to imprison Portia is a farcical one of muddle and misunderstanding in which Portia has ' "made nothing but trouble since before she was born" ' (*DH*: 10). In Anna's narrative, Portia's father is presented as an overgrown schoolboy gone to seed and her mother as a vulgar little thing. Their dignity is undermined in every possible way till even St Quentin is led to exclaim that her story curdles his blood. When he meets Portia, he questions Anna's text: ' "What a high forehead she's got . . . I wonder where she got that distinction. From what you say, her mother was quite a mess" ' (*DH*: 30; ellipsis mine). Anna's story is later rewritten by Portia herself and by Matchett who rescues Portia's father from Anna's demeaning account. Anna's narrative of Portia is unreliable and goes on being so. She is determined to write up both Irene and Portia as tarts: ' "she's Irene's own child, you know" ' (*DH*: 120).

In order to combat Anna's text and force her to participate in the one she has written for her, Portia has to become adept in reading the society in which Anna lives. She has, for instance, to learn how to read Anna's friend, Eddie. To Portia, Eddie appears natural, open and naïve. He is not: 'his apparent rushes of Russian frankness proved, when you came to look back at them later, to have been more carefully edited than you had known at the time' (*DH*: 62). Portia has no experience to go on in reading Eddie. As he tells her, she has to learn that a lover cannot replace the pre-oedipal closeness with the mother: ' "it's simply intolerable . . . because I said I loved you, you expect me to be as sweet to you as your mother" ' (*DH*: 281–2; ellipsis mine). Portia has misread Eddie completely. At the end of the novel, she walks around Eddie's room giving 'the impression of being someone who, having lost their way in a book or mistaken its whole import, has to go back and start from the beginning again' (*DH*: 277).

Her constant reiteration in their last scene together of phrases like 'I've got no way of telling' and 'I don't know what is unspeakable' underlines her bewilderment.

The only person who could help Portia interpret the text of grown-up life correctly is Anna. This is made clear at Waikiki where Portia dreams she is sharing a book with a little girl. The girl is Anna as she appears in Mrs Heccomb's sentimental portrait. Portia 'found she no longer knew how to read – she dare not tell Anna, who kept turning the pages over. She knew they must both read – so the fall of Anna's hair [cutting off communication between them] filled her with despair' (*DH*: 140-1). The dream registers Anna's refusal to help Portia 'read' life, but it also leaves Portia with a feeling of guilt: 'she had not been kind to Anna' (*DH*: 141). The dream is a turning-point. Portia ceases judging Anna or at least learns, in the words of Shakespeare's heroine, to temper justice with mercy. Portia begins to see that the withholding, cauterising mother may have her own vulnerability:

> That kitten, for instance – had it died? Anna never spoke of it. Had Anna felt small at day school? . . . Did Anna also, sometimes, not know what to do next? Because she knew what to do next, because she knew what to laugh at, what to say, did it always follow that she knew where to turn? Inside everyone, is there an anxious person who stands to hesitate in an empty room? (*DH*: 141; ellipsis mine)

Portia recognises the vulnerable child inside Anna that has been lost, or overlain, by a worldly mask.

What Portia must begin to do if she is ever to bridge the gap between the potentially motherly little girl cuddling the kitten and the grown woman who refuses to mother, is to see Anna as a separate person with her own history of suffering. The daughter must cease projecting her own needs on to the mother and enter into an intersubjective relationship with her: 'the need for *mutual* recognition, the necessity of recognizing as well as being recognized by the other . . . is crucial to the intersubjective view . . . mutual recognition, including the child's ability to recognize the mother as a person in her own right, is as significant a developmental goal as separation,' (Benjamin 1990: 23–4; ellipses mine).

This point is underlined by Major Brutt who suggests to Portia that she has been too stern a judge of Thomas and Anna and it is, in a sense, what everyone tells Portia in this last section, from Eddie's exclamation ' "My God we've got to live in the world" ' (*DH*: 282) to St Quentin who tells her that it does not do write things down just as they occur, facts must be glossed: ' "if one didn't let oneself swallow some few lies, I don't know how one would ever carry the past" ' (*DH*: 249). Portia agrees to give Anna and Thomas a second chance.

She sets them a test of the heart. The fact that it takes them so long to decide what to do, shows how far removed their life is from the spontaneous gesture.

Spurred on by the situation Portia has created, Anna makes some tentative steps towards empathy with her. In fact, though Anna is irritated and unnerved by Portia, throughout the book it is she who has noticed things about the girl to which others, including Thomas, have been blind. Anna notices when Portia has been crying; she knows that she and Matchett are in league and why; she understands all too well what Portia expects of her. As Thomas says at one point: ' "If you were half as heartless as you make out, you would be an appallingly boring woman" ' (*DH*: 242). Anna is not heartless, she simply lacks the courage to respond to Portia. In this final scene, she does go some way to acknowledging Portia's viewpoint in the speech beginning, ' "If I were Portia?" ' (*DH*: 312), speaking for Portia so well that St Quentin says in surprise: ' "This is all quite new, Anna. How much is the diary, how much is you?" ' (*DH*: 312). It is Anna, finally, who comes up with the solution of sending Matchett to fetch Portia.

By the end of the book, therefore, Anna has gone some way to acknowledging the 'daughter's' point of view. In sending Matchett, Anna admits her significance in Portia's life and the importance of the link between Windsor Terrace and the past. She also acknowledges, what Matchett has felt all along, that Portia is the heir to Windsor Terrace. The patriarchal mother accepts the 'daughter's' right to a place in the kingdom. But there are no facile solutions to the mother–daughter relationship; as Anna says: ' "I shall always insult her; she will always persecute me" ' (*DH*: 313), that is, Portia will always seek more affection from Anna than Anna can give. But at least the daughter's right to a viewpoint has been admitted. Uniquely in Bowen's work, the mother figure voluntarily renounces some of her power and, unusually for literature of this period, the daughter has in some small way changed the life of the mother. The needy daughter has written herself into a story and the resisting mother has in the end responded. Together mother and daughter have renegotiated the text of their relations.

However it is not a text that will be subversive in Irigaray's sense. Rather than rewriting the patriarchal text, Anna will show Portia how to live within it. There is a cost to this. Writing has given Portia access to power for the first time in her life. Her diary has seriously rattled the inhabitants of Windsor Terrace. But she cannot enter the 'male' world of authorship without losing some of her innocence. Indeed, if we are to believe St Quentin, Portia's innocence was lost the moment she took up the pen/phallus: ' "Style is the thing that's always a bit phoney," ' he says, ' ' "and at the same time you cannot write without style" ' (*DH*: 11). However plain Portia's writing may seem, the very fact of writing entails untruth, 'polishing up' the facts: ' "that's style," ' says St Quentin of the first sentence in her diary (*DH*: 11). When Portia deliberately destroys Major Brutt's sentimental text about Anna, the 'death of the heart' has already begun to set in for her. By the end of the book, she has become thoroughly disabused. She has seen her childhood through the eyes of Thomas and Anna, as funny and slightly despicable. She has seen Eddie renege on their shared private world. Her innocence, once lost, will be lost forever. As she tells Major Brutt: ' "This can't happen again" ' (*DH*: 292). From now on, Portia will learn to make compromises with the world. Her first compromise is to ask Major Brutt to marry her, seeking comfort after Eddie's betrayal with a man she trusts but does not love. In the same way Anna, let down by Pidgeon, had compromised with Thomas. In the patriarchy, the daughter's suffering repeats that of the mother. ' "Is this being grown up?" ' Portia asks Major Brutt (*DH*: 293).

In addition to loss of innocence, entry into language involves forgetting. To become a speaking/writing subject in the patriarchy means to betray the pre-oedipal union with the mother: 'Portia was learning to live without Irene, not because she denied or had forgotten that once unfailing closeness between mother and child, but because she no longer felt her mother's cheek on her own . . . or smelled the sachet-smell from Irene's dresses' (*DH*: 148; ellipsis mine). The narrator comments: 'The heart may think it knows better: the senses know that absence blots people out . . . We desert those who desert us; we cannot afford to suffer; we must live how we can' (*ibid.* ellipsis mine). Forgetting the pre-oedipal mother is the most heart-rending, because most inevitable, of Portia's compromises with the world.

Some of Bowen's heroines refuse to make that compromise. Cousin Nettie in *The Heat of the Day*, remains locked into silence, her 'madness' providing the excuse for her refusal to participate in the story of the woman in the Big House and provide an heir to continue the patriarchal tradition: ' "Here I am," ' she tells Roderick ' "and you can't make any more stories out of that" ' (Bowen 1949/1987: 214). In the same novel, Louie abandons her struggle with language and returns to her home in Kent where she recreates with her baby the silent relationship with the pre-oedipal mother. ' "I have no words" ' she tells Connie (*op. cit.* 145). ' "At home where I used always to be there never used to be any necessity *to* say" ' (*op. cit.* 246).

In *Eva Trout*, Eva, motherless since a baby, yearns for the wordless union with the pre-oedipal mother. Iseult, her teacher, starts to bring Eva into the symbolic by encouraging her to think rationally: ' "try joining things together: this, then that, then the other. That's thinking; at least, that's beginning to think" ' (*ET*: 62). But Eva clings to the silence of the womb and Iseult abandons her task, leaving Eva's identity unformed. She ' "sent me back again – to be nothing" ' (*ET*: 185). Eva retreats into silence and adopts a deaf-mute baby, Jeremy. For years they live together in wordless communication, 'near as twins in a womb' (*ET*: 188). In this way they can control their own text: 'They were within a story to which they imparted the only sense' (*ET*: 189). Returning to England, however, Eva's 'mistrust of or objection to verbal intercourse . . . began to be undermined . . . She was ready to talk' (*ET*: 188; ellipses mine). She plans to write herself into the patriarchal text by marriage to Henry. She has discounted the fact that by doing this, she is betraying her years with Jeremy: 'She had not computed the cost for him of entry into another dimension' (*ET*: 189). Jeremy punishes her for abandoning their pre-oedipal union by gunning her down. Eva never makes it into the symbolic; her last words reflect her continuing difficulty with language: ' "Constantine," asked Eva, "what is 'concatenation'?" ' (*ET*: 268).

When they do live in the symbolic, Bowen's women express dissatisfaction with language: 'Perhaps some day words will be different or there will be others,' thinks Emmeline in *To the North* (Bowen 1932/1945: 117). Or they enter language and culture at a tangent. Henrietta notices Naomi Fisher's 'peculiar idiom': 'Often when she spoke she seemed to be translating, and translating rustily. No phrase she used was what anyone could quite mean; they were doubtful, as though she hoped they would do' (*HP*: 19).

Nevertheless, though it cannot be on their own terms, women have no choice but to enter the symbolic. Bowen said memorably: 'it is not only our fate but our business to lose innocence, and once we have lost that it is futile to attempt to picnic in Eden' ('Out of a Book' (1946), reprinted in Bowen 1986: 50). The alternative to entering the symbolic is madness (Cousin Nettie), death (Eva) or a silence so total that it seems to erase all personality: in *The Heat of the Day*, Louie says, ' "From on and on like this not being able to say, I seem to get to be nothing" ' (Bowen 1949/1987: 246). Only in the symbolic can we speak as subject and it is only because we can speak that we can evoke the loss of our pre-symbolic existence.

Many of the stories of Bowen's heroines mirror her own. In a preface to her short stories, Bowen wrote: 'any fiction . . . is bound to be transposed autobiography' (Bowen 1986: 129; ellipsis mine). Silence was the keynote of Bowen's early life. As an only child living with her dreamy mother and her introspective, overworked father, she observed that: 'each ruled their private kingdom of thought . . . My parents did not always communicate with each other, and I did not always communicate with them' (Bowen 1942/1984: 9; ellipsis mine).

When she was seven, Bowen's father suffered a mental breakdown. Bowen was not told the full details about this. In fragments for an autobiography that was never completed, she speaks of 'the tension and mystery of my father's illness, the apprehensive silence or chaotic shoutings' (Bowen 1986: 270). One thinks of Leopold in *The House in Paris* wondering about the mystery surrounding his birth: 'Just how odd *is* all this?' (*HP*: 34). As a result of her father's breakdown, Bowen experienced more problems with language: she developed a nervous stammer.

Bowen and her mother moved to England where, wandering around from villa to villa on the Kent coast, they grew closer and more demonstrative. 'She was so much desolated that she unnerved me when anything went wrong between her and me,' Bowen was later to say (Bowen 1942/1984: 28). At each rented villa in which they lived, Florence and her daughter created a fantasy home, a 'pavilion of love' (Bowen 1986: 279), much as Portia and Irene do in *The Death of the Heart*. Unlike many of the authors dealt with here, Bowen's early experience was of positive maternal nurturing: 'She gave me – most important of all as a start in life – the radiant, confident feeling of being loved' (Bowen 1942/1984: 407). However her mother was unable to help her daughter to negotiate her way into adult life for when Bowen was thirteen Florence died. Again there was silence. Bowen was not encouraged, and did not allow herself, to talk of her feelings about her mother's death: 'I could not remember her, think of her, speak of her or suffer to hear her spoken of' (Bowen 1986: 290). In a cousin's opinion, Bowen never really got over Florence's death. One of the words she constantly had difficulty pronouncing was 'mother' (Glendinning 1977: 28).

Bowen was sent to live with her aunts, formidable women, very much at home with themselves and the world and very different from her dreamy, loving mother. Bowen described her aunt Maud as 'a very nasty looking-glass that made you look horrid' (Glendinning 1977: 28). Plunged into the company of her sharp-tongued aunts Bowen had, like Portia in *The Death of the Heart*, to come to terms with the grown-up world in which she now lived. Though she may have yearned for her mother her main priority was to gain adult status:

> Motherless since I was thirteen, I was in and out of the homes of my different relatives . . . Though quite happy, I lived with a submerged fear that I might fail to establish grown-up status. That fear, it may be, egged me on to writing . . . As far as I now see, I must have been anxious to approximate to my elders, yet to demolish them. (Bowen 1986: 121; ellipses mine)

Like Portia, Bowen had to write herself into grown-up life; out of the silences surrounding her father's illness and her mother's death, she had to create a text for herself. Reading Rider Haggard's novel *She* was a turning point: 'Writing . . . what it could do! That was the revelation; that was the power in the cave . . . The power of the pen' (Bowen 1986: 250; ellipses mine). Writing was a way of attaining the power of her elders while at the same time giving Bowen scope to 'demolish' their world which, however, as we have seen, she does only partially in her fiction. Her daughter figures may rebel against the patriarchal text for their lives but they are anxious not to be left outside it. Nevertheless, by replaying in so many of her novels the rebellion and confusion of adolescent girls on the verge of entering the text of grown-up life, she emphasises the strength of female resistance to that text.

According to her biographer, Bowen always thought of herself as a writer first and a woman second (Glendinning 1977: 91). And it was only as a writer that she felt able to inscribe herself securely into the symbolic: 'My writing, I am prepared to think, may be a substitute for something I have been born without – a so-called normal relation to society' (Bowen 1986: 223). The price for becoming an author, for entering the grown-up world on equal terms with her aunts, was betrayal of the symbiotic relationship she had had with her mother. Beginning with *The Death of the Heart,* Bowen's writing is increasingly haunted by this loss. In *The Little Girls* Dinah, looking for certainty, delves into her past life as a child living with her mother in their womb-like villa in Kent. She finds the past has vanished and is precipitated into a breakdown which threatens her identity: ' "there was nothing *there.* So, where am I now?" ' (Bowen 1963/1988: 163).

In widowhood, in an attempt apparently to recreate the happiness she had found with her mother, Bowen moved back to Hythe on the Kent coast. She wrote: 'I suppose I like Hythe out of a back-to-the wombishness, having been there as a child in the most amusing years of one's childhood – 8 to 13. But I can't see what's wrong with the womb if one's happy there, or comparatively happy there' (quoted in Glendinning 1977: 22). By taking up her pen, Bowen solved Karen's problem of how to enter the symbolic as 'something more' than a woman. As her life wore on, she came increasingly to lament that the cost of that entry was the betrayal of the pre-oedipal union with the mother.

5

Ivy Compton-Burnett: Tyrants, Victims and Camp

It seems to me that the real political task in a society such as ours is to criticize the working of institutions which appear to be both neutral and independent; to criticize them in such a manner that the political violence which has always exercised itself obscurely through them will be unmasked, so that one can fight them. (Michel Foucault in 'Human Nature: Justice versus Power' quoted in Rabinow 1991: 6)

In the light of this quotation, the novels of Ivy Compton-Burnett, though confined usually to the domestic sphere, are highly political. They provide a devastating insight into the psychopathology of Victorian family life and a critique of the patriarchal power structures underpinning it. The fact that her novels centre on the domestic sphere does not lessen their wider political implications for, in Chris Weedon's words: 'Resistance to the dominant at the level of the individual subject is the first stage in the production of alternative forms of knowledge' (Weedon 1992: 111). In Foucault the emphasis is always on the local struggles that undermine institutional power wherever the latter reveals itself – in offices, schools, prisons or the home.

In a patriarchy, as we have seen in Chapter 1, power structures work to ensure that the mother, and in the mother's absence, the daughter, sacrifice themselves to serve the father. The pointlessness of such sacrifice is the theme of Compton-Burnett's first novel, *Dolores* (1911). When Dolores, whose name identifies her as a suffering martyr, explains that she has given up her teaching post because her father needs her at home, the comments of Felicia, a fellow student, provide a gloss on her friend's actions: ' "My father needs me too. But he needs my help with the rent more" ' (*Dol*: 324). Felicia comes up with a simple and practical solution to Dolores's situation: she should have stayed in college and sent part of her salary home to pay for someone else to teach her half-sisters. 'The keynote of Dolores' nature,' the omniscient narrator tells us, 'was instinctive loyalty of service to that rigorous lofty thing, to which we give duty as a name . . . an unfaltering, unquestioning, it may soon be said, unreasoning service' (*Dol*: 44; ellipsis mine). The crucial word here is 'unreasoning'. Increasingly through the novel, Dolores's unremitting sacrifice of herself to people who do not value or even particularly need her sacrifice, causes misery not only to herself but also to others, so that the objects of her sacrifice come to look like her victims.

Mothers sacrifice themselves too. The life of Claverhouse's mother, devoted to the needs of her 'genius' son, will merge, we are told by the narrator, into 'the infinitude of unwritten history' (*Dol*: 188). When Claverhouse's wife dies in childbirth after nine months of unhappy marriage, her diary reveals 'the record of her hand of the hidden history of her wifehood' (*Dol*: 250). These women sacrifice their lives and it is a sacrifice which, like Dorothea's in *Middlemarch*, will go unacknowledged and uncelebrated in history. Unlike George Eliot, however, Compton-Burnett's omniscient narrator makes no attempt to get us to admire the hidden acts of self-sacrifice of these women; it is their wastefulness which is highlighted. In this way, to use Foucault's language, Compton-Burnett unmasks the violence that is exercised through that apparently neutral institution, the family.

In counterpoint to the dominant discourse of the patriarchy are the scenes between the women teachers at Dolores's college, modelled on Royal Hollo-way College, London, where Compton-Burnett studied classics. Here the daughters of the patriarchy have broken free to lead independent lives as professional women and the hierarchical structures of the patriarchy have given way to a more egalitarian mode of life. In contrast to the brooding Victorian pathos and strained sentimentality of the scenes in the homes of the Reverend Hutton and Sigismund Claverhouse, these women speak in bright, modern dialogue, foreshadowing the style of Compton-Burnett's inter-war novels, and they deconstruct Victorian stereotypes about gender divisions. ' "Cookery, you know, is the greatest attainment for a woman," ' says Miss Cliff, adding ' "I read it in a book, so of course it was true" ' (*Dol*: 99). ' "The students are increasing very quickly," said Miss Greenlow. "I don't know what the opponents of women's higher education would say to it." "I imagine that class has resigned its delusion that anything can be said for its view," said Miss Butler, in the casual manner which covers strong feeling' (*Dol*: 102-3). Once again Compton-Burnett brings practical reasons to bear as the opinion is expressed that, with women outnumbering men, there must always be some women able to support themselves, an argument which, as we saw in Chapter 1, gained prevalence after the war with the increase in the number of 'surplus' women.

This scene in the staff common room is a lighthearted but devastating defence of women's right to education and an illustration that even in a patriarchy, some women manage to practise reverse discourse and create a space for themselves: 'even where feminist discourses lack the social power to realize their versions of knowledge in institutional practices, they can offer the discursive space from which the individual can resist dominant subject positions' (Weedon 1992: 110–11). But in *Dolores* liberation for the daughters does not come about through a strengthening of the relationship with the mother for, as in Freud, the mother is seen as the point of obstacle in the daughter's bid for independence; it is the father to whom these women look for guidance in their professional lives. So Miss Butler defends women's right to education by stressing a daughter's paternal inheritance: ' "women are not descended only from women. Their heritage is from their fathers as much as their mothers. The development of one sex does not bear only upon that sex" ' (*Dol*: 104). In *Dolores*, Compton-Burnett reveals an attitude similar to that of Rose Macaulay who, as we have seen, modelled herself on her scholarly father in order to escape from her mother's domesticity into the wider professional world. In a patriarchy which silences the mother it is only from the father's example, Compton-Burnett suggests, that a daughter can learn to be independent. We may remember that Compton-Burnett's own father was a progressive and a radical in the field of medicine and allowed his daughter to study Latin and Greek with her brothers. In contrast to her ambivalent feelings towards her mother, Compton-Burnett loved her father very much despite his frequent absences from the family (Spurling 1984: 94, 233).

At the end of the novel, with a failed love affair behind her, Dolores returns to her old college to teach. Ironically the staff members, all older than herself, mistakenly regard Dolores as a modern woman who has spurned marriage in favour of pursuing her career: ' "She is the most sensible of us all," ' says Miss Cliff (*Dol*: 330). The self-sacrificing Victorian heroine is reluctantly transformed into a modern professional woman. It seems a fitting punishment for Dolores and underlines the fact that, contrary to what critics have often claimed, Compton-Burnett intended the novel to be subversive rather than supportive of the hierarchies.

In Compton-Burnett's third novel, *Brothers and Sisters* (1929), Andrew Stace is a patriarch whose views on women are highlighted in the first two sentences of the novel: 'Andrew Stace was accustomed to say, that no man had ever despised him, and no man had ever broken him in. The omission of woman from his statement was due to his omission of her from his conception of executive life' (*BS*: 1). Andrew's gender distinctions are immediately undermined as the narrator comments several times on the physical and emotional similarity between himself and his daughter, Sophia, a similarity to which

Andrew is blind: 'He never suspected her of a personality so like to his, never actually suspected her of one at all' (*BS*: 6).

The father's patriarchal attitudes lead directly to tragedy. Before her father's death, Sophia says: ' "I would not stoop to use absolute power like that. It shows how degrading absolute power can be" ' (*BS*: 16). After his death, she wrests control of the discourse by suppressing her father's will. As a wife and mother, Sophia founds her family's life on a secret: 'silence and secrecy are a shelter for power, anchoring its prohibitions' (Foucault 1990: 101). Sophia takes over management of the estate and maintains her adult children in a position of dependence, employing against them exactly the same tactic her father had used against herself – she denies them their subjectivity. ' "They don't feel what you imagine they are feeling," ' she tells her husband (*BS*: 94). By this means she asserts her power. As Jessica Benjamin has said: 'If the other denies me recognition, my acts have no meaning; if he is so far above me that nothing I do can alter his attitude toward me, I can only submit. My desire and agency can find no outlet, except in the form of obedience. We might call this the dialectic of control' (Benjamin 1990: 53). Sophia's children learn to adapt their moods to·hers.

Compton-Burnett's portrait of Sophia undermines inter-war media pro-paganda presenting mothers as naturally nurturing and caring. Far from being an Angel in the House, Sophia is cruel, autocratic and self-serving. As in *Dolores*, it is the relationship with the father which would seem to offer the children the best hope of freedom from tyranny but Sophia's husband either does not see or pretends not to notice her tyrannical ways. Dr Stace travels up to London to work and is therefore distanced from much of what goes on in the family home. The novel becomes thus, indirectly, an indictment of a system which encourages fathers' lack of participation in their children's upbringing.

Sophia is moulded by her father who in turn is moulded by the patriarchy. In this way, Compton-Burnett shows how difficult it is to think outside the dominant discourse: 'one is always "inside" power' (Foucault 1990: 95). In an interview, Compton-Burnett said of her characters: 'I think they are all in the grip of forces – economic and psychological and hereditary' (Compton-Burnett 1962: 108). This, perhaps, is the source of the forgiving attitude she displayed towards her tyrants. Unlike Rose Macaulay, Compton-Burnett is aware of the structures in which her mothers are trapped. The discourse that informs their behaviour is beyond any individual consciousness. As Foucault puts it:

> There is no power that is exercised without a series of aims and objectives. But this does not mean that it results from the choice or

decision of an individual subject; let us not look for the headquarters that presides over its rationality . . . the logic is perfectly clear, the aims decipherable, and yet it is often the case that no one is there to have invented them. (Foucault 1990: 95; ellipsis mine)

When Dr Stace dies, Sophia gives way to a sorrow that is entirely self-centred: 'Sophia's grief hung like a pall on the house, crushing its inmates with a load as if of guilt, that their sorrow was less great than hers' (*BS*: 145). Unrestrained by the presence of her husband, Sophia becomes histrionic and self-dramatising. And this is where Compton-Burnett's mother-as-tyrant shades off into camp for as wife, mother and widow, Sophia is always playing a role: 'Sophia in her extreme moments, when she suffered more than most, never ceased to listen to herself' (*BS*: 122). She is shown repeatedly rearranging her appearance to conform to the parts she wishes to play (*BS*: 148, 159). In her 'Notes on Camp' (1964/1983), Susan Sontag (who includes Compton-Burnett in her canon of Camp) emphasises the theatricality that is an inherent part of camp: 'Camp sees everything in quotation marks. It's not a lamp, but a "lamp"; not a woman, but a "woman". To perceive Camp in objects and persons is to understand Being-as-Playing-a-Role. It is the farthest extension, in sensibility, of the metaphor of life as theater' (Sontag 1964/1983: 109). Sophia is not a mother, but a 'mother'. She highlights her role-playing by referring to herself continually as 'Your mother'. Compton-Burnett thereby suggests there is a disjunction between the woman and the mother. The government and media of the inter-war period insisted that it was women's nature to be mothers, Compton-Burnett implies it is a role.

As often in Compton-Burnett's novels, it is the children who constitute the site of resistance to the dominant discourse. 'Discourse transmits and produces power; it reinforces it, but also undermines and exposes it, renders it fragile and makes it possible to thwart it' (Foucault 1990: 101). Their witty replies, asides, whispers that, in Natalie Sarraute's words, exist 'on the fluctuating frontier that separates conversation from sub-conversation,' ('Conversation and Sub-Conversation,' Burkhart 1972: 155), open up cracks and fissures in the dominant discourse which allow a muted discourse to emerge. They speak in the same style as the adults, in the precise, formal idiom of the classically educated, thus effectively dissolving hierarchies based on age (and inadvertently confuting the claim made by some French feminists that this sort of language can never be subversive). Dinah's weapons to defend herself against her mother are a tactical silence, wit, stoicism and self-knowledge. She realises that: ' "Power has never been any advantage to Sophia . . . It has worn her out, and everyone who would have served her" ' (*BS*: 182; ellipsis mine). But she also knows that all three children have become tainted through living under their mother's tyranny: ' "We have a terrible lot of Sophia in us. The way we understand Sophia shows that" ' (*BS*: 194). Sophia's children have become implicated in the dominant discourse against their will.

In her portrayal of Sophia Stace, Compton-Burnett shows that women are as capable as men of identifying with patriarchal values. Sophia may dominate the household but she does so in the service of the patriarchy: 'Sophia had her life in her husband, and her interest in her father's ambition to reclaim her lands. These things that were enough for her, were to suffice her children' (*BS*: 32). Here we see clearly the hierarchy – father-husband, wife, children. Compton-Burnett is never essentialist in her view of women. It is a constant assertion in her novels that each sex is capable of the behaviour of the other. This being so she is able to argue, through the portrait of Sophia, that the hierarchical nature of patriarchal power structures work to the detriment of men as well as women. The daughter imitates her father's exercise of power and this in turn wreaks havoc in the lives of her husband and her children, two of whom are sons.

Like Foucault, Compton-Burnett analyses the workings of power in an apparently neutral institution and, like Foucault also, she advocates no explicit programme of political action. The only lesson that might be drawn from her novels is that hierarchies must be done away with altogether. And this is in fact what happens at the end of *Brothers and Sisters*. When Andrew, Dinah and Robin finally leave Moreton Edge, it is less like Adam and Eve being thrown out of the garden of Eden, more like liberation from the patriarchy. The children will make a new life in London and they will not bring their grandfather's portrait with them. All through the novel, egalitarian brother-sister pairings have provided a reverse discourse to the dominant discourse of the patriarchy filtered through Sophia. Here I differ from Alison Light who in *Forever England* (1991) sees Compton-Burnett as radical on sexual matters but politically reactionary. The constant questioning of family power structures in her novels is in fact highly subversive of the political order embodied in the patriarchy. Because of this Rosalind Miles has called Compton-Burnett 'arguably one of the most political of writers on the twentieth-century scene,' (Miles 1987: 115).

Two later novels, *A Father and His Fate* (1957) and *The Last and the First* (1971) pick up the theme of the mother as tyrant. It is worth briefly looking at them for their resemblances to Compton-Burnett's inter-war novel. In *A Father and His Fate*, Eliza Mowbray is a self-centred woman whose widowhood, like that of Sophia Stace, casts a shadow over her children's lives. Eliza is given to self-pity and self-dramatisation. When one of her sons tells her: ' "You are born to be a figure in tragedy, Mother," ' she corrects him, ' "I *am* a figure in tragedy, my dear" ' (*FF*: 36). As in *Brothers and Sisters*, it is emphasised that motherhood is a role and one theatricalised to the extreme by Eliza. Indeed Eliza says that it is only one of the many roles she might have played: ' "Oh, there are many parts I could have filled, if I had had the chance, if I had had your opportunities. You don't know what is in your mother" ' (*FF*: 36). Like Elizabeth Bowen, Compton-Burnett suggests that her maternal tyrants are reduced to using motherhood as a way of gaining power denied to them by society. Both Bowen and Compton-Burnett thus highlight the dangers of confining women to the domestic sphere. Like Sophia Stace, Eliza Mowbray commands her children by denying their subjectivity (Benjamin's 'dialectic of control'): ' "The boys will not stay behind," said Eliza. "They do not need more wine. They are better without it." "Is that their view?" said her niece. "It is their mother's, and so theirs" ' (*FF*: 61). Eliza is, however, a minor character and her particular sort of tyranny is overshadowed by, though not without links with, that of her brother–in–law, Miles Mowbray, a hypocritical, sexist Victorian patriarch.

In her posthumously published novel, *The Last and the First*, Compton-Burnett returned to the plot of *Dolores*. Eliza Heriot's husband has handed power in the family to his wife and this is seen as the main cause of Eliza's tyranny. Given absolute power by her husband, it is not surprising Eliza rules absolutely. The tyrant mother is not wholly to blame. In an interview with John Bowen, Compton-Burnett said: 'I think there is a tendency for parents to misuse power, and I think there's always a tendency for power to be misused. Nothing's more corrupting than power. Very few people can stand it, I think' (Bowen 1979: 169). The case for balance of power within a family is clearly put at the end by Eliza's stepdaughter, Hermia: ' "When someone is taught through the years that anything she does must be right, it is no wonder if she comes to think that nothing she does can be wrong. In the end harm had to come of it" ' (*LF*: 142). Sir Robert accepts responsibility: ' 'The fault is mine" ' (*LF*: 142). Hermia agrees that both parents have been at fault though she adds, recognising the extent to which both have been caught up in a patriarchal discourse outside their control: ' "In another [sense] you are both of you innocent" ' (*LF*: 142). They are people, in Foucault's words, 'through whom power passes' (quoted in Rabinow 1991: 247).

As in *Dolores*, the solution for the daughter, Hermia, is to break free of the patriarchal structures which confine women to the home and earn her own living as a professional woman. ' "What I am showing is a resolve to live my own life according to myself," ' she declares (*LF*: 38). An unexpected legacy gives Hermia economic control over her family. The mother's power is overturned by the daughter. The Victorian hierarchies have been reversed, to the bewilderment of Sir Robert: ' "It is a daughter, a single woman, who holds the place. It is much to be on her, much to take from her, much to owe her in the end. We can hardly know our own thoughts" ' (*LF*: 127). But Hermia will not reproduce the old patriarchal hierarchies; instead, she redistributes her legacy fairly, according to people's needs.

In the portrayal of the tyrant mother in *The Last and the First*, as in *A Father and His Fate*, patriarchal society is blamed for allowing a strong and capable woman no scope for her energies other than to dominate her family. The narrator explains: 'Autocratic by nature, she had become impossibly so, and had come to find criticism a duty, and even an outlet for energy that had no other' (*LF*: 17). But these mothers' power is often just another name for service to the patriarchy. Eliza says: ' "What has my life been? Years of care and contrivance, of asking little for myself and accepting less, in order to serve your father and save the family home!" ' (*LF*: 106). As this passage reveals, Eliza is self-pitying and self-dramatising. Like Sophia Stace and Eliza Mowbray, she theatricalises her role: ' "Mater sees and hears herself," said Hermia. "That ends my pity for her," ' (*LF*: 24). The tyrant mother continues to camp it up.

These Compton-Burnett novels demonstrate the way in which the hierarchical structures of the patriarchal family allow the mother, if the father hands over authority to her, to wield absolute power. Her tyrant mothers are psychically locked into supporting existing power relations so that, anticipating Kristeva's description of the pseudo-masculine woman, they become 'guardians of the status quo, the most zealous protectors of the established order' ('Women's Time,' Moi 1986: 201). There is, though, another side to the patriarchal family: in the West at least it has been underpinned by Judeo-Christian idealisations of the self-sacrificing mother. This is the second aspect of Compton-Burnett's treatment of the mother figure in her inter-war fiction.

Compton-Burnett's own scepticism towards Christianity no doubt encouraged her deconstruction of its ideal of the self-sacrificing mother. In an interview with Elizabeth Taylor in 1957, Compton-Burnett explained: 'I was brought up perfectly ordinarily in the Church of England but when I was sixteen or seventeen my reason naturally rejected such nonsense. No good can come of it. Its foundations are laid in fostering guilt in people – well, that obviously makes it easier for our Pastors and Masters when we are young' (Spurling 1984: 64). To Kay Dick, she said: 'I don't think I ever believed in the sense that it meant anything to me . . . I thought it was a disagreeable and humiliating religion' (Dick 1983: 24; ellipsis mine). This was a position Compton-Burnett never abandoned. Satirical observations on religion are scattered throughout her novels. In *Pastors and Masters*, the sceptical Emily Herrick says of God: ' "And he had such a personality . . . Such a superior, vindictive and over-indulgent one. He is one of the best drawn characters in fiction" ' (Compton-Burnett 1925/1952: 32; ellipsis mine). In *Daughters and Sons*, France remarks: ' "The Almighty never had a daughter . . . He did not

risk feminine insight" ' (Compton–Burnett 1937/1961: 27; ellipsis mine) and
of her grandmother, she says: ' "If she were religious, she would not go [to
church]. She would have thought about her religion and lost it" ' (*op. cit.* 139).

In *Men and Wives* (1931), Harriet Haslam's Christian beliefs make motherhood an insupportable burden for herself and her family. The patriarchal, even
Old Testament, overtones of the opening scene where Sir Godfrey Haslam
surveys his property are promptly undercut by the arrival of his wife whose
fatigue and depression dominate the family breakfast. In her role of self-
sacrificing mother, Harriet has a particular way of playing on her family's
emotions so as to induce the maximum amount of guilt. This is the theme,
begun in *Dolores*, of the martyr as aggressor. Indoctrinated by her religion,
Harriet is incapable of separating her religion from her own wishes. She wants
to force her children to abandon what she sees as their self-indulgent ambitions
and live according to her creed. Her moods govern her children's lives: ' "It
isn't possible that all our lives should take shape from one person's pattern,"
said Griselda with tears in her voice' (*MW*: 71), incidentally making out a case
for children to be brought up by a variety of caretakers. Like Compton-
Burnett's tyrant mothers Harriet Haslam, the victim mother, is self-dramatising
and has more power than is good for her due to her husband's shuffling off of
responsibility for the family finances.

However, the reader is not without sympathy for Harriet. She subscribes to
the patriarchal religion of her husband but while this religion empowers him as
(nominal) head of the family, it only succeeds in enfeebling Harriet. She is not a
monster, but a woman bowed down by the stresses and strains of motherhood
and by the impossible demands placed on her by the belief system she has
adopted. As in the case of Compton-Burnett's tyrant mothers, Harriet is
innocent in so far as she is entangled in a discourse outside her control. The
narrator comments: 'Harriet's ambitions for her children were so confused
with her religious zeal, that her natural sense of values hardly emerged' (*MW*:
12). ' "I cannot help myself," ' she tells Gregory (*MW*: 16). Moreover, she is
right about her children: Jermyn's poetry will never amount to much,
Matthew will be betrayed by the predatory Camilla and Ernest Bellamy will
transfer his affections from Griselda to another woman.

By surrounding Harriet with comic characters such as the ineffectual,
garrulous Sir Godfrey and Agatha Calkin, a woman who plays at motherhood, and by having her neighbours, Sir Percy and Rachel Hardisty, discuss
Harriet's demands on her children in a humourous manner, Compton-Burnett
takes the sting out of her tyranny and shows her as a woman whose over-
serious approach to life makes her first and foremost a burden to herself. When
Rachel Hardisty remarks to her stepdaughter: ' "Mellicent, you must make up
to Jermyn for being told that poetry is not worth a sacrifice, that his mother

ought not to be sacrificed to it, when of course she ought. It is trying in such subtle ways to be told that you must not sacrifice your mother" ' (*MW*: 24), it sets Harriet in her proper context. Her brooding tyranny is not allowed to disturb the wit and pointedness of the dialogue. The analysis of Harriet's character shades off into playfulness and camp and the reader who wishes to adopt a judgemental attitude is thwarted. As Sontag has said: 'Camp taste is, above all, a mode of enjoyment, of appreciation – not judgement. Camp is generous. It wants to enjoy. . . . Camp taste is a kind of love, love for human nature. It relishes, rather than judges . . . People who share this sensibility are not laughing at the thing they label as "camp", they're enjoying it. Camp is a tender feeling' (Sontag 1983: 119; ellipses mine).

Tortured by her failure to coerce her loved ones to live up to her standards for them and by guilt that she is to blame for this failure, Harriet violates her beliefs by attempting to take her own life. Thus Christian ideology is shown as defeating its own ends. While she is away in a nursing home recovering from her breakdown, her family at first attempt to lead their lives as she would have wished but six months later finds them happily following their own purposes. Under the influence of the Christian ideal of motherhood, Harriet has overrated her importance in her family's life. As she says to Rachel: ' "Rachel, my husband and children! They can do without me" ' (*MW*: 199). When she returns to her family, she makes an effort to change her outlook and accept them for what they are but she is unable to let things be (Compton-Burnett thought people did not change much). She cannot reconcile their behaviour with what she perceives as God's will:

> 'I will gather myself together,' said Harriet. 'I will gird on my armour; I will stand up to the fray. I will fight my husband and children, my best beloved. That is what I have before me.' 'Is it worth it, apart from the sound of it?' [Rachel Hardisty asks] . . . 'Well, God's will be done, or rather your will be done, Harriet.' (*MW*: 202; ellipsis mine)

Rachel understands that while Harriet is trapped by her beliefs, they also underpin her bid for power. Her role of martyred mother becomes an act of self-assertion. Her frequent proclamations of guilt are a way of affirming her identity. Commenting on the position of Western women in *The Gospel According to Women*, Karen Armstrong suggests that: 'Guilt makes a woman feel she is important and that her actions count and have a significance which, in reality – where women are so often thrust on to the sidelines of life – they simply do not have,' (Armstrong 1996: 218). Harriet's sense of her mission as a Christian mother ultimately drives her eldest son to matricide – another comment on the self-defeating ends of Christian ideology when pushed to the extreme.

Men and Wives is essentially a comedy, or a tragi–comedy, rather than a tragedy and, as such, ends on an ironic note. Matricide as a way of checking the mother's power does not work for Harriet's death effectively brings about the events in her children's lives she so much desired. As Rachel says: ' "Harriet was always a fortunate woman" ' (*MW*: 278). The irony is that Harriet, entangled in her system of beliefs, was unable to perceive her good fortune. She did not recognise the idealism which led Matthew to devote himself to medical research and Jermyn to poetry. *Men and Wives* is a powerful illustration of the way in which Christian ideals about motherhood can get in the way of good mothering.

Compton-Burnett's analysis of the burdens placed by Christianity on women and on mothers in particular, is remarkably prescient, foreshadowing more recent feminist writing. In 'About Chinese Women', Kristeva speaks of the double bind in which Christianity places women: 'Christianity does associate women with the symbolic community, but only provided they keep their *virginity*. Failing that, they can atone for their carnal *jouissance* with their martyrdom' (Moi 1986: 145–6). Marina Warner makes a similar point in *Alone of All Her Sex* where she describes how the figure of the Virgin Mary was slowly transformed over the centuries till she became 'an effective instrument of asceticism and female subjection' (Warner 1985: 49). Warner explains: 'Mary establishes the child as the destiny of woman, but escapes the sexual intercourse necessary for all other women to fulfil this destiny . . . By setting up an impossible ideal, the cult of the Virgin does drive the adherent into a position of acknowledged and hopeless yearning and inferiority' (*op. cit.* 336–7; ellipsis mine). In Kristeva's words, the Virgin Mary becomes an 'ideal totality that no individual woman could possibly embody' ('Stabat Mater', Moi 1986: 171). Kristeva and Warner are describing the Catholic religion, but other writers have shown that the same twin burden of guilt and idealism is placed upon women in the Church of England: 'she is a martyr because she has to die to herself daily,' says Karen Armstrong of the nineteenth-century Protestant wife and mother (Armstrong 1996: 291).

Compton-Burnett returns to this theme of the mother burdened down by Christian beliefs in two later novels, *Elders and Betters* and *Parents and Children*. In *Elders and Betters* (1944), Jessica's Christianity casts a cloud over her whole family. Ironically, because of the sensitivity of Jessica's moral conscience, she becomes absorbed in analysing her own moral failings and neglects to spend time with her children. Once again, the Christian ideal of motherhood is shown to get in the way of good mothering. Jessica acknowledges the strains of her position: ' "I wish I could be clearer," said Jessica, putting her hand to her head. "I get too many people on my mind, and do justice to none. I am afraid the little ones need more guidance; there are hours in the day when I scarcely know where they are. And then I feel that your father is missing me, and that his claim is the first [note the father's priority over his children in a patriarchy]. I am not worthy of my place" ' (*EB*: 43). Her son, Terence, replies: ' "No one could be but a martyr . . . And martyrs are more pleased with themselves than you could ever be" ' (*EB*: 44; ellipsis mine). Terence's reply underlines the impossibility of the role his mother is expected to play in the Judeo-Christian scheme of things. Jessica's religion fosters in her a sense of guilt which in turn leads to her unhealthy concentration on herself to the neglect of her children. The victim mother is as self-obsessed as the tyrant mother.

Because Jessica is trapped in a discourse conventional to her culture, it is easy for Anna to manipulate her. By couching her condemnation in religious terms, Anna induces Jessica to believe her family will be better off without her. Jessica is a good illustration of the way in which maternal thinking can result in chronic self-denial if attentiveness to the needs of others is not matched by a need for self-preservation. She accepts martyrdom for her family's sake: ' "I must free them by any means in my power. I must make any sacrifice, even that of sin. I will not flinch from anything that gives them freedom" ' (*EB*: 156). Once again Christianity is shown to be an illogical religion, defeating its own ends. Compton-Burnett's portrayal of Jessica Calderon is an astonishing and harrowing indictment of the burden the Judeo-Christian heritage places upon mothers and the debilitating effect of the internalisation of religious beliefs.

Parents and Children (1941) is almost a paradigm of an Ivy Compton-Burnett novel about motherhood. Eleanor Sullivan shares the religious beliefs of Harriet and Jessica and she also shares Harriet's ambitions for her children and Jessica's nervousness and uncertainty in dealing with them. Eleanor wants to come first with her children but, in accordance with the practice of the upper middle classes of her era, has handed over the care of the younger children to their nurse who is consequently better loved by them. Eleanor is caught in a double bind: her society expects her to sacrifice herself to her children, but it has also established the practice of using nannies to take over the nurturing role, thus distancing her from understanding them. Successful mothering becomes almost impossible on these terms. Since her society does not allow her to infringe on male activities in the public sphere, Eleanor is left with too much time on her hands. She continually chivvies and harasses her children, demanding to know if they are spending their time usefully and always dissatisfied with their answers. On several occasions she reduces the younger ones to tears.

Eleanor's lack of success as a mother is determined partly by the social structures in which she has to live and partly by her own character. As her husband points out, she hardly differentiates between her children. Like many of Compton-Burnett's maternal monsters Eleanor has no time for anyone else's point of view, regarding her children as extensions of herself. When Hatton tells Honor that Eleanor loves her, Honor replies: ' "She feels I belong to her" ' (*PC*: 243). If Compton-Burnett wished to persuade her readers that, contrary to media propaganda, the mothering instinct is not natural to all women she could scarcely have created a more effective character to prove her point than Eleanor Sullivan. Eleanor is not entirely unsympathetic, however. She is trapped by circumstances in her in-laws' house where patriarchal hierarchies prevail. It is revealed to be a house built on hypocrisy and exploitation. The lives of the Marlowes who were conceived in South America provide a subtle comment on British imperialism which treats both foreigners and women as second-class citizens. Fulbert has 'a full respect for the woman's sphere, but was glad it was not his own' (*PC*: 9). Eleanor is forced to chivvy her sons into working because their father ran through her money in his failed attempt to establish himself as a barrister. Eleanor's incomprehension of her children and her harassment of them both have their source in the social structures in which she is obliged to live.

Eleanor is also trapped by her society's gender arrangements. In an interesting exchange with her daughter Luce, she declares: ' "I might prefer to be your father" ' (*PC*: 101). Fathers were allowed to have a more distant relationship with their children. As Regan says: ' "Things are not the same to men . . . Their family is only a part of their life" ' (*PC*: 201; ellipsis mine). This is the type of relationship Eleanor, in marrying Ridley and setting up house separately from her children, seems about to engineer for herself but she is well aware that society's expectations of a mother demand more than this and she is conscious of her failure. She tells her children: ' "I have never had faith in myself as a mother" ' (*PC*: 215). Eleanor's gender is a disadvantage to her whereas Sir Jesse's is an advantage. Though by the end of the book he too is revealed as a neglectful parent of his three illegitimate children, his gender and status in the patriarchy enable him to avoid having to face up to his failings.

Daughters in Ivy Compton-Burnett's novels may, like Luce Sullivan, support their mother or, more frequently, like Tullia in *Elders and Betters*, side with their father against their mother, or they may, like Dolores, take their dead mother's place only to find themselves supplanted later by their father's second wife. The mother–daughter relationship is central to one inter-war novel, *Daughters and Sons* (1937). In this novel, the Ponsonby household is ruled by two matriarchs, eighty-five-year-old Sabine Ponsonby and her daughter, Hetta. When a family friend, Dr Chaucer, remarks that: 'the old patriarchal system is nobly exemplified' in the Ponsonby family, he immediately perceives his mistake and corrects himself, 'or shall we say matriarchal?' (*DS*: 146). Yet, in a way, Dr Chaucer is not mistaken. Unlike the egalitarian community described by Jane Harrison (see Chapter 7), this matriarchy, with its hierarchical system of power, is remarkably similar to the patriarchal system. Sabine, though she loves her daughter Hetta above everyone else, says: ' "A woman takes the second place . . . I came second to my husband and was content to do so" ' (*DS*: 267–8; ellipsis mine). Her patriarchal attitude succeeds in suppressing the mother's story:

> Sabine never spoke against her daughter-in-law, though she was incapable of seeing her the fitting mate for her son . . .To marry a husband, live with him in intimacy and isolation, bear him children for survival or burial, and die in the effort to continue in this course, appeared to her an honourable history, dignified in life and death. So, prevented from speaking against her, she never spoke of her, and had established the rule. (*DS*: 6–7; ellipsis mine)

In this matriarchy 'rooted in the same hierarchical dynamics of power and oppression as the patriarchal system' (Gentile 1991: 98) the nurturing mother is silenced.

Sabine's daughter, Hetta, rules the Ponsonby household antagonising her nephews and nieces and causing even her brother to have moments of rebellion. Observing her, her niece, France, remarks that none of the rest of them should ever be permitted to exercise power because, having being brought up under a tyranny, they have unwittingly absorbed the knowledge of how to abuse it. ' "It would be good to have power," ' observes one of her brothers. ' "No, we should use it," said France. "No one can stand it. None of us could: think of the stock we come of" ' (*DS*: 45). Like so many other children in Compton-Burnett's work, they have become entangled in a discourse not of their choosing. France's sister Clare's urge to power is already apparent to Sabine (*DS*: 47). And twelve-year-old Muriel cannot think except in terms of hierarchies.

Like other characters in Compton-Burnett's novels who try to live for others, Hetta is shown to have vastly overestimated her own importance; the family can happily manage without her, as they realise when she fakes her own death. One of the constant themes of Compton-Burnett's work is that women will have to learn to give up the illusion of maternal omnipotence. On this point, she anticipates Irigaray who has said: 'we need to say goodbye to maternal omnipotence (the last refuge) and establish a woman-to-woman relationship of reciprocity . . . That is an indispensable precondition for our emancipation from the authority of fathers' ('Women-Mothers, the Silent Substratum', in Whitford 1991a: 50; ellipsis mine). Like Irigaray, Compton-Burnett underlines the fact that the fantasy of maternal omnipotence is linked, not with the ancient matriarchy as described by Jane Harrison and others, but with the hierarchical structures of the patriarchy.

What is interesting and new in this novel is the relationship between Sabine and her daughter Hetta. Hetta is the only person who does not fear Sabine. Hetta is the only person to whom Sabine, the tyrant, occasionally, submits. She is aware of her daughter's sacrifice in remaining single in order to look after her brother's children. When John remarries, a marriage largely engineered by Sabine for financial gain, and Hetta is in danger of being replaced in the household, Sabine feels guilt over her daughter's wasted years of self-sacrifice. She expresses remorse for having helped her son at the expense of her daughter, rebelling now against the patriarchal hierarchy in which sons are valued more highly than daughters: ' "Why do women think of men? Why do mothers think of sons, when they have their daughters? Men can think of themselves. She was a woman and helpless. She has been sacrificed to others, my daughter" ' (*DS*: 246). The shock is so great that after Hetta's return, Sabine lapses into senility. She dies at the moment of realising that Hetta is going to marry Dr Chaucer: 'she looked on something which both seared and satisfied her soul, and then, with a sound almost of a satisfied sigh, relapsed with a single shudder' (*DS*: 284–5), joining other fictional mothers (Mrs Ramsay, Mrs Michaelis) who die after seeing their daughters safely married off. The themes in this novel – the daughter at home, empathy between mother and daughter, the mother's wish to see her daughter married off – are ones which recur in women's fiction of the inter-war period, but treated in quite a different way for here, the mother recognises and regrets the daughter's sacrifice: ' "She lived for us all and we did nothing for her, nothing" ' (*DS*: 246).

There are two sorts of mothers in Compton-Burnett's inter-war novels: the mother as tyrant and the mother burdened by guilt. Both mothers are presented as trapped in discourses outside their control, discourses they are likely to hand on to their children. When women do achieve power they are shown to be as capable as men of wielding it tyrannically. Michel Foucault has said: 'Power is tolerable only on condition that it mask a substantial part of itself' (Foucault 1990: 86). By unmasking the way power operates in the patriarchal family, Compton-Burnett shows how intolerable it is. She reveals the dangers both to men and women of the patriarchal constructs of motherhood.

Like Elizabeth Bowen, Compton-Burnett highlights the empty patriarchal codes in which women's energies are trapped but, unlike Bowen, Compton-Burnett suggest new plots for women. As we have seen, some daughters (the teachers in *Dolores*, Hermia in *The Last and the First*) do escape their mothers' entrapment in domesticity and establish an independent, professional life for themselves outside the patriarchal structures. By demonstrating the bad effect of hierarchical power structures both on women who adopt them (Sophia Stace, Sabine) and women who are oppressed by them (Harriet, Jessica,

Eleanor), Compton-Burnett's novels implicitly (and sometimes explicitly) argue for doing away with hierarchies altogether, either in a women's community, as at the end of *Dolores*, or in brother–sister pairings, as at the end of *Brothers and Sisters*. In *More Women than Men*, Maria Rosetti gives up her baby and finds fulfilment as a teacher and in her relationships with women. She is not condemned for this, neither does she condemn herself. She has sufficient self-knowledge to judge that she would not have made a good mother. She tells her son: ' "You seem as if you had suffered harm, but you have had great kindness in your life. Many people have done their utmost for you. I have done it, and will do it now. My utmost is to tell you that I am glad that you cannot see me as your mother" ' (Compton-Burnett 1933/1948: 220). In this conversation between Maria and her son, Compton-Burnett puts forward the strikingly modern idea that a good mother may be one who recognises her lack of mothering skills and provides an alternative nurturer for her child.

In none of these plots does the mother–daughter relationship feature as empowering; rather the mother's example is an obstacle which the daughter must overcome if she is to gain her freedom. In *The Last and the First*, it is suggested that Hermia derives her wish for independence, which is opposed by her stepmother, from her father. She is described as bearing 'the strongest likeness to the father' (*LF*: 17) and possesses 'a look of being personally unusual, inherited from her father' (*ibid.*). And Compton-Burnett's novels provide little hope for women who wish to become wives and mothers in a way that does not replicate the old patriarchal structures. In *Men and Wives*, Mellicent has to choose between writing poetry or becoming Jermyn's wife. She chooses poetry. The intelligent, likeable and married Rachel Hardisty who looks on her single years as her happiest, congratulates Mellicent on escaping marriage: ' "Well, a selfish life is lovely, darling," said Rachel. "It is awful to be of use" ' (*MW*: 264). In *A God and His Gifts* when it is suggested to her that marriage might mean a fuller life, Rosa Lindsay replies tartly: ' "I don't want the things it would be full of" ' (Compton-Burnett 1963: 5). As Hilary Spurling has said: 'Few writers have celebrated the single state more cordially than Ivy' (Spurling 1984: 285).

Compton-Burnett's novels provide a critique of the Victorian notion of separate spheres which the government and media of the inter-war years were seeking to reaffirm. By displaying the patriarchal power structures at work in family life, Compton-Burnett reveals the way in which the outer world impinges on the domestic. Again and again her novels show that there is no safe haven from the spirit of aggression and power-seeking fostered in the public life of the patriarchy. She anticipates Jessica Benjamin's statement that: 'Although their [gender conservatives'] ideal is the structure of gender polarity, which upholds masculine rationality and autonomy in the public world and honors feminine nurturance in the home, the masculine principle cannot in fact be contained in public life. It inevitably threatens to exceed these limits and devalue the cherished haven of home' (Benjamin 1990: 199–200). Public and private life cannot be kept separate. So Foucault says: 'When I think of the mechanics of power, I think of its capillary form of existence, of the extent to which power seeps into the very grain of individuals, reaches right into their bodies, permeates their gestures, their posture, what they say, how they learn to live and work with other people' (from an interview with J. L. Brochier, quoted in Diamond and Quinby 1988: 6). Ivy Compton-Burnett's novels anticipate quite startlingly Foucault's analysis of the way power operates. Her mothers imitate the patriarchal behaviour of the outer world so well that the home is no longer a nurturing haven.

How seriously can we take Compton-Burnett's tyrant mothers? In her 'Notes on Camp' Susan Sontag points out that time may enhance the campiness of a work of art. This is what has happened to Compton-Burnett's novels. Her maternal tyrants, stagey and histrionic in their own time, seem increasingly extravagant and fantastic. They demand to be judged on their own terms. The world of her novels operates according to laws of its own: her tyrants arouse in the reader a gasp of admiration that has nothing to do with conventional moral criteria. In *A Father and His Fate*, Ursula says of Eliza: ' "I grant her superhuman qualities. Her self-esteem and insistence on support for it are above the human scale" ' (*FF*: 64).

Nevertheless, histrionic and stagey, even camp as these maternal monsters seem, some of them bear a close resemblance to Compton-Burnett's own mother. The Compton-Burnett household was dominated by their strong-willed, irascible mother. Before her marriage, Katharine Compton-Burnett had been a lively, sociable woman. Afterwards, her seven children and five stepchildren kept her confined to the home and to a role for which she was not naturally suited. Compton-Burnett commented: 'She loved us but she didn't like us very much' (Spurling 1984: 38). Having handed over the day to day care of her children and her house to servants and rarely seeing people outside her own family, their mother's pent-up, frustrated energy vented itself, like Eleanor's in *Parents and Children*, on harassing her children.

Like many of the children in her novels, the Compton-Burnett children looked for maternal feeling to their nurse, Minnie. Their father worked away during the week, returning home only at weekends. The recurrence of the situation in her novels where the father hands over authority to the mother shows how deeply marked Compton-Burnett had been by her kindly, tolerant father's absences from the family. She early learned to retreat into herself and observe the emotional turmoil going on around her. Juliet Compton-Burnett gives us an image of her sister standing by the window, twisting the blind cord round and round while the rest of the children rampaged through the schoolroom. She said: 'I think Ivy observed everything that happened in everybody's life and mind all the time she lived in Hove' (Spurling 1984: 187).

When Dr Burnett died in 1901 Katharine Compton-Burnett, like Sophia Stace in *Brothers and Sisters*, gave way to hysterical fits of weeping. She practised severe economies, discouraged visitors and never again went out of mourning. She lived, and forced her children to live, according to a strict routine which never varied. The burden of their mother's grief fell heaviest on the two eldest children, Guy and Ivy, and after Guy's death in 1905, on Ivy alone. Isolated with her four younger sisters in the big house in Hove, she was well placed to observe the effects of maternal tyranny. The whole household lived under the shadow of their mother's grim widowhood and terrible rages.

After her mother's death in 1911 Compton-Burnett did not, as might have been expected, escape to a new and liberating life in London. She stayed on in Hove tyrannising over the lives of her young sisters just as cruelly as their mother ever had. Having lived so long under a tyranny she had absorbed her mother's way of behaving. Her sister Vera commented: 'There always *had* been a tyrant – she inherited the position, [literally true since their mother's will stipulated that Ivy was entitled to be head of the household] and she used it' (Spurling 1984: 192). For four years Compton-Burnett, seemingly unable to alter the family structure she had inherited from her mother, kept her sisters' accounts, oversaw their education, dealt out their allowances and regulated their daily lives. One of her sisters was later to say, inadvertently illustrating the extent to which all human beings are caught up in discourse not of our own making: 'Those were years in which Ivy wasn't master of herself – something was mastering her, and it wasn't the best part of her' (Spurling 1984: 192). Compton-Burnett was caught in an ideological trap and only released from it by her sisters' rebellion.

The years after 1915 were spent in prolonged convalescence. Compton-Burnett had learned to recognise and fear in herself her mother's passionate will and tendency to tyrannise. She never again attempted to recreate the kind of authority she had exercised over her sisters. In the light of this family background a comment made by Compton-Burnett in an interview given in 1962 is significant: ' "I've seen people who were tyrannised over as children being careful not to be tyrants themselves" ' (Compton-Burnett 1962: 110).

As a novelist Compton-Burnett's imagination was to draw again and again on this childhood world. Even in her posthumously published novel, *The Last and the First*, the mother, Eliza, bears a physical and temperamental resemblance to Compton-Burnett's mother. Like Katharine Compton-Burnett, Eliza favours her own children and resents the presence of her stepchildren. The eldest, Hermia, is clearly modelled on Compton-Burnett's eldest stepsister,

Olive, who died in 1963, the year Compton-Burnett started planning *The Last and the First*. Like Olive, Hermia refuses to submit to her stepmother's tyranny and escapes the family home to teach in a school. In an episode Compton-Burnett later cancelled, Eliza is publicly humiliated. Hilary Spurling comments that the handwriting in the manuscript of this scene is 'huge, wild, fierce, lurching diagonally across the page' (Spurling 1984: 540). Was this cancelled scene Compton-Burnett's final act of vengeance against her mother? Or was she punishing those aspects of her mother (the urge to tyranny) she knew were present in herself? What this last novel shows is the way in which Ivy Compton-Burnett continued to be haunted by memories of her mother to the very end of her life – and haunted too by the thought that she had inherited her mother's tyrannical nature and was involved in a discourse she would never break out of. If she put herself into her daughter figures, she put herself also into her tyrant mothers.

After her mother's death, Ivy Compton-Burnett endured the death in the First World War of a much-loved brother, Noël, the double suicide of two younger sisters in mysterious circumstances, the break-up of the family home and what seems to have been a prolonged depression brought on by these traumatic events. Sharing a flat with Margaret Jourdain helped bring stability to Compton-Burnett's life and provided the peace and security necessary to nurture her career as a writer. Against this background, protected from further emotional upsets, she was able to plunge again and again into her childhood memories. Later in life she described a writer's work in the following way: 'We have to dig it out of our insides . . . I think I feel on the whole that something's there trying to get out . . . It's sort of trying to get out and wants help' (Dick 1983:14; ellipses mine). The exhaustion she invariably felt on the completion of a novel (Spurling 1984: 379) shows how deep this 'digging' went.

Speaking of the period in which most of her novels are set (roughly 1888 to 1902) Compton-Burnett told John Bowen: 'People were much more individual and much more powerful than they are now' (Bowen 1979: 169). There is a sense here and in other remarks made by her that Compton-Burnett found life duller after 1915 when the household at Hove was dissolved and her family went its separate ways. Reacting against the emotional traumas she had endured, she seems deliberately to have constructed a life of self-protective dullness. Even her physical appearance stagnated. Perhaps this deliberately chosen tameness was another reason why her imagination continually went back to those early years, circling round and round the problem of inherited tyranny and the power of the family to inflict damage. As Susan Sontag has said: 'The relation between boredom and Camp taste cannot be overestimated,' (Sontag 1983: 117).

At the same time as she was appalled by them, Compton-Burnett admired her tyrants, she enjoyed watching them exercise their power and was surprised when readers disliked them: ' "they don't seem to me such monsters as they do to other people," ' she commented (Compton-Burnett 1962: 106). In a body of work which elevates tolerance and charity as the supreme virtues, few of her characters are condemned outright. Compton-Burnett remains true to the Camp tradition which admires extravagance and eccentricity without moralising: 'Camp is the consistently aesthetic experience of the world. It incarnates a victory of "style" over "content," "aesthetics" over "morality," of irony over tragedy' (Sontag 1983: 115). Not many of Compton-Burnett's novels are pure tragedies. The downfall or the survival of her tyrants is viewed with equal irony.

Compton-Burnett had been through too much in her younger years to want to condemn. In a letter dated 24 March 1913, she wrote: 'Real charity and a real ability never to condemn – the one real virtue – is so often the result of a waking experience that gives us a glimpse of what lies beneath things' (Spurling 1984: 246). Her 'waking experience' came from the emotional dramas she witnessed early in her life. To come to terms with them, she evolved a style that allowed her to treat a serious subject lightly without rendering it negligible. In so doing she found, like other writers in this study, though perhaps less obviously, a way to heal painful memories of her childhood, in particular her relationship with her mother. As R. F. Kiernan says in his study of the camp novel: 'Camp invites a sophisticated, amoral mode of laughter that recognizes it might be critical but elects to be uncritically affectionate, not in a spirit of perversity, but for the psychic relief that such amorality and such release of affection afford' (Kiernan 1990: 16).

6

Jean Rhys: The Empty Mirror

she pushed me away, not roughly but calmly, coldly, without a word, as if she had decided once and for all that I was useless to her . . . I was old enough to look after myself. 'Oh, let me alone,' she would say, 'let me alone,' and after I knew that she talked aloud to herself I was a little afraid of her.' (*WSS*: 17; ellipsis mine).

This is Antoinette Cosway's account of her mother's reaction to a spontaneous expression of love on Antoinette's part.

In *After Leaving Mr Mackenzie* (1930) Julia Martin, sitting by the bed of her dying mother, remembers that when she was a very young child:

Her mother had been the warm centre of the world. You loved to watch her brushing her long hair; and when you missed the caresses and the warmth you groped for them . . . And then her mother — entirely wrapped up in the new baby — had said things like, 'Don't be a cry-baby. You're too old to go on like that. You're a great big girl of six.' And from being the warm centre of the world her mother had gradually become a dark, austere, rather plump woman, who, because she was worried, slapped you for no reason that you knew. So that there were times when you were afraid of her; other times when you disliked her. (*AL*: 77; ellipsis mine)

A similar emotional trajectory — the daughter trying to attract the mother's attention, the mother growing increasingly indifferent and even hostile, the daughter becoming afraid of her mother — is described in both novels with the addition, in *After Leaving Mr Mackenzie*, that the daughter has been displaced in her mother's attentions by a new child. What is apparent from both accounts is that a daughter looking at such a mother will be unable to derive a positive sense of identity from her. The healthy relationship with the mother that was suggested by Irigaray to be so necessary for the daughter's liberation is missing. Studying Jean Rhys's novels we will encounter daughters who, lacking a positive sense of identity and a positive relationship with their mothers, nevertheless have to negotiate a place in the patriarchal society in which they find themselves. We will be moving between the novels for there is a quality of interchangeability between Rhys's heroines which invites us to deal with her novels as a continuum rather than treating them as separate works; indeed it can be argued that Rhys's heroines represent different stages in the life of the same woman.

In his chapter 'Mirror-role of Mother and Family in Child Development' (*Playing and Reality* 1971), D. W. Winnicott extends Lacan's notion of the mirror phase to include specifically the mother's face: 'In individual emotional development *the precursor of the mirror is the mother's face*' (Winnicott 1971: 111). According to Winnicott, when a child looks into its mother's face, her expression tells the child something about its identity: 'What does the baby see when he or she looks at the mother's face? . . . ordinarily, what the baby sees is himself or herself. In other words the mother is looking at the baby and *what she looks like is related to what she sees there*' (Winnicott 1971: 112; ellipsis mine). When the mother's face does not reflect the infant, but instead 'reflects her own mood or, worse still, the rigidity of her own defenses', the baby will look 'and not see [itself]' (*ibid.*). Winnicott adds: 'This brings a threat of chaos' (*op. cit.* 113). To Winnicott's theories can be added Roland Barthes's *A Lover's Discourse* (1977), a work which is remarkably illuminating when read in conjunction with Rhys's accounts of women in love. Barthes says: 'the gratifying Mother shows me the Mirror, the Image, and says to me: "That's you." But the silent Mother does not tell me what I am: I am no longer established, I drift painfully, without existence' (Barthes 1977/1990: 168). As we shall see, this is a state suffered by many of Rhys's heroines.

In Winnicott, the mother figure represents the first mirror into which a girl-child looks to discover her identity; he speaks of 'the mother's role of giving back to the baby the baby's own self' (Winnicott 1971: 118). In the passage from *Wide Sargasso Sea* quoted above, Antoinette looks into her mother's face and finds only indifference. Later, after her mother's descent into madness, Antoinette visits her to say that her son, Pierre, is dead. ' "But I am here, I am here," I said, and she said, "no," quietly. Then "No no no" very loudly and flung me from her' (*WSS*: 40). The daughter looks and receives no sense of who she is from her mother: 'She looked away from me, over my head just as she used to do' (*WSS*: 147).

In *After Leaving Mr Mackenzie*, Julia's mother does not even recognise her:

'The sick woman looked steadily at her daughter. Then it was like seeing a spark go out and the eyes were again bloodshot, animal eyes. Nothing was there' (*AL*: 71). The daughter has searched for her identity in her mother's face and found emptiness where her reflection should be: 'it felt empty, and she was bewildered, as though some comfort that she had thought she would find there had failed her' (*AL*: 89). Julia's exclusion from her mother is exacerbated by her sister Norah who, replaying her earlier displacement of Julia at birth, sends her out of the room saying their mother is upset by 'anybody strange' (*AL*: 72).

Winnicott explains that a baby whose mother is an inadequate mirror 'will grow up puzzled about mirrors and what the mirror has to offer' (Winnicott 1971: 113). In the failure of the early mother–daughter relationship lies the origin of all those moments when the Rhys heroine looks into the mirror, not out of vanity, but to discover her identity and affirm her existence. Anna in *Voyage in the Dark* (1934) often finds herself looking at a stranger: 'I walked up to the looking-glass and put the lights on over it and stared at myself. It was as if I were looking at somebody else' (*VD*: 21). Worse still, Antoinette in *Wide Sargasso Sea* lacks a mirror and therefore an identity: 'There is no looking-glass here and I don't know what I am like now . . . What am I doing in this place and who am I?' (*WSS*: 147; ellipsis mine). Lacking the validating glance of a mother, the Rhys heroine continually looks to her mirror for approval. A case described by Winnicott is pertinent here. He recounts the history of a seriously depressed woman who found her depression could only be lifted by the act of making up her face in the mirror. He adds: 'What is illustrated by this case only exaggerates that which is normal. The exaggeration is of the task of getting the mirror to notice and approve. The woman had to be her own mother' (Winnicott 1971: 114).

The failure of the early mother–daughter bond is made explicit in *After Leaving Mr Mackenzie* and in Rhys's post-war novel, *Wide Sargasso Sea*, but it is arguable that this failure lies at the heart of Rhys's other inter-war novels where the heroines, lacking protection and any secure sense of self, drift without purpose in a hostile society. In her chapter 'Jean Rhys: Race, Gender and History,' Maggie Humm judges, as I do, that the lost mother is 'Rhys's organising motif' (Wisker 1994: 48) but Humm focuses particularly on *Wide Sargasso Sea* and the issue of race. By contrast, in this chapter, I would like to examine the failed mother–daughter relationship in the light particularly of theories put forward during the inter-war period by Karen Horney and Melanie Klein.

In her lecture, 'The Neurotic Need for Love', published in 1937, Karen Horney locates one source of the neurotic's need for love in the failure of the early mother–child relationship: 'The early history of these persons shows indeed that they did not get enough love and warmth from their mothers . . .

the neurotic need for love is the expression of a persistent longing for the love of a mother, which was not freely given in early life' (Horney 1967: 254; ellipsis mine). Such people are left with a lifelong need to be loved in order to feel secure and raise their self-esteem. Horney explains: 'these people suffer from an increased basic anxiety and their whole life shows that their unending search for love is but another attempt to assuage this anxiety' (*op. cit.* 255). As if under a compulsion, they start one sexual relationship after another in order to allay 'a feeling of helplessness in a hostile and overpowering world' (*op. cit.* 258).

Many of the traits of the neurotic delineated in Horney's lecture can be applied to Rhys's heroines. In Rhys's first novel, *Quartet* (1928), Marya becomes aware of her basic anxiety when Stephan is arrested: 'It was a vague and shadowy fear of something cruel and stupid that had caught her and would never let her go. She had always known that it was there – hidden under the more or less pleasant surface of things. Always. Ever since she was a child' (*Q*: 28). To allay her anxiety and her feeling of being alone in 'a malignant world' (*Q*: 28), Marya starts a relationship with Heidler about whom she feels ambivalent and then, when he abandons her, she has a sexual encounter with a stranger.

In Rhys's third novel, *Voyage in the Dark*, Anna's relationship with her harsh stepmother, Hester, has left her with a persistent sense of failure. Hester has brought Anna to England and wants to make an English lady out of her. She has the sort of voice that says to Anna: 'I have spoken and I suppose you now realise that I am an English gentlewoman. I have my doubts about you' (*VD*: 50). Anna's failure to be accepted by the English is seen by Hester as a moral failing. Like the mothers of Antoinette and Julia, Anna's stepmother offers no positive sense of identity to Anna and, by sneering at her West Indian background, leaves her with an inner emptiness.

The opening pages of *Voyage in the Dark* replay the daughter's primary, reluctant separation from the mother/mother country and establish Anna as lost and alone: 'It was as if a curtain had fallen, hiding everything I had ever known. It was almost like being born again' (*VD*: 7). Comforting memories of her Dominican home and her surrogate mother, the black servant girl, Francine, surface from time to time through the novel, interrupting the chronological narrative with Kristevan 'women's time'. Anna recalls Francine nursing her through a fever, her songs and stories and her straightforward, natural approach to menstruation compared with Hester's awkwardness. These memories press against the main narrative, as in Kristeva the semiotic presses against the symbolic. But Francine comes from a different race; Anna knows that she distrusts her for being white. Separated by race and now by geography, Francine is powerless to provide the maternal nurturance Anna seeks.

Cut off from her West Indian roots, Anna manifests what Horney terms the neurotic's 'insatiable' need for love as she searches for someone to mother her and take care of her. The type of society in which she lives encourages Anna's search for love for it is a society in which women are valued only insofar as they are able to attract a man. When Anna and her friend Maudie are insulted by a man in the street, Maudie says: ' "He wouldn't have said a word if we'd had a man with us" ' (*VD*: 42). Anna's low self-esteem is exacerbated by the fact that, in order to attract a man, she has to conform to male ideas of femininity. She knows that: 'People laugh at girls who are badly dressed' (*VD*: 22). She becomes entangled in the patriarchal discourse on femininity that governs and controls the shape and appearance of women's bodies. This discourse, as we have seen in Chapter 1, was particularly virulent during the inter-war period. Looking into men's eyes Anna sees herself reflected back as object, her body divided into separate parts. With the aid of fashionable clothes, make-up, perfume, Anna builds up an insecure and shallow identity based on male social and sexual values.

In S. Lee Bartky's chapter 'Foucault, Femininity, and the Modernization of Patriarchal Power' (Diamond and Quinby 1988: 61–109), many of Bartky's comments on the way in which women learn in a patriarchy to police their own bodies so that they conform to the feminine construct are relevant to Rhys's heroines. Bartky concludes: 'In contemporary patriarchal culture, a panoptical male connoisseur resides within the consciousness of most women: they stand perpetually before his gaze and under his judgement. Woman lives her body as seen by another, by an anonymous patriarchal Other' (Diamond and Quinby 1988: 72). Under Walter's gaze, Anna feels 'so nervous about how I looked that three-quarters of me was in a prison, wandering round and round in a circle. If he had said that I looked all right or that I was pretty, it would have set me free. But he just looked me up and down and smiled' (*VD* : 66). A typical Rhys heroine, Anna internalises male values and becomes 'other' to herself.

In a hostile world the precarious identity Anna has constructed for herself is easily shattered by a chance rude remark. As Horney explains: 'In the neurotic, the need for love is increased. If a waiter or a newspaper vendor are less friendly than usual, it may spoil his mood' (Horney 1967: 245). 'The damned way they look at you,' thinks Anna about girls behind desks in hotels, 'and their damned voices, like high, smooth, unclimbable walls . . . closing in on you' (*VD*: 126; ellipsis mine). Anna's priorities resemble those of a very young child: survival and protection. Partly this childishness is socially constructed: Anna is living in a society where women are excluded from power and responsibility. But her childlike submission to her lovers is also Anna's way of protecting herself against anxiety. Horney explains the neurotic reasons thus: ' "If I give in, always do what people expect, never ask for anything, never resist – then nobody will hurt me" ' (Horney 1967: 258). When Walter leaves her money after sleeping with her, Anna means to protest: 'But when I went up to him instead of saying, "Don't do that," I said, "All right, if you like – anything you like, any way you like." And I kissed his hand' (*VD*: 33–4).

In her search for a surrogate mother, Anna seems at first to have struck lucky with Walter Jeffries, an archetypal Englishman who appears to provide the protection she craves and who, because of his Englishness, satisfies her stepmother's standards which Anna has internalised. Anna acts like a child with her lover, running away from him to hide in another room where the atmosphere is womb-like: 'In this room too the lights were shaded in red; and it had a secret feeling – quiet, like a place where you crouch when you are playing hide-and-seek,' (*VD*: 21). Like a child, she seeks out comforting places and things. The dressmaker's shop in Shaftesbury Avenue is another womb-like place. From there, with Walter's money, Anna will be born again: 'Out of this warm room that smells of fur I'll go to all the lovely places I've ever dreamt of. This is the beginning' (*VD*: 25).

Anna lives for the moment when her lover/mother will send for her. In *A Lover's Discourse*, Roland Barthes vividly describes the search for the mother in the lover and the lover's anxious wait for the mother's return: 'The being I am waiting for is not real. Like the mother's breast for the infant, "I create and re-create it over and over, starting from my capacity to love, starting for my need for it" ' (Barthes 1977/1990: 39; the quotation is from Winnicott). Barthes says: 'I madden myself by the thought that at a certain (imminent) hour I shall have to leave, thereby running the risk of missing the healing call, the return of the Mother' (*op.cit.* 38–9). Similarly Anna in her rooms in Adelaide Road, walks up and down, thinking of Walter and waiting for the telegraph-boy. Her life, like that of Barthes's lover, becomes organised around love. '*I-love-you* has no usages. Like a child's word, it enters into no social constraint . . . It is a socially irresponsible word' (Barthes 1977/1990: 148; ellipsis mine). Anna gives up work and any real connection with the outside world. Life becomes a round of restaurants and drinks and kisses in taxis, 'anything might happen' (*VD*: 64).

Anna is not alone among Rhys's heroines in attempting to recreate the pre-oedipal world with her lover. In *Quartet*, Marya believes she has found a mother figure in her husband, Stephan, who makes her feel like a 'petted cherished child' (*Q*: 20). He criticises her clothes with authority and knows her better than she knows herself: 'She sighed deeply like a child when a fit of crying is over, lit a cigarette and smoked it slowly, luxuriously. It was extraordinary, but there it was. This was the only human being with whom she had ever felt safe or happy' (*Q*: 104). When Stephan is sent to prison, Marya turns to Heidler who seems also to offer her protection: ' "I want to comfort you. I want to hold you tight – and safe – d'you see. Safe!" ' he tells her (Q: 62). Similarly, in *Wide Sargasso Sea*, Rochester seems to offer Antoinette safety when he rocks her 'like a child' and sings to her (*WSS*: 70).

This quest of Rhys's heroines for the mother/lover is reminiscent of Portia's relationship with Eddie in Bowen's novel, *The Death of the Heart*. Portia looks to Eddie to be a nurturing mother and in the end he fails her: as Barthes points out, the lover is always 'an insufficient Mother' (Barthes 1977/1990: 57) because he is concerned primarily with his own happiness or unhappiness. Unlike the mother, the lover demands things in return for his love: 'Yet, within this infantile embrace, the genital unfailingly appears; . . . the logic of desire begins to function, the will-to-possess returns, the adult is superimposed upon the child' (*op.cit.* 104; ellipsis mine). The lover substitutes the phallus for the mother (*op.cit.* 173) and falls short of the mother's self-abnegation: 'the Mother who loves enough (protective and generous), around whom the child plays, while she peacefully knits or sews . . . like those obliging natives who show you the path but don't insist on accompanying you on your way' (*op. cit.* 137; ellipsis mine). For Rhys's heroines this kind of selfless, nurturing love is impossible to find from men: Rochester is frightened by Antoinette's demands; Heidler flees Marya's emotional pressure; Stephan rejects Marya when he learns of her affair with Heidler. 'Women look to men to mother them but remain bereft' (Eichenbaum and Orbach 1992: 36).

Cracks soon appear in the mother/child relationship between Walter and Anna. He holds back on her, refusing to talk about himself or visit her in her rooms. Maudie says he is ' "the cautious sort, is he? . . . It's not such a good sign when they're like that" ' (*VD*: 39; ellipsis mine). His house is not a warm, maternal place for Anna. It 'sneers' at her. Walter talks about her 'predecessor' (she was not, then, his only child). The final shattering of the image of Walter as mother/lover comes at the end of the scene where he tells Anna he cannot see her any more and she feels like dying and he says: ' "I shouldn't wonder if I got ill with all this worry" ' (*VD*: 85).

The loss of Walter reawakens an earlier loss. Anna is propelled back in time to her mother's death: 'The candles crying wax tears and the smell of stephanotis and I had to go to the funeral in a white dress . . . they said so young to die' (*VD*: 83; ellipsis mine). Instinctively Anna realises that she lacks the maternal nurturing which enables a daughter to negotiate and survive heterosexual relationships. She retreats to her hotel room and soothes herself with memories of bathing in a pool on her family's West Indian estate. Like a child in a womb she lies without moving, hearing time slide past her, 'like water running' (*VD*: 97). Water is often a maternal symbol in Rhys and it runs through *Voyage in the Dark*, comforting Anna or reminding her of her early loss. Walking along a street she hears a piano playing 'a tinkling sound like water running. I began to walk very slowly because I wanted to listen. But it got farther and farther away and I couldn't hear it any more. "Gone for ever," I thought. There was a tight feeling in my throat as if I wanted to cry' (*VD*: 10).

Lacking the mother's presence Anna, in a neat illustration of Lacanian theory, begins to write, embarking on a long letter of explanation to Walter. Before she can finish it, she finds herself pulled back into the world of heterosexual relations by the predatory Edith. She drifts into prostitution, becomes pregnant and has an abortion which, in the original ending of the novel (reprinted in *The Gender of Modernism* ed. B. Kime Scott), kills her. In the revised version, written at the insistence of Rhys's publishers, Anna recovers and will return to the patriarchal order ready, in the words of her doctor, ' "to start all over again" ' (*VD*: 159). In the original version, which Rhys herself preferred and which is more consistent with the underlying theme of the novel, Anna remains forever a child. She dies in the pre-oedipal world, hallucinating about her past. Not a very positive ending, perhaps, but in view of the contrast built up in the novel between cold, hypocritical England and the warmth of Anna's memories of her West Indian island, the thought that she dies surrounded by these memories rather than surviving to suffer again makes the original ending paradoxically the more optimistic. In the original Anna frees herself by retreating to the pre-oedipal world, whereas in the revised version she remains forever the patriarchal victim.

When the affair with Walter breaks up, Anna not only loses a lover but fails to live up to the standards of Englishness she has internalised from her stepmother. The result is a massive loss of self-esteem, leading to depression. In her illuminating article, 'Women and Schizophrenia: The Fiction of Jean Rhys' (1979), Elizabeth Abel finds that Rhys's heroines manifest several specific symptoms of schizophrenia including apathy, obsession, a sense of unreality, detachment from the body. It has been suggested, notably by R. D. Laing, that schizophrenia can be caused by parents' failure to instil or support a sense of autonomy in their children, preferring them, particularly female children, to be compliant and passive. Abel argues that: 'There is a continuum between the general lack of confidence produced in women by cultural attitudes and the radical lack of sense of self characteristic of schizophrenia' (Abel 1979: 169). Nevertheless, despite the strength of Abel's argument and bearing in mind that the difference between schizophrenia and depression is notoriously difficult to assess, I would categorise Rhys's heroines not as schizophrenic, but as depressive.

In *Voyage in the Dark* Anna thinks: 'I wish I were old and the whole damned thing were finished; then I shouldn't get this depressed feeling for nothing at all' (*VD*: 78). This type of generalised depression is shared by other Rhys heroines: in *Good Morning, Midnight* (1939), Sasha cries 'for myself, for the old woman with the bald head, for all the sadness of this damned world, for all the fools and all the defeated' (*GMM*: 25). In *After Leaving Mr Mackenzie*, Julia is prey to random 'fits of melancholy when she would lose the self-control necessary to keep up appearances' (*AL*: 21); 'a feeling of foreboding, of anxiety, as if her heart were being squeezed, never left her' (*AL*: 45).

The theories of Melanie Klein are relevant here. In her paper, 'Mourning and Its Relation to the Manic-Depressive States,' presented to the British Society in 1938, Klein describes the depressive as someone who has failed to negotiate successfully the infantile depressive position:

> Unpleasant experiences and the lack of enjoyable ones, in the young child, especially lack of happy and close contact with loved people, increase ambivalence, diminish trust and hope and confirm anxieties about inner annihilation and external persecution; moreover they slow down and perhaps permanently check the beneficial processes through which in the long run inner security is achieved. (Mitchell 1991: 150)

She adds: 'The manic-depressive . . . [has] been unable in early childhood to establish their internal "good" objects and to feel secure in their inner world' (*op. cit.* 173; ellipsis mine). The predisposition to depression is likely to be reinforced, according to Klein, if early disappointments in the love-object are repeated later in life. In Anna's case, the relatively commonplace event of a middle-aged business man breaking off his affair with a chorus girl triggers fear and anxiety that were already latent: 'And I saw that all my life I had known that this was going to happen, and that I'd been afraid for a long time. There's fear, of course, with everybody. But now it had grown, it had grown gigantic; it filled me and it filled the whole world' (*VD*: 82).

Klein's description of the depressive provides an explanation for all those moments of emptiness experienced by Rhys's heroines, those moments of 'inner annihilation'. 'Qui est là? Qui est là?' asks the parrot in *Wide Sargasso Sea* and his cry is echoed by Antoinette's mad mother, but there is never any answer. Julia feels ' "as if all my life and all myself were floating away from me like smoke and there was nothing to lay hold of – nothing" ' (*AL*: 41). As in Klein's account of the depressive, the Rhys heroine has feelings of persecution by the world at large. In *Quartet*, Marya walks down the street 'certain that every woman she passed was mocking her gleefully and every man she passed was mocking her contemptuously' (*Q*: 117). Julia in *After Leaving Mr Mackenzie* 'wondered why the maid had looked at her with unfriendly eyes. But hadn't she always suspected, ever since she knew anything, that human beings were – for no reason or for any reason – unfriendly?' (*AL*: 114–5). Here, Klein's theories blend with Karen Horney's theory of the neurotic's abnormal fear of rejection.

In *After Leaving Mr Mackenzie*, Julia is another Rhys heroine whose life has been permanently affected by the failure of her early relationship with her mother. Julia's story is one of loss – loss of her husband, her son, her wealthy lover – but at the heart of it is the loss of her mother. This loss has left Julia with a yearning to confide in women about her life: to the artist Ruth, to the dark woman in Modigliani's painting, to the slim woman behind the counter in a café. 'I felt that it was awfully important that some human being should know what I had done and why I had done it' (*AL*: 40). She confides in Ruth but Ruth does not believe her account of her life and Julia is left with an even frailer sense of identity. It is her mother who will be the final judge of her life, she thinks, as she waits by her dying mother's bed in the hope of some sign of acceptance: 'Supposing that her mother knew her or recognised her and with one word or glance put her outside the pale, as everybody else had done. She felt a sort of superstitious and irrational certainty that if that happened it would finish her; it would be an ultimate and final judgement' (*AL* 69). Soon after her mother's death Julia begins to be afraid: 'The idea of staying alone in the dark room was horrible to her, and as she dressed she twice looked suddenly and fearfully over her shoulder' (*AL*: 103). After her hysterics on the landing, she explains to Horsfield: ' "I thought it was – someone dead . . . catching hold of my hand" ' (*AL*: 120; ellipsis mine). Julia was afraid of her mother when she was alive and now she has begun to be fearful of her mother's ghost. It is only another step before the Rhys heroine will internalise her mother's voice and it will become the voice of her super-ego. Once again, Klein is relevant.

In her paper, 'The Psychogenesis of Manic–Depressive States' (1935), Klein speaks of 'the severity of the super-ego in the melancholic,' (Mitchell 1991: 123). As we saw in Chapter 2, Klein believed that the super-ego arises at an earlier stage than Freud had assumed. She argued that the super-ego is implanted in the child by the mother: 'the internalization of an injured and therefore dreaded breast on the one hand, and of a satisfying and helpful breast on the other, is the core of the super-ego' ('The Psycho-analytic Play Technique,' in Mitchell 1991: 50–1). According to Klein, the phantasies and impulses underlying paranoid and manic-depressive anxieties stem from the internalisation of an attacked and therefore frightening mother. In turn this gives rise to a harsh super-ego. This is interesting in view of what we know of Julia's perception of her mother as frightening and judgemental but it is in Rhys's later novel, *Good Morning, Midnight*, that we first hear the voice of the Rhys heroine's internalised mother, her super-ego, directly – as a superior, judgemental voice in Sasha's head.

Sasha has survived a breakdown at the cost of a hardening of the heart and a loss of feeling which she deliberately fosters: 'I'm a bit of an automaton, but sane, surely – dry, cold and sane' (*GMM*: 10). However, Sasha is not a successful automaton: memories, odd snatches of music, brief moments when she trusts another human being, keep breaking in on her. For Sasha has two selves: the self that feels a natural, instinctive movement towards other people and the self that is cautious and raises a self-protective barrier of indifference between herself and other human beings. We are reminded of Horney's description of the neurotic as 'someone who is starving [for love], but whose hands are tied behind his back' (Horney 1967: 251).

Sasha's neurotic need for love is most clearly seen in her relationship with René, which consists of a series of advances and retreats on her part. At one moment she thinks: 'I don't know what it is about this man that seems to me so natural, so gay – that makes me also feel natural and happy' (*GMM*: 130). At the next, she thinks: 'what's it matter to me what his story is? I expect he has a different one every day' (*GMM*: 142). Sasha's fear of responding to René fits Horney's description of the neurotic who has a 'fear of love in any form . . . Essentially, these people protect themselves against their enormous fear of living, their basic anxiety, by keeping themselves all closed up and they maintain their feeling of security by withholding themselves' (Horney 1967: 251–2; ellipsis mine). Sasha tells René: 'You want to know what I'm afraid of? All right, I'll tell you . . . I'm afraid of men – yes, I'm very much afraid of men. And I'm even more afraid of women. And I'm very much afraid of the whole bloody human race" ' (*GMM*: 144; ellipsis mine).

The complex final scene of the book shows Sasha being torn between her awakening emotions for René: 'My mouth hurts, my breasts hurt, because it hurts, when you have been dead, to come alive' (*GMM*: 153) and the 'high, clear, cold voice' (*ibid.*) inside her which tells her that he is only after her money. Aloud, this is the voice she uses to push him away: ' "Everybody's got their living to earn, haven't they? I'm just trying to save you a lot of trouble" ' (*ibid.*). Inside, she thinks: 'Don't listen, that's not me speaking. Don't listen. Nothing to do with me – I swear it' (*ibid.*). Under the pressure of her awakening feelings, Sasha becomes aware of an alien voice inside her. When René leaves, she curls up into the foetal position and cries: 'I cry in the way that hurts right down, that hurts your heart and your stomach. Who is this crying? The same one who laughed on the landing, kissed him and was happy. This is me, this is myself, who is crying. The other – how do I know who the other is? She isn't me' (*GMM*: 154).

The punitive, judging voice then takes over, reminding Sasha that René is expecting her to pay to have sex with him, that the man next door must have heard everything, that René has most likely taken all her money. But the voice is proved wrong: René has not taken her money. 'I knew, I knew,' she says, 'That's why I cried' (*GMM*: 156). Sasha's instincts have been proved right. It was the judging voice that was wrong. With a lot of drink, she is finally able to make that voice go: 'Damned voice in my head, I'll stop you talking . . . I am walking up and down the room. She has gone. I am alone' (*GMM*: 157; ellipsis mine). Relying on her instincts now, Sasha wills René to return but, in keeping with the black humour of the book, when the door opens the wrong man comes through it, it is the travelling salesman. Nevertheless, she accepts him as her fate. She had listened to her judging voice and that voice drove René away. She will not let it drive the salesman away: 'I look straight into his eyes and despise another poor devil of a human being for the last time' (*GMM*: 159). She reaches out to the travelling salesman, confident now of her ability to repair her relations with others.

An understanding of the voices in Sasha's head is vital to our understanding of this novel, particularly the much disputed final scene. We have seen that Sasha finally gets rid of the voice in her head (her internalised mother). Given the punitive, judgemental nature of this voice, this would seem to be a good thing, but nothing in this novel is unambiguous, there are good and bad sides to everything. Lavatories, for example, are sordid, but they are also places of refuge where women come to repair their self-esteem, hug their mother, fortify themselves for the world outside (*GMM*: 10). It may seem right that Sasha gives up despising others and welcomes the salesman. On the other hand, she has hated and feared this man. He is scarcely human, being 'as thin as a skeleton' (*GMM*: 13) and is often likened by Sasha to a ghost. In another light, her acceptance of him, this degraded human being, may be seen as representing her lowest ebb.

For her mother's voice is her conscience, a protection against the world. For example, it is true that Sasha is attracted to René and that he knows it. This leaves her vulnerable. Only her inner voice protects her against him, making her afraid to trust him, strengthening her against him, as can be seen in the following lines:

> 'I knew you really wanted me to come up – yes. That was easy to see,' he says. I could kill him for the way he said that, and for the way he is looking at me . . . Easy, easy, free and easy. Easy to fool, easy to torture, easy to laugh at. But not again. Oh no, not again . . . You've been unkind too soon. Bad technique. 'Hooray,' I say, 'here's to you. It was sweet of you to come up and I was very pleased to see you. Now you've got to go.' (*GMM*: 150-1; ellipses mine)

Punitive, judgemental, the mother's voice is also protection for her daughter in the world of heterosexual relations, instilling in her whatever pride in herself she still possesses. Losing that protection, Sasha is at the mercy of her instincts and at the mercy of the world; hallucinating, in a dream-like state with the control of her ego and super-ego partly relaxed, she gives in to her instincts and accepts the travelling salesman – her best instincts, or her worst? The ending, like most of Rhys's endings, is ambiguous but it seems at least possible, in the light of Klein's theories of the internalised mother, to read the novel as an illustration of the importance of the mother's voice as protection for the daughter in the heterosexual world.

There is another side to the mother's story in *Good Morning, Midnight* for, running beneath the chronological narrative, are Sasha's memories of her own failed motherhood. Her son is born in 'a place for poor people' (*GMM*: 50) and after his birth Sasha's main worry is how to find the money to feed him. Her feelings towards the baby are ambivalent: 'Do I love him? Poor little devil, I don't know if I love him. But the thought that they will crush him because we have no money – that is torture' (*ibid.*). The baby eventually dies. Motherhood has proved impossible for Sasha. The midwife binds her body in bandages so that there will be no mark left of her maternity, fatal in a society where Sasha survives by her looks. Indeed, Sasha's memories of her baby are sandwiched between thoughts about having her hair dyed: 'Tomorrow I'll be pretty again' (*GMM*: 48). Nothing shows so clearly how the patriarchy stifles the mother's desire. Obliged to depend financially on men, the Rhys heroine literally cannot afford motherhood. In *After Leaving Mr Mackenzie* Julia tells Mr James: ' "When you've just had a baby, and it dies for the simple reason that you haven't enough money to keep it alive, it leaves you with a sort of hunger" ' (*AL*: 80). The mother's hunger for her dead baby pulses against the main narrative in *Good Morning, Midnight*. The mother's voice is muted, it is forced to be in the kind of society presented in Rhys's fiction, but it is present nevertheless in Sasha's memories.

Wide Sargasso Sea was published in 1966 and therefore falls outside our period. However, according to Carole Angier, a first version was already in existence before 1940 (Angier 1990: 372) and some mention of the novel is necessary in order to complete our account of the mother–daughter story in Rhys's work. *Wide Sargasso Sea* is a daughter's protest against a 'mother' text, Charlotte Brontë's *Jane Eyre*. Rhys said of Brontë's novel: 'I was vexed at her portrait of the "paper tiger" lunatic, the all wrong creole scenes' (Rhys 1984: 262). *Wide Sargasso Sea* is a daughter's attempt to affirm her identity against yet another 'mother' who has withheld the vital validating gaze: 'White West Indians . . . have a side and a point of view' (Rhys 1984: 297; ellipsis mine).

In this last novel Antoinette is haunted by the memory of her dead mother, Annette. She is condemned by others to identify with her mother's madness before she has had time to discover her own identity: ' "They say she worse than her mother, and she hardly more than a child," ' Daniel Cosway tells Rochester (*WSS*: 103). We have seen (above, p.108) that Antoinette fails to gain a secure sense of identity from her mother. The reason now becomes clear: Annette's own identity has been undermined by the colonial discourse in which she is trapped. As a white Creole, suspected by both Europeans and blacks, she lacks a positive identity to transmit to her daughter. Antoinette has never known who she is. She tells Rochester: ' "It was a song about a white cockroach. That's me. That's what they call all of us who were here before their own people in Africa sold them to the slave traders. And I've heard English women call us white niggers. So between you I often wonder who I am and where is my country and where do I belong and why was I ever born at all" ' (*WSS*: 85). The wilderness in which mother and daughter live, unlike the mother's garden in Rose Macaulay's novel, *The World My Wilderness*, is not a happy place but a place of uncertainty, isolation and fear.

In her final dream, as commentators have pointed out, Antoinette's fate merges with that of her mother. Antoinette finally learns her identity in a mirror; she is mad, like her mother: 'I went into the hall again with the tall candle in my hand. It was then that I saw her – the ghost. The woman with the streaming hair. She was surrounded by a gilt frame but I knew her' (*WSS*: 154). Antoinette has recovered her maternal inheritance but it is one that is allowed no place in the symbolic order. The ending of *Wide Sargasso Sea*, like that of *Good Morning, Midnight*, is ambiguous. Antoinette's identity has become merged in her mother's. Has she found her identity, or lost it forever? We do not know for certain. What is certain is that, unlike Irigaray, Rhys sees no possibility of subversion of the symbolic order through identification with the mother; for Antoinette, such identification brings exclusion and self-destruction. As in Kristeva the maternal is a place of madness and dreams: 'the call of the mother . . . troubles the word: it generates hallucinations, voices, "madness" ' ('About Chinese Women' Moi 1986: 156–7; ellipsis mine).

There is, however, another mother–daughter story in this novel. Antoinette has a surrogate black mother, Christophine, whose nurturing care is foreshadowed in Francine's care of Anna in *Voyage in the Dark*. Christophine's protective love rescues Antoinette from her loneliness and provides her with a playmate. Later, she tries to patch up the damage done to her by Rochester. But just as Francine cannot protect Anna in her journey through white patriarchal society, so Christophine is defeated by Rochester who invokes the twin arms of the patriarchy, the law and the police, when he threatens Christophine with arrest and informs her that Antoinette's possessions now legally belong to him.

Nevertheless, the mother is given a voice in this novel. The maternal world of Granbois where 'only the magic and the dream are true' (*WSS*: 138) presses against and disturbs Rochester's patriarchal narrative, unnerving him. It is a place of song, of patois, a language he does not understand and finds 'horrible' (*WSS*: 71) and of female desire which appals him: 'She'll moan and cry and give herself as no sane woman would' (*WSS*: 136). He finds the atmosphere frightening: 'everything round me was hostile' (*WSS*: 123). Yet when he leaves he knows he will long for this place for the rest of his life: 'however far I travel I'll never see a lovelier' (*WSS*: 135). Though mother–daughter relationships are powerless in this novel to defeat the symbolic order, yet by presenting a warm, nurturing counter-balance to Rochester's world, Rhys points up what is lacking in his world.

It could be argued that there are in fact two mother–daughter stories in Rhys's fiction. In the patriarchal, 'master' narrative, none of the mothers are able to provide their daughters with an identity strong enough to counter the patriarchal discourse and some, as we have seen in the case of Hester in *Voyage in the Dark*, actively endorse the patriarchal discourse. The daughter is separated from the mother and has to make her own way in the world of heterosexual relations. In the case of Julia and Sasha, so fragile and insecure is the daughter's position that she is unable to be a successful mother herself.

Running beneath this master narrative, fragmenting and disrupting it, is the daughter's yearning for a pre-oedipal world of song and dreams and memories. By evoking this world, Rhys suggests there is an identity for women other than the one laid down by the patriarchy. It may be stifled but it can still dimly be heard and its roots, as in Irigaray and Cixous, lie in women's lingering bond with the pre-oedipal world. In this way Rhys's fiction moves beyond the analyses of her contemporaries, Horney and Klein, to anticipate the writings of the French feminists.

All her life Rhys wrote and rewrote the story of a woman rejected by her mother and then by her lovers and haunted by memories of the lost maternal bond. It was her own story. While one would want to avoid any simple correlation between Rhys's life and the events in her books, it seems undeniable that the emotional states she describes so vividly in her novels were ones she herself had experienced. She admitted in an interview: 'there is very little invention in my books' (Vreeland 1979: 224).

The roots of the failure of the initial mother–daughter bond lie in the circumstances of Rhys's birth. Carole Angier's biography tell us that Rhys was born, in 1890 on the island of Dominica, exactly nine months after the probable date of an elder sister's death. In other words, Rhys was conceived in order to compensate her mother for the death of her sister. In her chapter on 'Motherhood, Motherliness, and Sexuality', Helene Deutsch comments: 'A motherly woman can replace one child by another only when she has resolved the loss of the first by an adequate period of mourning . . . An unresolved mourning, unresolved because of the strength of the sense of guilt, prevents the growth of motherly feelings for a new child' (Deutsch 1945: 51; ellipsis mine). Angier adds: 'a child with a mourning mother . . . can be left with a lifelong sense of loss and emptiness, of being wanted by no one and belonging nowhere; of being nothing, not really existing at all' (Angier 1990: 11; ellipsis mine).

In Rhys's case, this sense of emptiness was compounded when she was five

by the birth of her youngest sister: 'she was now the baby, the spoilt and
cherished one. I didn't hate her for supplanting me . . . but I think that my
loneliness was very sudden. I was now expected to look after myself,' she wrote
in the autobiographical fragment *Smile Please* (Rhys 1979/1981: 26; ellipsis
mine). Both the dead sister and the new sister were called Brenda. Sandwiched
between these two births, conceived to make up for the loss of the elder,
displaced by the younger, as Norah displaces Julia at their mother's bedside,
Rhys must have found it hard to trust in a secure maternal love. She was forced
to mother herself, to be an adult, too soon; in *Good Morning, Midnight*, Sasha
says: 'I've never been young. When I was young I was strained-up, anxious.
I've never been really young. I've never played' (*GMM*: 130).

Like Julia and Antoinette, Rhys became 'afraid' of her mother but also
desperately sought affection from her: 'Even after the new baby was born there
must have been an interval before she seemed to find me a nuisance and I grew
to dread her. Another interval and she was middle-aged and plump and
uninterested in me. Yes, she drifted away from me and when I tried to interest
her she was indifferent' (Rhys 1979/1981: 43). As we have seen, in 'Mourning
and its Relation to Manic-Depressive States' (1940), Klein suggests that lack of
pleasurable experiences of being mothered leaves a child unable to conquer her
inner anxieties. From being a pretty, curly haired, dimpled infant Rhys had
grown, by the age of nine, tall, thin and pale. She seems already to have
become prey to that depression which was to haunt her for the rest of her life.
She neglected her appearance and was filled with self-disgust: 'I was wearing an
ugly brown holland dress, the convent uniform, and from my head to my black
stockings which fell untidily round my ankles, I hated myself' (Rhys 1979/
1981: 20).

Rhys's fragile sense of identity was made even less secure by the colonial
situation in which she found herself. Her mother's family, the Lockharts, had
been plantation and slave owners in Dominica since the late eighteenth
century. Now, though the slaves had been freed and most of the land had
been lost, the blacks still felt hostile to these 'white cockroaches'. And wealthy
whites despised these impoverished Creole families and called them 'white
niggers'. Like Annette in *Wide Sargasso Sea*, Minna Lockhart lacked a positive
identity to transmit to her daughter. In *Smile Please*, Rhys writes of her
rejection by her mother country in terms very similar to her rejection by her
mother: 'It's strange growing up in a very beautiful place and seeing that it is
beautiful. It was alive, I was sure of it . . . I wanted to identify myself with it, to
lose myself in it. (But it turned its head away, indifferent, and that broke my
heart)' (Rhys 1979/1981: 81; ellipsis mine). Neither mother nor mother
country gave Rhys any positive sense of identity

It was Rhys's mother who, like Hester in *Voyage in the Dark*, tried to implant in her daughter a belief in the superiority of all things English. According to Carole Angier, Rhys 'always thought of her mother as her English parent, the one who set high standards, and who didn't love her because she failed them' (Angier 1990: 34). In a notebook, Rhys wrote: 'I will never succeed in England. Never' (*op. cit.* 373). She saw English people as cold, judging and hypocritical. Given that her mother had implanted in her daughter a belief in the superiority of all things English, it was inevitable that Rhys would fall in love with a stereotypical Englishman. Lancelot Smith was wealthy, well-connected and he had been educated at Eton and Cambridge. As Rhys says in *Smile Please:* 'He was like all the men in all the books I had ever read about London' (Rhys 1979/1981: 114). He was the model for Anna's first lover, Walter Jeffries. Like Anna, Rhys felt when the relationship with Smith ended, that she had failed to live up to her mother's standards of Englishness. And in *Good Morning, Midnight,* the concentration on the anti-English theme, which might otherwise seem thematically redundant, can only be explained in the context of Rhys/Sasha's struggles against the voice of the mother and the standards she had imposed on her daughter. Resisting that voice, Sasha takes every opportunity to show up the English as pompous, indifferent, a fatally flawed race: 'He makes a little speech about English hypocrisy. Preaching to the converted' (*GMM*: 110).

Yet this harsh, judgemental internalised voice of the mother is not Rhys's final word. In the portrait of Minna in *Smile Please*, a more vulnerable woman is revealed to us, a woman who was left on her own to bring up her children by a husband preoccupied with his work, a woman who had money worries and whose husband was extravagant and flirted with other women. Her daughter catches glimpses of her solitariness: 'Behind her silence she looked lonely, a stranger in a strange house' (Rhys 1979/1981: 45). She often lost her temper. The image builds up of a thwarted life – indeed this is the word Julia uses in *After Leaving Mr Mackenzie* to describe her mother transported, as Rhys's mother was, from a hot country to cold, grey England, at the end of her life. The daughter's recognition of the mother's vulnerability achieves fullest expression in Rhys's post-war novel, *Wide Sargasso Sea*, in the description of Annette Cosway, despairing victim of a colonial system, suspected by both whites and blacks.

All her life, like the neurotic described by Horney, Rhys looked for something or someone to fill up the empty space inside her. She never found anyone who could fulfil that need, at least on a permanent basis. No one could. The heroine of 'The Sound of the River' tells herself: 'Nobody's going to comfort you . . . you ought to know better' (Rhys 1968/1972: 132; ellipsis mine). And Rhys was unable to give that comfort to anyone else: her failed relationship with her mother left her unable to mother her own children adequately. Her son died as a baby, possibly as a result of neglect (Angier 1990: 112–3). Her daughter was largely brought up by other people. As we have seen, motherhood is never a success for the Rhys heroine. Anna has an abortion. The sons of Julia and Sasha die as babies, leaving both women seemingly completely unmarked. 'I was never a good mother,' Rhys said (Angier 1990: 113). A comment by her daughter tellingly reveals Rhys's inability to project herself as a mother: ' "I've never been able to see my mother as a real person. What I've seen is her likeness in a looking-glass" ' (*op. cit.* 590). Her daughter is a significant absence in Rhys's fiction. She could bear to write of her mother, her lovers, her dead son, but not of her failure to be a good mother to Maryvonne.

Rhys was more fortunate than her heroines: there was one thing she could do for herself and that was write out her sadness. In *Smile Please*, Rhys describes how, in the aftermath of her affair with Lancelot Smith, she went out and bought some exercise books. 'Now that old table won't look so bare, I thought' (Rhys 1979/1981: 129). For the next few weeks she wrote obsessively: 'I remembered everything that had happened to me in the last year and a half. I remembered what he'd said, what I'd felt. I wrote on until late into the night, till I was so tired that I couldn't go on, and I fell into bed and slept' (*ibid.*).

The pen was Rhys's purchase on the symbolic order. Writing gave her the confidence to stand up to her landlady. Eventually it was to earn her money, far more than any of her husbands were ever able to give her. Unlike her heroines, Rhys was able to enter the symbolic on her own terms and not simply as the 'other' of the male imaginary. Paradoxically, though she wrote about women as victims, Rhys's writings and her life can be seen as empowering. Because her heroines are logical, if extreme, manifestations of ideals of femininity, her anatomising of 'the feminine' becomes in itself a powerful social critique. And she was able, as we have seen, to articulate women's bond with the pre-oedipal world as a counterweight to the symbolic.

In the fragment 'From a Diary: at the Ropemakers' Arms,' Rhys said: 'I must write. If I stop writing my life will have been an abject failure' (Rhys 1979/1981: 163). To her daughter she wrote: 'It is my only thing. All I can do' (Angier 1990: 480). Like Anna in *Voyage in the Dark*, Rhys wrote initially for herself and not for a public. Writing was as much an act of healing for Rhys as it was for Compton-Burnett: 'I found when I was a child that if I could put the hurt into words, it would go. It leaves a sort of melancholy behind and then it goes' (Vreeland 1979: 224). By writing, Rhys was able to make herself whole: 'I have given myself up to something which is greater than I am. I have tried to be a good instrument. Then I'm not unhappy. I am even rather happy' (Angier 1990: 374). Her books gave Rhys the only identity she could be sure of; they were her way of mothering herself.

7

Virginia Woolf: Retrieving the Mother

In *A Room of One's Own* (1929) there is a symbolic moment when, having been excluded from the library of a male college, Woolf comes across 'the formidable yet humble' figure of 'the famous scholar', Jane Harrison, walking on the terrace (*RO*: 21). In Chapter 1, we saw that the inter-war period was a time when anthropologists such as Harrison (1850–1928) were pursuing matriarchal myths. In her *Prolegomena to the Study of Greek Religion*, published in 1903, Harrison shows how in Greek mythology the mother came to be robbed of her power. Demeter and Kore, Mother and Maid, were not, originally, two women but two aspects of one goddess, woman before and after maturity. In the Homeric Olympus the Maid became split from the Mother and the power of the goddess became weakened. The Earth-goddess's attributes were distributed amongst various maiden goddesses (Athene, Aphrodite, Artemis, etc.) and this led to a privileging of the Maid over the Mother. Harrison comments: 'Zeus the Father will have no great Earth-goddess, Mother and Maid in one, in his man-fashioned Olympus' (Harrison 1922: 285).

Harrison's account clearly locates the power of the patriarchy in the separation of the daughter from the mother and the consequent suppression of the mother. In this, she anticipates the writings of Irigaray by several decades. In 'Women-Mothers, the Silent Substratum of the Social Order', Irigaray states: 'the whole of our western culture is based upon the murder of the mother. The man-god-father killed the mother in order to take power' (Whitford 1991a: 47). According to Harrison, the Homeric patriarchal Olympus emphasised the individual, competition and heroism in war. 'On the other hand the worship of the Mother emphasizes the group, the race and its continuance rather than the prowess of the individual, it focuses on the facts of fertility and the fostering of life' (Harrison 1924: 63). In Harrison's account, matriarchal society is communal, co-operative and life-giving; it encourages women's independence and creativity and egalitarian relations between women and men. As in Irigaray, the matriarchal world nurtures women's creativity which is stifled in a patriarchy. The buried great goddess is a symbol of the buried artist in all women.

Woolf met Jane Harrison several times and in an article on 'The Intellectual Status of Women', she lists Harrison as one of the great women of history (Woolf 1978b: 339). Scholars (Barrett 1987, Shattuck 1987, Cramer 1993) have pointed to Jane Harrison as a major intellectual influence on *Between the Acts*. In this chapter I would like to look at the whole of Woolf's *oeuvre* in the light of Harrison's project of uncovering an earlier matriarchy. I am not necessarily suggesting always a conscious influence. We know (Abel 1983: 180) that Woolf was reading Jane Harrison's works around the time that she wrote *Mrs Dalloway* (1925) and that her library contained a copy of Harrison's *Ancient Art and Ritual* (1918) inscribed to Woolf by Harrison and dated 1923. What I am proposing is that reading Harrison confirmed for Woolf certain ideas she had been groping towards for years.

Woolf had personal reasons for wanting to retrieve the buried maternal world. One was connected with her anxieties of authorship. Growing up, it was to her father, Leslie Stephen, that Woolf had looked for guidance in her reading and he was her role model in her profession as woman of letters (Gordon 1992: Chapter 6). Yet she was a woman, on the other side of the sexual divide from her father; she needed to find a female artistic heritage and a way of writing that would not entail abandoning the mother. Even her choice of pen reflected this: 'Here I am experimenting with the parent of all pens – the black J., *the* pen, as I used to think it . . . because mother used it' (Woolf 1977: 208; ellipsis mine). Woolf's mother, Julia Stephen, wrote children's short stories and essays, including an essay on the management of sick rooms and Noël Annan detects a tone of voice in Stephen's *Notes for Sick Rooms* similar to that in Woolf's essays (Annan 1984: 103).

Woolf had reasons also for wishing to give the mother a public voice in the patriarchy where, in Adrienne Rich's words: 'The absence of respect for women's lives is written into the heart of male theological doctrine, into the structure of the patriarchal family, and into the very language of patriarchal ethics' (Rich 1977: 269). Woolf knew, from her own experience of sexual abuse, that the society in which she lived was dangerous for women. The daughter's safety and sense of self-worth depended on the empowerment of the mother as a counterweight to the father. Harrison's project of uncovering an earlier matriarchy fitted in with Woolf's personal need to oppose the power of the patriarchy.

Virginia Woolf's first published novel, *The Voyage Out* (1915), opens with a scene in which a mother, Helen, weeps for her children in the presence of her uncomprehending husband and then spends dinner 'promoting men's talk' (*VO*: 13), as she has been trained to do. The way in which, in a patriarchy, maternal instincts are buried in the interests of the father is clearly demonstrated.

Rachel Vinrace's mother is another buried mother in *The Voyage Out*. She died years ago and has had her personality veiled and idealised by Rachel's pair of patriarchal aunts who have presented her to Rachel as 'very sad and very good' (*VO*: 187), that is, as the Victorian model of what a woman should be, much as Leslie Stephen built up Julia in his *Mausoleum Book* to be an idealised figure of womanhood. It is only through talking with Helen that Rachel gains access to the real personality of her mother, a more spirited individual than her aunts have led her to believe. There is a sense of a lifting of a burden on Rachel. It was a burden Woolf herself struggled with: in the autobiographical sketch 'Reminiscences' (written in 1908) she speaks of the 'unpardonable mischief' Leslie Stephen had done his offspring 'by substituting for the shape of a true and most vivid mother, nothing better than an unlovable phantom' (Woolf 1990: 53). We may remember Jane Harrison's account of the Homeric Olympus where: 'Goddesses became projections of male desires and fears and lost their power to provide women with models of autonomy and strength' (Cramer 1993: 173–4).

The Voyage Out is an account of Rachel's attempt to enter the text of grown-up life, the symbolic order. In this respect, she can be compared to several of Elizabeth Bowen's daughter figures, particularly Portia in *The Death of the Heart*. Although Rachel is twenty-four, she appears to Helen to have a mental age of about six. She has not yet mastered language: 'Rachel read . . . with the curious literalness of one to whom written sentences are unfamiliar, and handling words as though they were made of wood' (*VO*: 123; ellipsis mine). She responds to Terence Hewet's questions about womanhood with non-verbal communication:

> ' "Every woman not so much a rake at heart, as an optimist, because they don't think." What do you say, Rachel?' . . . Rachel said nothing. Up and up the steep spiral of a very late Beethoven sonata she climbed, like a person ascending a ruined staircase . . . '. . . query, what is meant by the masculine term, honour? – what corresponds to it in your sex? Eh?' Attacking her staircase once more, Rachel again neglected this opportunity of revealing the secrets of her sex. (*VO*: 298; ellipses mine)

Rachel's silence is illustrative of the way in which women's lives in general have remained unwritten. Terence thinks they should be written about, but for

Rachel, words are inadequate: ' "They're sheer nonsense!" Rachel exclaimed. "Think of words compared with sounds!" ' (*VO*: 299).

To help her gain a foothold in the symbolic, Rachel has two surrogate mothers: Clarissa Dalloway and Helen Ambrose. Neither in the end are able to provide Rachel with maternal nurturing strong enough to withstand the discourse of the patriarchy. Clarissa explains about marriage to Rachel but is unable to protect the girl from the sexual advances of her own husband. Helen tries to educate Rachel intellectually and sexually but she is an ambivalent mother figure. She feels no particular empathy for women and there is something threatening in the way she presides over her niece's union with Terence Hewet. Over the speechless, passive body of Rachel, Terence and Helen kiss, affirming the marriage plot into which Rachel is now inscribed.

As time passes, Rachel begins to be dissatisfied with this plot: 'she wanted many more things than the love of one human being' (*VO*: 309). Given the paucity of plots available to the pre-war heroine, the only refuge Rachel can find from patriarchal marriage is death. Abandoning her attempt to enter the symbolic governed by men, Rachel retreats into the protection of the maternal *chora*:

> She fell into a deep pool of sticky water, which eventually closed over her head. She saw nothing and heard nothing but a faint booming sound, which was the sound of the sea rolling over her head. While all her tormentors thought that she was dead, she was not dead, but curled up at the bottom of the sea. There she lay, sometimes seeing darkness, sometimes light, while every now and then someone turned her over at the bottom of the sea. (*VO*: 348)

Rachel has become a foetus in the womb, lapped around and protected by the waters of the foetal sac. One could compare Woolf's early memory of the nursery at St Ives and 'lying in a grape and seeing through a film of semi-transparent yellow' ('Sketch of the Past,' Woolf 1990: 74), hearing the waves break against the shore and 'feeling the purest ecstasy I can conceive' (*op. cit.* 73).

If language arises in the absence of the mother, Rachel's failure to master language may be seen as a refusal to be cut off from the mother, a refusal which becomes permanent through her illness and death. Did Woolf, like Elizabeth Bowen, feel that in order to enter the world of language and culture on equal terms with men, she was being forced to betray the memory of her mother? In her biography of Woolf, Lyndall Gordon adduces as one of the aspects of Woolf's periods of madness, a rebellion against the language and the standards her father had instilled in her — what Gordon refers to as 'the constant friction of inner perception against standard expression' (Gordon 1992: 59) and what we may term an awareness of the mother's language pressing against the father's. From the beginning, then, Woolf's fiction displays an unwillingness to abandon the mother. The very first scene of her first published novel demonstrates the way in which patriarchal social structures suppress the mother in favour of the father and it is a novel where the daughter chooses silence and death in preference to entering the father's world.

In *Mrs Dalloway* (1925), the mother's power has been destroyed by war: 'so prying and insidious were the fingers of the European War, [they] smashed a plaster cast of Ceres' (D: 77). Almost everyone in *Mrs Dalloway* is cut off from the mother. Bourton is a place which holds warm maternal memories for Clarissa because of her love for Sally Seton but she is separated from it when her brother inherits the house from their father. Bourton becomes a symbol of what, in Jane Harrison's account, happens to the mother in a patriarchal culture: she is taken over by fathers and sons, separated from her daughter and buried.

Septimus Warren Smith has cut himself off from the mother, leaving home 'because of his mother; she lied' (D: 76). He attempts to cultivate manliness and suppress the body. He thwarts Rezia's urge to maternity and, by bringing her to England, cuts her off from her female past in Italy. In England Rezia is entirely robbed of her power to nurture and is easily discounted by Dr Holmes: 'He could see her, like a little hen, with her wings spread barring his passage. But Holmes persevered. "My dear lady, allow me . . ." Holmes said, putting her aside' (D: 132). This society's suppression of the mother is apparent even in the lives of minor characters: Sir William Bradshaw forbids childbirth, Moll Pratt's motherly gesture towards the Prince of Wales is discouraged by a constable.

Beneath the patriarchal structures of the society presented in *Mrs Dalloway* lies a maternal inheritance so deeply buried that, as in Jean Rhys's novels, it lingers in the minds of the characters only as a faint, far-off memory, surfacing occasionally in dreams, imagery of waves and flowers, an old beggar woman's semiotic babble and in brief moments of sympathy between women, as in the following passage:

> [Lady Bruton's] inquiry, 'How's Clarissa?' was well known by women infallibly to be a signal from a well-wisher, from an almost silent companion, whose utterances (half a dozen perhaps in the course of a lifetime) signified recognition of some feminine comradeship which went beneath masculine lunch parties and united Lady Bruton and Mrs Dalloway, who seldom met, and appeared when they did meet indifferent and even hostile, in a singular bond. (D: 95)

No words are spoken: in a patriarchy it is inevitable that the bond between women will, more often than not, be a silent one. As Kristeva puts it in 'Stabat

Mater': 'Women doubtless reproduce among themselves the strange gamut of
forgotten body relationships with their mothers. Complicity in the unspoken,
connivance of the inexpressible . . . The community of women is a community of dolphins' (Moi 1986: 180–1; ellipsis mine).

Clarissa has internalised her society's suppression of the mother – her first
reference to her daughter Elizabeth shows her repressing her maternal instincts:
'(but one must economize, not buy things rashly for Elizabeth)' (*D*: 7). She is as
much Maid as Mother: we are told that she possesses 'a virginity preserved
through childbirth,' (*D*: 29). Her relationship with her daughter, patriarchal
and possessive, has not awakened the mother in her. Peter Walsh thinks of her
as 'unmaternal' (*D*: 169). Clarissa must retrieve her maternal inheritance in
other ways, through her relationships with women and through rediscovering
the mother in herself. As Cixous has said: 'The mother, too, is a metaphor. It is
necessary and sufficient that the best of herself be given to woman by another
woman for her to be able to love herself and return in love the body that was
"born" to her' (Cixous in Marks and de Courtivron 1981: 252). It is to women
Clarissa looks for a clue as to how to negotiate life in the patriarchy – hence her
fascination with dowagers like Lady Bruton and Lady Bexborough who
represent dignity and strength and the capacity to survive in a patriarchal
society. Rejection by Lady Bruton leaves Clarissa feeling unattractive and
sexless: 'Narrower and narrower would her bed be' (*D*: 29).

Since she searches for her identity through other women, it is they who
inspire Clarissa's deepest feelings of love or hate. About her feelings for Miss
Kilman Clarissa realises: 'That was satisfying; that was real . . . She hated her;
she loved her' (*D*: 155; ellipsis mine). Miss Kilman's integrity as a single woman
points up the extent to which the position Clarissa has achieved for herself
within society has involved compromise: 'She had schemed; she had pilfered.
She was never wholly admirable' (*D*: 164). At the same time, Miss Kilman
represents a masculine will to domination and possession that Clarissa rejects.
By contrast, the elderly woman opposite going quietly upstairs to bed seems to
hold out the promise that it is possible for women in a patriarchy to achieve
independence and 'privacy of the soul' (*D*: 113).

Clarissa is also searching to give expression to the mother inside herself,
difficult to do in a society where any expression of the mother has to be
suppressed. Her relationship with Sally Seton begins the process, awakening
protective, maternal feelings on Clarissa's part: 'The strange thing, on looking
back, was the purity, the integrity, of her feeling for Sally. It was not like one's
feeling for a man. It was completely disinterested and besides, it had a quality
which could only exist between women . . . It was protective, on her side' (*D*:
32; ellipsis mine). With Sally, Clarissa glimpses the possibility of living life
outside the patriarchy in a bond with another woman, but they are forced apart

by Peter's 'determination to break into their companionship' (*D*: 33). The ancient matriarchy, a community of women, is glimpsed and then destroyed as Peter interrupts their kiss. Adrienne Rich has spoken of 'the societal forces which wrench women's emotional and erotic energies away from themselves and other women and from women identified values' (Rich 1980: 35). Nevertheless, the relationship with Sally has gone some way to awakening the maternal impulse in Clarissa. Her role as society hostess will take her further.

Both Peter Walsh and Richard Dalloway mock Clarissa's hostess role but, as the Lacanian moment when Clarissa confronts her own image in her dressing-table mirror makes clear, it is her role as hostess, drawing people together, which gives her her identity:

> That was her self – pointed; dart-like; definite. That was her self when some effort, some call on her to be herself, draw the parts together, she alone knew how different, how incompatible and composed so for the world only into one centre, one diamond, one woman who sat in her drawing-room and made a meeting-point, a radiancy no doubt in some dull lives, a refuge for the lonely to come to, perhaps . . . (*D*: 34–5)

Peter and Richard are wrong to despise Clarissa's hostess role for, in a patriarchal society, it is one way in which she can express her maternal impulses to bring people together, to create a work of art, 'an offering; to combine, to create' (*D*: 109), both inside and outside time. It is through her party that Clarissa expresses her maternal impulses and becomes, finally, herself. 'It is Clarissa, he said. For there she was' (*D*: 172). Her parties are not an assertion of power, but instead express communal values. In that sense, they may be seen as a lingering remnant of Harrison's matriarchal society.

Significantly, it is at the party that Clarissa's mother is mentioned for the first and only time in the novel. Tears come into Clarissa's eyes when she is compared to her mother by that fairy godmother, Mrs. Hilbery. The maternal moment between Clarissa and Mrs Hilbery is interrupted, as always in *Mrs Dalloway*, by the demands of the patriarchy. Two of her male guests are quarrelling and Clarissa must pacify them. Nevertheless, embattled as she is in a patriarchal, matricidal society, Clarissa has succeeded in finding a way of expressing her maternal impulses to create and connect. Because of this, she is able to take Septimus's death, empathise with it and turn it into something meaningful: 'Death was defiance. Death was an attempt to communicate,' (*D*: 163). As in Jane Harrison's description of the matriarchy Clarissa, the mother defeating death, stands for continuance of the race. Woolf herself felt similarly maternal after completing her biography of Roger Fry: 'What a curious relation is mine with Roger at this moment – I who have given him a kind of shape after his death . . . I feel . . . as if I were intimately connected with

him: as if we together had given birth to this vision of him: a child born of us'
(25 July 1940 in Woolf 1953/1981: 322; ellipses mine).

In the portrait of Clarissa Dalloway, Woolf shows how one fragile and rather
vulnerable 'bird-like' woman, beleaguered in a patriarchal society, adopting
the patriarchal daughter's role of society hostess, yet manages to turn that role
into an expression of her self and her maternal instincts. Clarissa has traits in
common with Julia Stephen as described by her daughter. They share an ability
to bring people together and create an atmosphere; they are able intuitively to
seize hold of people's characters: 'she stamped people with characters at once,'
says Woolf of her mother in 'Reminiscences' (Woolf 1990: 42). Compare the
description of Clarissa in *Mrs Dalloway*: 'Her only gift was knowing people
almost by instinct' (*D*: 10). Clarissa shares Julia Stephen's scepticism, and her
determination, since there is no God, to relieve suffering, 'this atheist's religion
of doing good for the sake of goodness' (*D: 70*).

As we have seen, from the first, Woolf wished to find a way of writing that
would not entail abandoning the mother. Always defensive about her child-
lessness, in *Mrs Dalloway* Woolf found her likeness to her mother, not through
having children of her own, but in perceiving that Julia Stephen's creativity
bore similarities to that of the artist. Julia's creativity, like Clarissa's, involved
drawing people together and creating a 'moment', a work of art. Woolf had
been told repeatedly that Stella and Vanessa resembled her mother but that she
resembled her father. In Clarissa Dalloway she creates a character she is able to
share with her mother. 'I alternately laugh at her and cover her, very
remarkably, with myself', she wrote of Clarissa (Woolf 1953/1981: 83).
Hence the importance of the pivotal moment when Mrs Hilbery compares
Clarissa to her mother. In *Mrs Dalloway*, Woolf thinks her way back to a
mother who can affirm her daughter's artistic vocation.

Finding a likeness between her mother and the artist in the act of creation
freed the artist in Woolf, helping her surmount her fear that writing was an act
that unsexed her and isolated her from the world of women (on this, see
Showalter 1977/1982: 270-1). It is precisely through creating that Woolf
rejoins her mother. So she is able to write in her diary that *Mrs Dalloway* 'seems
to leave me plunged deep in the richest strata of my mind. I can write and write
and write now: the happiest feeling in the world' (Woolf 1953/1981: 75).
Since writing was no longer an act that betrayed the mother, in her next novel,
Woolf could afford to allow her memories of Julia Stephen to surface.

It is a commonplace of critical writing on *To the Lighthouse* (1927), from
Hermione Lee to Minow-Pinkney, to say that in order to fulfil herself as an
artist, Lily Briscoe has to deconstruct the rigid Victorian gender identities. In
order to become a painter, to enter the symbolic order, these critics argue, Lily
has to identify with the father and repress her bodily needs; Mrs Ramsay's

example of self-sacrifice and selflessness can only block Lily as an artist. What is not so commonly noticed is that Mrs Ramsay herself to some extent deconstructs her own role, that is, she expresses doubts and dissatisfaction about the gender role into which she has been forced. *To the Lighthouse* is not only the daughter's story. The voice of the mother can be heard as well.

Mrs Ramsay's dissatisfaction with her role as mother is apparent right from the start. She is first presented as a typical Victorian mother, preaching to her daughters the superiority of the male sex: 'Indeed, she had the whole of the other sex under her protection; for reasons she could not explain, for their chivalry and valour, for the fact that they negotiated treaties, ruled India, controlled finance; . . . and woe betide the girl – pray Heaven it was none of her daughters! – who did not feel the worth of it' (*TL*: 11; ellipsis mine). Immediately after this, however, there is a change:

> They must find a way out of it all. There might be some simpler way, some less laborious way, she sighed. When she looked in the glass and saw her hair grey, her cheek sunk, at fifty, she thought, possibly she might have managed things better – her husband; money; his books. (*TL*: 11–12)

Mrs Ramsay's tone has changed from triumph to exhaustion and uncertainty about her role. Then she pulls herself together: 'But for her own part she would never for a single second regret her decision, evade difficulties, or slur over duties' (*TL*: 12). Nevertheless, for a moment, a fracture has appeared in Mrs Ramsay's role, revealing that she is not entirely at ease with it.

Similarly, a few pages later, reviewing her charitable work (which she has in common with Julia Stephen), Mrs Ramsay ends on a note of dissatisfaction. She carries a notebook of statistics in her bag, 'in the hope that thus she would cease to be a private woman whose charity was half a sop to her own indignation, half a relief to her own curiosity, and become, what with her untrained mind she greatly admired, an investigator elucidating the social problem' (*TL*: 14). She longs, in other words, for a professional training and expresses admiration for Lily's independence which is, partly, the independence of the professional woman: 'There was in Lily . . . something of her own which Mrs Ramsay liked very much indeed' (*TL*: 96; ellipsis mine).

Though she has often been seen as the embodiment of maternal self-sacrifice, Mrs Ramsay clearly expresses the frustrations of being a mother: 'They came to her, naturally, since she was a woman, all day long with this and that; the children were growing up; she often felt she was nothing but a sponge sopped full of human emotions' (*TL*: 34). She finds it a relief when the children are in bed, 'For now she need not think about anybody. She could be herself' (*TL*: 60). By pointing up these cracks and fissures in Mrs Ramsay's maternal persona, Woolf counters Leslie Stephen's reverential account in the *Mausoleum*

Book of her mother as a sort of Victorian secular saint and retrieves the real woman behind the patriarchal myths.

Mrs Ramsay has doubts, too, about her defence of marriage. Is she simply trying to vindicate her own choice, she wonders? ' she was driven on, too quickly she knew, almost as if it were an escape for her too, to say that people must marry; people must have children. Was she wrong in this, she asked herself' (*TL:* 58–59). Her doubts about marriage resurface from time to time: 'No happiness lasted; she knew that' (*TL:* 62). She thinks of Minta and Paul as 'these people entering into illusion' (*TL:* 93). When Lily later holds against Mrs Ramsay the fact that the Rayleys' marriage has failed, we have to remember that the mother was there first with her unspoken doubts about the match.

There are other occasions when the Victorian myth of motherhood seems an illusion to Mrs Ramsay. Rose's adoration makes her feel inadequate: 'what Rose felt was quite out of proportion to anything she actually was' (*TL:* 77). At the very moment when she might be expected to feel most at one with the myth, sitting down to dinner with her family around her, Mrs Ramsay expresses a sense of dissatisfaction with her role: 'But what have I done with my life? thought Mrs Ramsay, taking her place at the head of the table' (*TL:* 78). Her role is breaking down, there is a discrepancy between what she is doing (feeding her family) and what she is feeling (resentment, indifference). However, her awareness of the fact that she is faltering in her role, cannot be expressed: 'But this is not a thing, she thought, ladling out soup, that one says' (*TL:* 79). The mother's desire cannot be expressed in the symbolic. Mrs Ramsay rouses herself to bring the party back into harmony: 'for if she did not do it nobody would do it' (*ibid.*). Nevertheless, the momentary fissure between her self and the role she is expected to play highlights the fact that Mrs Ramsay *is* playing a part. Despite what the myth of motherhood says, it is not easy or natural for her to create harmony; it requires an effort of the will as great as that required of Lily in painting her picture.

Though she is deeply sexist, high-handed, a worshipper of masculine intelligence, there have been moments of doubt when Mrs Ramsay questioned her role and felt uncomfortable in it. Her self-questioning provides a window on to the future when the next generation, her daughters, will go further in deconstructing the Victorian myth of motherhood. Whether Woolf is expressing here her own thoughts on the mothering role or whether she dimly felt Julia Stephen's dissatisfactions is an open question. Certainly Julia Stephen was a woman who on the surface fully endorsed her society's view of the proper role for women (De Salvo 1991: 45).

As in *Jacob's Room*, the mothering task is defeated by war. Mrs Ramsay's eldest son, Andrew, is killed in the First World War and she herself dies, casually and disconcertingly, in brackets. When there is no mother present to mirror back her infant's gaze, there is a loss of human identity. Objects reign in the house in the Hebrides. The mirror on the wall reflects only light: 'Once the looking-glass had held a face . . . now, day after day, light turned . . . its clear image on the wall opposite' (*TL*: 120; ellipses mine). Then, gradually, the mother reasserts herself, comically in the figure of old Mrs McNab; mystically in the coming of spring, in dreams, in the light from the lighthouse softly caressing the empty house, 'gliding gently as if it laid its caress and lingered stealthily and looked and came lovingly again' (*TL*: 124). The house is rescued from the ravages of time.

In Woolf's earlier novels, Rachel Vinrace, Katharine Hilbery, Clara Durrant, Elizabeth Dalloway, are all daughter figures who fail to establish themselves securely in the symbolic order. Elizabeth Dalloway, for instance, is described as inarticulate, 'a hyacinth sheathed in glossy green' (*D*: 109). She realises that in order to have the career she wishes she will have to do battle with her mother and align herself with her father. Lily Briscoe is the first of these daughter figures to succeed in inscribing herself into the symbolic without betraying the mother. She recognises that the qualities which make up Mrs Ramsay's maternal thinking – self-forgetfulness, attention to detail – are also the qualities she needs as an artist: 'Mrs Ramsay making of the moment something permanent (as in another sphere Lily herself tried to make of the moment something permanent) – this was of the nature of a revelation. In the midst of chaos there was shape' (*TL*: 151). Here an insight – the artist's resemblance to the mother – gained in *Mrs Dalloway* is repeated and developed. Mothering and art have a similar goal, giving shape to the moment, and Mrs Ramsay's achievements remain in Lily's mind like a work of art. Compare Woolf's comment on Julia Stephen in 'Reminiscences': 'All lives directly she crossed them seemed to form themselves into a pattern and while she stayed each move was of the utmost importance' (Woolf 1990: 42). In order to become an artist and enter the symbolic order, Lily must identify with the father but she must not lose touch with the mother's voice.

Lily is conscious of the difficulties of recovering the maternal legacy. She lives in a society where the mother's knowledge is buried: 'she imagined how in the chambers of the mind and heart of the woman . . . were . . . tablets bearing sacred inscriptions, which if one could spell them out would teach one everything, but they would never be offered openly, never made public' (*TL*: 50; ellipses mine). In addition to burying the maternal legacy, this society has turned the mother into a patriarchal icon. In order to paint Mrs Ramsay and her child, Lily has to get behind sentimentalised versions of the mother to the real Mrs Ramsay: 'the thing itself before it has been made anything' (*TL*: 178).

In the same way as Lacan shows language arising in the absence of the mother, so Lily's painting is an attempt to compensate for the loss of the mother's body. Unlike Lacan, however, Lily sees her art not as a replacement for the mother but as an attempt to get back to her and recover her female artistic heritage. At the height of Lily's anguish, Mrs Ramsay comes in a vision to console her. It is a reversal of the Demeter–Persephone myth: the daughter's desire raises her 'mother' from the dead. The mother is not, as in Freud and Lacan, a regressive influence who must be defeated if art and civilisation are to flourish (indeed Bankes sees Mrs Ramsay as a civilising influence in whose presence 'barbarity was tamed, the reign of chaos subdued,' *TL*: 48). The mother is, as in Cixous, the source of the daughter's art. Thoughts of Charles Tansley and of Mr Ramsay impede Lily's art; Mrs Ramsay, on the contrary, inspires it: ' "Mrs Ramsay! Mrs Ramsay!" she repeated. She owed this revelation to her' (*TL*: 151).

Writing to her sister after reading *To the Lighthouse*, Vanessa underlined the fact that Woolf had managed to get beyond the child's point of view and see their mother as a subject in her own right: 'It was like meeting her again with oneself grown up and on equal terms and it seems to me the most astonishing feat of creation to have been able to see her in such a way' (11 May 1927, quoted in Gordon 1992: 39). Having retrieved her mother in *To the Lighthouse* and perceived the importance of her influence on her as a writer, increasingly Woolf began to hear the generalised voice of the mother as she wrote: 'Often now I have to control my excitement as if I were pushing through a screen; or as if something beat fiercely close to me. What this portends I don't know . . . Often it is connected with the sea and St Ives' (from her diary 13 June 1923, quoted in Gordon 1992: 178–9; ellipsis mine).

In *The Waves* (1931), the six characters share their creator's awareness of the mother's language pressing against the symbolic. Bernard thinks:

> But it is a mistake, this extreme precision, this orderly and military progress; a convenience, a lie. There is always deep below it, even when we arrive punctually at the appointed time with our white waistcoats and polite formalities, a rushing stream of broken dreams, nursery rhymes, street cries, half-finished sentences. (*W*: 172–3)

He desires to be able to express this maternal semiotic: ' "I begin to long for some little language such as lovers use, broken words, inarticulate words" ' (*W*: 161). To convey pain, particularly: 'for pain words are lacking. There should be cries, cracks, fissures, whiteness . . . interference with the sense of time, of space' (*W*: 178; ellipsis mine).

In her diary, Woolf wrote of *The Waves* that she wanted to 'make prose move . . . as prose has never moved before; from the chuckle, the babble to the rhapsody' (7 January 1931, Woolf 1953/1981: 162; ellipsis mine). The mother's language is represented in the text by interspersed descriptions of waves breaking upon the shore which continue after the individual lives of the characters have ended. In an early draft, waves and mothers are indistinguishable as the characters are born out of the waves:

> Wave after wave, endlessly sinking and falling as far as the eye can stretch. And all these waves have been the prostrate forms of mothers, in their flowing nightgowns, with the tumbled sheets about them holding up, with a groan, as they sink back into the sea, innumerable children. (*Waves*, Holo. Draft I, quoted in Roe 1990: 113)

In the book's opening description of the birth of the world, there is a revisioning of *Genesis* as a woman brings light to the world. The voices of the six characters are individualised but, as one would expect in a world presided over by a mother-goddess, it is the characters' sense of shared humanity that is stressed: ' "We melt into each other with phrases," ' says Bernard. ' "We are edged with mist" ' (*W*: 11). This is at the beginning, before the patriarchal social structures have begun to close round the characters making Bernard, for one, feel that language must compensate him for the loss of the pre-oedipal union: 'I must make phrases and phrases and so interpose something hard between myself and the stare of the housemaids, the stare of the clocks, staring faces' (*W*: 20). As he enters further into life, Bernard grows dissatisfied with the limitations of personal identity: 'that persistent smell . . . one's identity' (*W*: 77; ellipsis mine). Susan also longs to get rid of the social identity imposed on her at school, to 'take out whatever it is I have made here; something hard' (*W*: 36). Rhoda hates 'all detail of the individual life' (*W*: 71). She exists on the margins of the symbolic in 'the white spaces that lie between hour and hour' (*W*: 138). She dreams of drowning in waves where 'everything falls in a tremendous shower, dissolving me' (*W*: 139). Rhoda lives so closely to the maternal rhythm of the waves that she scarcely succeeds in establishing an identity in the symbolic order.

For all six characters the memory of the mother remains, pressing against the symbolic. Even for Louis who leaves school eager to embrace the patriarchal society ('blessings be on all traditions,' *W*: 39) 'the problem remains . . . Flowers toss their heads outside the window . . . I hear always the sullen thud of the waves' (*W*: 39; ellipses mine). Neville says: ' "We are in that passive and exhausted frame of mind when we only wish to rejoin the body of our mother from whom we have been severed" ' (*W*: 157). They are six individuals, but aspects of one being, 'a many-faceted flower' (*W*: 155), a maternal image that recurs in the novel (*W*: 85, 154). Only as part of the whole, do these characters' lives have meaning. 'As I talked I felt "I am you". This difference we make so much of, this identity we so feverishly cherish, was overcome,' Bernard thinks (*W*: 195). Thus Woolf expresses the communal values which, according to

Jane Harrison, are part of a matriarchy. In the world of the flirtatious Jinny, women are rivals for men's attention. In the world of Susan, the mother, 'women kiss each other' (*W*: 42).

Towards the end of *The Waves*, Woolf seems actually to have been writing in some kind of semiotic trance: in her diary she describes reeling 'across the last ten pages with some moments of such intensity and intoxication that I seemed only to stumble after my own voice, or almost, after some sort of speaker (as when I was mad) I was almost afraid, remembering the voices that used to fly ahead' (7 February 1931, Woolf 1953/1981: 165). Here Woolf is explicit about the connection between the voices she heard when she was mad (which may, as we have seen, have been produced by her unconscious straining against conventional discourse), and her creative experiments in writing in a way that was more closely in tune with the mother's voice. In a letter to Ethel Smyth, dated 28 August 1930, speaking of *The Waves*, Woolf explained: 'I am writing to a rhythm and not to a plot' (Woolf 1978b: 204). As Minow-Pinkney comments in relation to *The Waves*: 'Her constant though strictly speaking impossible aim is to write about what escapes the symbolic order' (Minow-Pinkney 1987: 163).

The Waves is, as Minow-Pinkney suggests, a poetic vision, outside the socio-temporal order. In the last decade of her life, Woolf sought to frame a public voice for herself and to give expression to women's values in a world increasingly dominated by power-hungry demagogues. To do this, Woolf needed to bring the maternal genealogy into the symbolic; in other words, attempt in literature a task similar to that performed in anthropology by Jane Harrison. In her essay, 'Professions for Women,' Woolf describes the process of 'letting her imagination sweep unchecked round every rock and cranny of the world that lies submerged in the depths of our unconscious being' (Barrett 1979: 61). In *The Years* (1937), the story of the Pargiter family from the 1880s to the 1930s, Woolf attempts to excavate this buried matriarchy.

In 1880, the household of the Pargiter family is typically Victorian and patriarchal. Colonel Pargiter dominates his children and their mother is sick and dying. Indeed, she is barely articulate: 'her sentences were more broken than usual . . . she seemed to be fumbling for words' (*Y*: 21; ellipsis mine). This is the buried mother of the Victorian age. Even when the relationship between mother and daughters is positive, like that between Eugenie and her daughters, the mother–daughter *jouissance* (dancing round the bonfire or telling stories) is always liable to be interrupted by men. Their first mother–daughter scene is broken up by Colonel Pargiter, the second by Digby. Woolf demonstrates the way Victorian patriarchal structures intervened to weaken the mother–daughter bonding. The Italian mirror that Eugenie bequeathes to her daughters is 'blurred with spots' (*Y*: 128); Rose Pargiter's portrait gathers dirt after her death. The maternal inheritance is veiled.

As the novel moves into the twentieth century, the social structures become more fluid. The Pargiter household is broken up. There is less stress on hierarchical relationships, more on egalitarian ones between siblings. Characters become conscious that identity is not fixed: 'What's "I"?' asks Sara (*Y*: 108). 'What would the world be . . . without "I" in it?' wonders Martin (*Y*: 185; ellipsis mine). The First World War hastens this dissolution of identity: 'it was the war,' Eleanor thinks, 'things seemed to have lost their skins; to be freed from some surface hardness; even the chair with gilt claws, at which she was looking, seemed porous' (*Y*: 220). The characters drink to a new world and Nicholas prophesies a new communal way of life, rather than living as they do, 'Each in his own little cubicle' (*Y*: 227). But the Victorian mother is still unintegrated into the symbolic order: Rose's portrait remains uncleaned (*Y*: 122).

In the final section, 'Present Day,' where, significantly, the mother's portrait has been cleaned and restored, this sense of community which, as we have seen, is the mark of a matriarchal society, is emphasised by several of the characters. 'Where does she begin, and where do I end?' wonders Peggy, driving through London in a cab with her aunt Eleanor (*Y*: 255). The prophet of revolution is Eleanor's nephew, North, who envisages a post-individualist future: 'Why not down barriers and simplify? . . . To keep the emblems and tokens of North Pargiter . . . but at the same time spread out, make a new ripple in human consciousness, be the bubble and the stream, the stream and the bubble – myself and the world together' (*Y*: 312; ellipses mine). Though North and his sister Peggy try to describe a life lived communally, they have difficulty finding the words to articulate their vision: 'he felt that he had been in the middle of a jungle; in the heart of darkness; cutting his way towards the light; but provided only with broken sentences' (*Y*: 313). Peggy, too, feels that: 'There was the vision still, but she had not grasped it. She had broken off only a little fragment of what she wished to say' (*Y*: 298). Brother and sister share a pessimism as to the success of the project. Fear, North realises, will always separate people. Unable to come to grips with the future he drifts off into a consoling dream.

But the future does erupt into the novel at the end, in the shape of two working-class children who sing their hideous song. 'There was something horrible in the noise they made. It was so shrill, so discordant, and so meaningless' (*Y*: 327). The semiotic babble that erupts here is not soothing but threatening. This new language is no adequate replacement for the old. The novel ends, as far as the future is concerned, on a note of pessimism and menace. Knowledge is fragmented, stories never get finished, communication falters. 'There must be another life,' thinks Eleanor, 'This is too short, too broken. We know nothing, even about ourselves' (*Y*: 325).

This pessimism is continued in *Between the Acts* (1941). The portrait of the lady in yellow, the Olivers' unofficial ancestress, has no name. Presiding over an empty room, she leads the eye 'into silence' (*BA*: 33). She is the absent mother, the lost ancestress. Lucy Swithin, a maternal figure who claims kinship with the woman in yellow, is investigating humanity's primeval origins. She frequently defies the authority of her patriarchal brother, Bart: 'For she belonged to the unifiers; he to the separatists' (*BA*: 90). She soothes William Dodge with her semiotic babble, 'an old child's nursery rhyme to help a child' (*BA*: 57). But Lucy is trapped by her adherence to a patriarchal religion. She wears a gleaming gold cross on her breast. Looking at it, Dodge wonders: 'How could she weight herself down by that sleek symbol? How stamp herself, so volatile, so vagrant, with that image?' (*BA*: 59).

Like Lucy, Isa is weighed down by stereotyped feminine roles: 'she loathed the domestic, the possessive; the maternal' (*BA*: 20). When she tries to escape these roles she falls into another trap, the myth of romantic love, endowing Haines, a gentleman farmer, with all the attributes of the romantic hero. Partly Isa's failure is a failure of language. There are words to describe her feelings for Haines (' "In love," ' *BA*: 16) and for her husband (' "The father of my children," she added, slipping into the cliché conveniently provided by fiction,' *ibid*.), but, in common with other mothers in Woolf, Isa can find no words to articulate her true feelings as a mother (as opposed to the idealised patriarchal version of motherhood): 'what feeling was it that stirred in her now when above the looking-glass, out of doors, she saw coming across the lawn the perambulator; two nurses; and her little boy George, lagging behind?' (*BA*: 16). There is no suggestion that these women will escape. At the end of the novel, Isa is doomed to repeat the age-old fight between fox and vixen: 'Love and hate – how they tore her asunder! Surely it was time someone invented a new plot' (*BA*: 158).

In her diary, Woolf describes her methods in *Poyntz Hall* (the original name for the novel): ' "I" rejected: "We" substituted . . . "We" . . . the composed of many different things . . . we all life, all art, all waifs and strays – a rambling capricious but somehow unified whole' (Woolf 1953/1981: 276; ellipses mine). Woolf's vision of 'a unified whole' is shared by Miss La Trobe. Her pageant is a mixture of songs, rhymes and music that at times becomes a semiotic babble: 'It didn't matter what the words were; or who sang what. Round and round they whirled, intoxicated by the music' (*BA*: 73). Music brings the audience together. 'I hear music, they were saying. Music wakes us. Music makes us see the hidden, join the broken' (*BA*: 91). Like North, La Trobe envisages a post-individualist future where the individual will be absorbed into the community and into the pattern of history.

But La Trobe has to struggle to hold on to her vision of 'a recreated world' (*BA*: 114). Indeed at times it fails her: 'Beads of perspiration broke on her forehead. Illusion had failed. "This is death," she murmured, "death" ' (*BA*:

105). The audience is held together only by her vision; in the interval, the refrain that runs through their minds is 'Dispersed are we' (*BA*: 75). At the end of the pageant, they drift off into their separate lives and the refrain is repeated. The music degenerates into a cacophony of broken sounds: 'the tune changed; snapped; broke; jagged' (*BA*: 134). Mirrors are held up to the audience, not maternal mirrors conferring wholeness and identity, but malicious mirrors designed to show the audience in their worst light, fragmented and disparate. Miss La Trobe lacks Clarissa Dalloway's gift for unifying and reconciling.

In the end, La Trobe despairs of her vision and seeks deliberately to sabotage it: 'how's this wall . . . which we call, perhaps miscall, civilization, to be built by (here the mirrors flicked and flashed) orts, scraps and fragments like ourselves?' (*BA*: 138; ellipsis mine). For a moment an anonymous tune from the gramophone (the voice of the Mother?) unites the audience:

> The whole population of the mind's immeasurable profundity came flocking . . . Compelled from the ends of the horizon; recalled from the edge of appalling crevasses; they crashed; solved; united . . . Was that voice ourselves? Scraps, orts and fragments, are we, also, that? (*BA*: 139; ellipses mine)

But 'the voice died away' (*ibid.*). The waves withdraw. La Trobe feels the pageant has been a 'failure' (*BA*: 153). Her meaning has not been understood.

Between the Acts operates largely through parody and in the figure of Miss La Trobe, Woolf satirises both herself as artist and many of her most cherished beliefs. Entertaining though *Between the Acts* is, it is as if Woolf's trust in herself and her vision was breaking down. Three months before her death, she wrote in her diary: 'the idea came to me that why I dislike, and like, so many things idiosyncratically now, is because of my growing detachment from the hierarchy, the patriarchy' (Woolf 1953/1981: 341). Her difficulty was in finding a discourse to oppose that of the patriarchy. In *Three Guineas* (1938) she suggests that women should unite together in a Society of Outsiders; but the war and the rise of fascism seem to have made Woolf despair of ever creating a society which would reflect the values women have acquired as a result of their exclusion from power. In *Women's Fiction of the Second World War*, Gill Plain suggests that Woolf is attempting in *Between the Acts* 'to write herself out of time' and that she does this by envisaging 'a pre history – a space outside the symbolic order of the father's history' (Plain 1996:136). I would characterise this 'pre history' as the matriarchy and I agree with Plain that Woolf's strategy for writing herself out of the war largely fails in this novel.

Between the Acts shows how women have become psychically locked into supporting the existing power relations. Isa and Lucy start to discuss the possibility that we are all part of one another 'when the gentlemen came in'

(*BA*: 158). Their talk never gets started. If there is another society, a matriarchal one, lurking on the margins of the patriarchy, these women are powerless to retrieve it (and women like Manresa, with their worship of the dominant male, will work actively to counter it). In the end, La Trobe sinks down into the primeval swamp of the semiotic: 'Words rose above the intolerably laden dumb oxen plodding through the mud. Words without meaning – wonderful words' (*BA*: 155-6). But the words never get spoken. La Trobe has been unable to bring the mother's language into speech, she has been unable to retrieve the maternal legacy. To paraphrase Irigaray, the foundations of the patriarchy remain unshaken.

It is clear that Woolf's treatment of the maternal inheritance is more sustained than that of any other author discussed in this study. In the yearning after the lost mother, her work shows similarities with that of Jean Rhys. Both authors try to recreate the mother's presence and both are strongly aware of the buried mother's world pressing against the father's. For both women their identity as writers depends, not on cutting themselves off from the mother's world, but in trying to retrieve it. Woolf is at her greatest in those works which recreate the mother's voice (*To the Lighthouse*, *The Waves*).

Woolf foreshadows later feminist thinking on the importance of recognising the mother as a subject in her own right (Mrs Ramsay) and on the importance of establishing a maternal genealogy. In her essays, particularly *Three Guineas* and *A Room of One's Own*, she encourages women to think back through their mothers and to revalorise motherhood. In *Three Guineas*, she suggests that motherhood is a profession and as such is entitled to payment. The ideal education she envisages will be founded on matriarchal values: 'The aim of the new college . . . should be not to segregate and specialize, but to combine' (Woolf 1992: 200; ellipsis mine).

For much of her life Woolf was obsessed by her mother's memory. Julia Stephen died when Woolf was thirteen. As Woolf herself realised, for a mother to die at this crucial stage, before the daughter has achieved the detachment necessary to view her mother as a being separate from herself, can profoundly mark a daughter's life. She explained to Vanessa: 'dying at that moment, I suppose she cut a great figure on one's mind when it was just awake' (letter quoted in Roe 1990: 64). Woolf remained haunted by her mother's image: 'Until I was in the forties [that is, until she wrote *To the Lighthouse*] the presence of my mother obsessed me. I could hear her voice, see her, imagine what she would do or say as I went about my day's doings' (*op.cit.* 89). As Lidoff points out, the early loss of her mother before she was able to establish a separate identity, accounts for Woolf's recurring difficulty in establishing a sense of self (Lidoff 1986: 43-59). Again, there are parallels with Jean Rhys's heroines whose lack of positive experiences of maternal mirroring leave them with a fragile sense of identity. Woolf was always hungry for maternal affection and in her most important relationships with women she acted like a daughter in relation to a mother. She wrote, for instance, of Vita Sackville-West that she 'lavishes on me the maternal protection which, for some reason, is what I have always most wished from everyone' (Woolf 1978b: 118).

When, in *To the Lighthouse*, Woolf solved the problem of how to see her mother as an individual in her own right, her mother ceased to haunt her. In 'A Sketch of the Past,' she explains: 'I suppose that I did for myself what psycho-analysts do for their patients. I expressed some very long felt and deeply felt emotion. And in expressing it I explained it and then laid it to rest' (Woolf 1990: 90). But she had still not solved the problem of how to inscribe the mother's voice into the symbolic order. Without this, the daughter is left vulnerable in a patriarchal society. As we have seen, Woolf had personal reasons for knowing this. After her mother's death, her half-brother, George Duckworth, began to abuse her sexually ('22 Hyde Park Gate', Woolf 1990: 193). The abuse only ended when Woolf had a breakdown and was sent away to recover. She was cared for by Violet Dickinson. In 'The Magic Garden', a work Woolf wrote after her recovery, she describes an idyllic world without men. In Violet's garden, women are protected; there is freedom, peace, joy, sisterhood. Here, for the first time, Woolf glimpsed what living in a matriarchy might be like. The vision of a matriarchal world in Woolf's fiction is not merely political but expresses a deep personal need to find protection.

That Woolf's vision of a matriarchal society failed her in the end was partly due to the historical circumstance of the outbreak of war. The unfinished manuscript, *Anon*, begun on 18 September 1940, seems to have been yet another attempt to assert a common vision of history – but there was no community any more, 'no public to echo back,' as she wrote in her diary on 24 July 1940 (Woolf 1953/1981: 321). Given over to militarism, civilisation had moved further away from the wholeness and security provided by the nurturing mother. Woolf now doubted the daughter's ability to preserve the maternal legacy. And with the loss of her maternal heritage came doubts about her ability as a writer: 'But shall I ever write again one of those sentences that give me intense pleasure?' she wrote in her diary on 26 February 1941, a month before her death.

Partly, too, Woolf's failure was due to the disturbing memories she was recovering of the abuse she had suffered as a child. She began writing 'A Sketch of the Past' on 18 April 1939 and continued writing it up to 17 November 1940, that is, until four months before her death (De Salvo 1991: 126–133). For the first time she remembered that the abuse had started before her mother died when, as a small child, she had been sexually assaulted by Gerald Duckworth (Woolf 1990: 77). In other words, her mother had been powerless to protect her daughter against men's violence. 'She began to think that there might be no cure for the womanliness bred by manliness' (Gordon 1992: 272).

As a writer Woolf was always attempting to recapture that sense of wholeness and safety she had experienced, all too briefly, in her mother's presence, 'the mother of her earliest childhood, whose silence seemed to answer questions that were never asked' (*ND*: 410). In 'A Sketch of the Past', Woolf links the moment at St Ives when she saw a flower as part of a whole and still connected to the nurturing earth, with her motivation as a writer 'to put the severed parts together' (Woolf 1990: 81). She said, 'It is only by putting it into words that I make it whole; this wholeness means that it has lost its power to hurt me' (*ibid.*). These words are a striking echo of Jean Rhys's description of the way she sought to heal herself through her writing (see above p.124). Towards the end of her life, Woolf's efforts to recapture that sense of wholeness both in her own life and in the society around her failed. Unable to recreate the safety of her mother's presence, that 'panoply of life' (Woolf 1990: 92), she chose instead to return to her in death, playing out a regression that is foreshadowed in *The Voyage Out*.

> For a woman, the call of the mother is not only a call from beyond time, or beyond the socio-political battle . . . this call troubles the word: it generates hallucinations . . . I think of Virginia Woolf, who sunk wordlessly into the river, her pockets weighed down with stones. Haunted by voices, waves, lights, in love with colours. (Kristeva 'About Chinese Women', Moi 1986: 157; ellipses mine)

8

Dorothy Richardson: The Artist's Quest

Nothing happens. It is just life going on and on. (May Sinclair)

Everything going into Dorothy Richardson's mind is summoned forth again complete in every detail, with nothing taken away from it – and nothing added. (Katherine Mansfield)

I suppose the danger is the damned egotistical self; which ruins Joyce and Richardson to my mind. (Virginia Woolf)

A very curious experiment in autobiography. (H. G. Wells)

If I have much more of this bloody steamship, I shall begin to write like Dorothy Richardson. (H. G. Wells in a letter to Rebecca West, 1921, on board the S.S. *Adriatic*)

Few women writers have attracted so much hostile criticism as Dorothy Richardson, partly because few have attempted such an ambitious project as *Pilgrimage*. As Virginia Woolf said in her review of *The Tunnel*, we clamour for a new way of writing and then complain when we get it: 'We want to be rid of realism, to penetrate without its help into the regions beneath it, and further require that Miss Richardson shall fashion this new material into something which has the shapeliness of the old accepted forms. We are asking too much' (Barrett 1979: 191).

Pilgrimage is shapeless and formless, but not as shapeless and formless as some critics have suggested. Our judgement of *Pilgrimage* has been distorted by the reactions of Richardson's contemporaries. Reading *Pilgrimage* volume by volume (and not having access to the final volume, *March Moonlight*), early reviewers like May Sinclair were unable to see the work as a finished whole and were quick to apply labels such as 'stream-of-consciousness' and 'impressionism'. Richardson always disliked the description 'stream-of-consciousness,' (Fromm 1977: 232). What she claimed to be doing was offering 'a feminine equivalent of the current masculine *realism*' (Richardson's foreword to *Pilgrimage*: 9; my emphasis). There is, in fact, a plot in *Pilgrimage* and it is one in which the mother is central. Daughter of a powerless mother who never succeeded in finding a satisfactory role for herself, Miriam is on a quest to learn how to express herself as a woman and an artist in the patriarchal, gender divided society of, roughly, 1890 to 1915.

Miriam's quest can be set within the framework of Helene Deutsch's theories about women's psychology. Miriam's search for a discourse of maternity that will not reproduce the law of the father echoes Deutsch's widening of the term motherhood in *The Psychology of Women*, volume 2, where she states: 'A woman need not have given birth to a child in order to be motherly . . . motherliness can also be turned toward indirect goals' (Deutsch 1945: 47; ellipsis mine). This redirection of motherhood 'toward indirect goals', provides, as we shall see, a conclusion to *Pilgrimage*. Moreover, Miriam's prolonged attachment to her mother and her oscillation between mother and father illustrates Helene Deutsch's thesis, set out in volume 1 of *The Psychology of Women* (1944) and later borrowed by Nancy Chodorow in *The Reproduction of Mothering*, that the oedipal triangle lasts late into a woman's life since a woman never entirely breaks with her mother:

> It is erroneous to say that the little girl gives up her first mother relation in favour of the father. She only gradually draws him into the alliance, develops from the mother-child exclusiveness toward the triangular parent-child relation and continues the latter, just as she does the former, although in a weaker and less elemental form, all her life . . . The ineradicability of affective constellations manifests itself in later repetitions. (Deutsch 1946: 162; ellipsis mine)

As in Deutsch's theory, in Richardson's *roman fleuve* the pattern of the emotional triangle set by her relationship with her parents will be repeated again and again in Miriam's life.

Miriam Henderson sees her inheritance as deeply divided. From her father she inherits intellectual curiosity and a fastidious Puritan temperament. From her mother she inherits a more instinctive approach to life and a deep distrust of facts: 'Don't go so deeply into everything, chickie. You must learn to take life as it comes. Ah-eh, if I were strong I could show you how to enjoy life' (*Pointed Roofs*: 169). Miriam dwells at length on this dual inheritance in *Revolving Lights*. She feels the two sides are so sharply contrasting that they will end by tearing her apart: 'She was the sport of opposing forces that would never allow her to alight and settle. The movement of her life would be like a pendulum' (*RL*: 246). She can belong wholly neither to her mother's world nor to her father's, illustrating Deutsch's thesis that the early triangular parent-child relation is never entirely given up by the girl: 'Only the principal part changes: now the mother, now the father plays it' (Deutsch 1946: 162). This divided inheritance is reinforced for Miriam by the rigid gender divisions of the society in which she lives, so that she comes to think of herself as an outsider, accepted neither by the world of women nor by the world of men.

The younger Miriam is more strongly drawn to the world of men. She dislikes the narrow complacency of women: 'those hateful women's smiles – smirks – self-satisfied smiles as if everybody were agreed about everything. She loathed women' (*Pointed Roofs*: 21). Her mother, treated with contempt by her husband, is a helpless victim of patriarchal society and no help to a daughter who wishes to gain access to the symbolic order: 'mother did not know. She had no reasoning power. She could not help because she did not know' (*Pointed Roofs*: 169). Miriam resents her mother's efforts to force her into society's construct of femininity: 'The love of God was like the love of a mother; always forgiving you, ready to die for you, always waiting for you to be good. Why? . . . The things one wanted one could not have if one were just tame and good' (*Honeycomb*: 391; ellipsis mine). As in the novels of Macaulay and Compton-Burnett, it is the father who represents for his daughter freedom from the claustrophobic world of women and access to the symbolic order which, for Miriam, means access to the wider world of the intellect and politics.

Miriam finds it a relief that 'Pater knew how hateful all the world of women were and despised them. He never included her with them; or only sometimes when she pretended, or he didn't understand' (*Pointed Roofs*: 22). The last few words of this quotation point to the ultimate failure of Miriam's relationship with her father. In treating her as a surrogate son he approaches their relationship from a masculine standpoint and fails to take into account her feminine consciousness. Later Miriam realises that her father deliberately chose not to take her to the public talks and lectures he attended in London. Like most of the men in this deeply divided society, he wishes to retain power through making knowledge exclusive; he will share it with his daughter, but only on his terms. Though in women's fiction of this period daughters may look to fathers for help in establishing their identity, these fathers are very often presented as failing their daughters, either because they are too remote (as in the novels of Compton-Burnett) or because they wish to make their daughters conform (in Antonia White's quartet) or simply because, as in Woolf's case, the daughter recognises that as a woman she needs to recover her female inheritance. This is what happens to Miriam.

For, despite her loathing of the feminine stereotype to which her mother conforms, Miriam cannot help siding emotionally with her mother rather than with her father. She imagines what her mother's married life must have been like in a household dominated by an autocratic husband: 'that neighing laugh had come again and again all through the years until she sat meekly, flushed and suffering under the fierce gaslight, feeling every night of her life winter and summer as if the ceiling were coming down on her head' (*Backwater*: 234–5). This early sympathy with her mother against her father, despite all he can offer her, is part of the dawning of Miriam's feminine consciousness which in turn will lead her to discover her identity both as a woman and an artist.

So profound is her empathy with her mother that Miriam feels she would make a better husband to her than her father has: 'She laughed towards her mother and smiled at her until she made her blush. Ah, she thought proudly, it's I who am your husband. Why have I not been with you all your life? . . . all the times you were alone; I know them all. No one else knows them' (*Honeycomb*: 456; ellipsis mine). This is a remarkable illustration of Nancy Chodorow's thesis that a child makes up to the mother for the emotional needs unmet by her husband: 'Women come to want and need primary relationships to children. These wants and needs result from wanting intense primary relationships, which men tend not to provide both because of their place in women's oedipal constellation and because of their difficulties with intimacy' (Chodorow 1978: 203). Listening to her parents argue, Miriam hears her mother's 'tearful, uncertain voice' and thinks: 'Don't mother . . . don't, don't . . . he can't understand . . . Come to me!' (*Honeycomb*: 460; ellipses mine) As we saw in Chapter 2, there is an analogous emotional triangle in Radclyffe Hall's novel, *The Unlit Lamp* (1924), where the daughter supplies the mother with the sympathy and attention she fails to get from her husband and behaves towards her mother as if towards a lover. Similarly, when her mother tells her she is the only one who understands how she feels, Miriam smokes for the first time in her presence and generally acts like a flirtatious lover (*Honeycomb*: 474).

Mrs Henderson's mental stability deteriorates and Miriam accompanies her to the seaside in the hope that the sea air will improve her health. Miriam tends to her mother day and night, listening to her laments over a wasted life: ' "It's no use . . . I am cumbering the ground" ' (*Honeycomb*: 485; ellipsis mine). She hears her mother's despair break out in a kind of semiotic babble: 'In the room yellow with daylight a voice was muttering rapidly, rapid words and chuckling laughter and stillness . . . It was a trust; triumphing over everything. "*I* know," said a high clear voice "*I* know . . . I don't deceive myself" . . . rapid low muttering and laughter . . . It was a conversation. Somewhere within it was the answer. Nowhere else in the world' (*op. cit.* 487; ellipses mine). Her mother's suicide confirms Miriam's observation that the patriarchy's construct of femininity is deadly for women: 'Mother – almost killed by things she could not control, having done her duty all her life . . . doing thing after thing had not satisfied her . . . being happy and brave had not satisfied her. There was something she had always wanted, for herself . . . even mother' (*Honeycomb*: 472; ellipses mine). The mother's rage becomes a determining factor in daughter's quest for identity.

Her mother's death makes more poignant Miriam's later observations of the damage done to women's lives by gender divisions. Miriam's refusal to give up the bond with her mother means that she will try to find a way of articulating her mother's (and all women's) needs. There is a parallel here with some of Virginia Woolf's heroines: Clarissa Dalloway dimly recognising her maternal inheritance, for example, or Miss La Trobe seeking to recover the mother's language. In creating characters who find their identity in their refusal to be cut off from the mother's world and who seek to articulate the mother's desire, both Woolf and Richardson anticipate Irigaray's declaration that: 'we must not once more kill the mother who was sacrificed to the origins of our culture. We must give her new life . . . We must refuse to let her desire be annhilated by the law of the father. We must give her the right to pleasure, to *jouissance*, to passion, restore her right to speech, and sometimes to cries and anger' (Whitford 1991a: 43; ellipsis mine).

Her mother's suicide leaves Miriam with a sense of failure: she has failed to provide her mother with sufficient mothering to prevent her from taking her own life. Rachel Blau du Plessis argues that this failure accounts for the intense maternal drive Miriam later displays with men (Du Plessis 1985: 144). Her mother's death also leaves Miriam with a recurring sense of loneliness (*Interim*: 326). She tells Michael Shatov: 'If I could have her back for ten minutes I would gladly give up the rest of my life' (*Deadlock*: 220). The horror of the memory of her mother's death, which is always associated for Miriam with a particular spot in London, is not finally exorcised until *Dawn's Left Hand* (155–6).

Miriam's determination to gain access to the masculine world of knowledge means that her feminine side develops quite slowly: in a rigidly gendered society, she continues to be suspicious of the social construct of femininity. Most of all, she despises those women who, like Mrs Corrie, act the part of hostess. 'That was feminine worldliness, pretending to be interested so that pleasant things might go on . . . Feminine worldliness then meant perpetual hard work and cheating and pretence' (*Honeycomb*: 388; ellipsis mine). At the same time, Miriam begins to wonder whether women have some superior wisdom and whether the reason why she hates women is because she is a failure as a woman, being instead 'a sort of horrid man' (*Honeycomb*: 404). This, she comes to realise, would be worse and it is at Mrs Corrie's that she first learns about masculine worldliness and how deeply unsatisfactory it is for a woman to attempt to imitate men.

Miriam is excited when she enters Mr Corrie's study for the first time. Here is 'a sort of deep freedom,' she thinks (*Honeycomb:* 366). The owner of this study will be someone who can relate to her intellectual needs. But when she tries to participate in the men's discussion of Darwin, her subversive behaviour offends both men and women. She realises that there is a social construct of masculinity which limits and blinkers Mr Corrie as much as his wife is limited and blinkered by trying to live up to the social construct of femininity: 'Masculine worldliness meant never being really there; always talking about things that had happened or making plans for things that might happen' (*op. cit.* 388). She realises that 'mannishness' which had seemed to her 'mighty and strong and comforting' after being 'mewed up with women' all her life, can in reality be 'utterly imbecile and aggravating' (*op. cit.* 423).

Miriam's dissatisfaction with the world of men and her search for some kind of alternative remind us of Cixous's warning: 'If we enter society to become men, we have lost everything' (Conley 1984: 135). Is there any way out of this dilemma? Can a woman enter the symbolic order without becoming a pseudo-male? Cixous suggests that it is a hard task:

> Can one win? Only on condition that upon entering society one does not identify with men but that one works on other possibilities of living, on other modes of life, on other relations to the other, other relations to power, etc., in such a way that one also brings about transformations in oneself, in others, and in men. That is a long project. (Conley 1984: 136)

This is the 'long project' on which Miriam now embarks – to find 'other possibilities of living'.

Not surprisingly, since she refuses to conform to her society's understanding of what a woman should be and since she has learned that she cannot simply imitate men, Miriam has difficulty establishing a sense of identity. She rediscovers 'herself, the nearest, most intimate self she had known,' through reading Ouida's novels. 'It was not perhaps a "good" self, but it was herself, her own familiar secretly happy and rejoicing self – not dead' (*Backwater:* 282). She goes on to examine her large, rather masculine hands which throughout *Pilgrimage* are an important aspect of her identity: 'they were her strength. They came between her and the world of women' (*op. cit.* 283). Thus she sways between her secret bond with the world of women (Ouida's novels) and her separation from the social construct, woman. Indeed, with other women, Miriam can sometimes feel like a man – with her mother, as we have seen, with Miss Dear (*The Tunnel:* 243), with Miss Holland (*The Trap:* 412, 428). However, she is not quite like a man – reading to Miss Dear: 'She felt that in some way she was like a man reading to a woman, but the reading did not separate them like a man's reading did' (*The Tunnel:* 261). Miriam is something in between a man and a woman: 'I don't like men and I loathe women', she says (*Pointed Roofs*: 31). Her society offers her a limited range of identities.

In London, Miriam begins to recognise the great gulf separating men and women in her society. They speak different languages and, since the man will never understand the woman's, the woman 'must, stammeringly, speak his. He listens and is flattered and thinks he has her mental measure when he has not touched even the fringe of her consciousness' (*The Tunnel*: 210). Watching a performance of *The Merchant of Venice*, she feels the attractions of a woman's world, apart from men: 'How much more real was the relation between Portia and Nerissa than between either of the sadly jesting women and their complacently jesting lovers' (*The Tunnel*: 187). The value of this intimacy between women has been underestimated by male writers, she realises. Science, art and religion in this gender divided society collude in insisting on the inferiority of women: 'Life is poisoned, for women, at the very source' (*The Tunnel*: 222). Whereas 'If women had been the recorders of things from the beginning it would all have been the other way round' (*The Tunnel*: 251 and see *Deadlock*: 218). She wants a relationship with a man but since she cannot play the feminine part for long, her relationships with conventional men will always break down (though she will continue to be attracted by them – Densley, Guerini, Richard Roscorla). She decides she must live alone: 'Women who had anything whatever to do with men were not themselves. They were in a noisy confusion, playing a part all the time' (*Interim*: 321). Like Woolf, she decides that freedom for a woman is 'a cold clear room to return to' (*ibid.*).

Coming up against the conventional man, Miriam begins to be more tolerant of women. She makes several observations about the drudgery and lack of prospects of the working woman's life. Women are expected to do all the unselfish jobs and then are despised for this. Observing Mrs Bailey, a mother figure, she learns about women's ability to create atmospheres. The relationship between Mrs Bailey and Miriam is very like that between Mrs Ramsay and Lily Briscoe in that the maternal legacy is ambivalent. Miriam does not want to be Mrs Bailey, for Mrs Bailey has no concept of scholarship or freedom. On the other hand, she possesses some gift, some intuition about life, which Miriam herself lacks and which she perceives to be an essential part of a woman's nature: 'Where did women find the insight into personality that gave them such extraordinary prophetic power?' (*Deadlock*: 37). Miriam is opposed to feminism ('an insult to womanhood', *Deadlock*: 219) precisely because of women's strength and ability to create atmospheres. As in *Mrs Dalloway* and *To the Lighthouse*, in *Pilgrimage* this ability to create atmospheres is seen as a woman's art, equal to men's, and involving self-realisation. Amabel will be shown to possess the gift to perfection (*MM*: 59–67).

Before long Miriam discovers limitations in less conventional men. Male writers, she finds, have always been convinced of the inferiority of women: 'Even Emerson . . . positive and negative, north and south, male and female . . . why *negative*?' (*Deadlock*: 51; ellipses mine). Miriam's question foreshadows Cixous's deconstruction of the binary oppositions which work to the disadvantage of women. Male thinkers, Miriam realises, have constantly invented intellectual systems: 'those everlasting mannish explanations of everything which explain nothing' (*Deadlock*: 111). Her own father tried to live according to one such theory (Herbert Spencer's). Miriam rejects this approach to life and in doing so remains loyal to her maternal legacy: as we have seen, it was Miriam's mother who instilled in her a distrust of facts. One might compare Her Gart in H. D.'s *Her*, similarly torn between her father and her mother and realising that: 'Words of Eugenia [her mother] had more power than textbooks, than geometry, than all of Carl Gart [her father] and brilliant "Bertie Gart" as people called him. Bertrand wasn't brilliant, not like mama. Carl Gart wasn't brilliant like Eugenia,' (H.D. 1981/1984: 89).

Miriam meets Michael Shatov, an unconventional man whom she thinks could be her intellectual companion; but because Michael shares Orthodox Judaism's view that women find their highest calling in being wives and mothers it is impossible for Miriam to marry him. Even with Michael she would always be solitary. She understands him, but he does not understand her female consciousness: 'His happiness was, she now recognised, hearing his voice, different from hers . . . they were too separate' (*Deadlock*: 202; ellipsis mine). This is even before she learns about Michael's past (he has frequented prostitutes) when she comes up against the truth about men: that though they may say they respect women, this does not stop them abusing them. Miriam finds herself at a dead end ('deadlock'). The man whom she thought could be her life's companion has failed her. She eventually forgives Michael with a maternal embrace, but this does not relieve her own feeling of loneliness: ' "Poor boy," she murmured, gathering him as he sank to his knees, with swift enveloping hands against her breast . . . This was the truth behind the image of woman supported by man. The strong companion was a child seeking shelter; the woman's share an awful loneliness. It was not fair' (*Deadlock*: 212; ellipsis mine). As a woman, she can nurture a man but he, because of his upbringing in a culture which has taught him to repress emotion, cannot nurture her.

One part of Miriam's personality now begins to express itself, through her translations. She has a moment of epiphany, a recognition that from now on life will be less important to her than writing: 'Nothing would matter now that the paper-scattered lamplit circle was established as the centre of life . . . Held up by this secret place, drawing her energy from it, any sort of life would do that left this room and its little table free and untouched' (*Deadlock*: 134; ellipsis mine). This satisfies one part of her personality: her 'masculine mind' (*RL:* 236) has found a purpose in life. But her emotional life has yet to be resolved.

Miriam's relationship with Hypo Wilson will crystallise certain things for her in this regard. In their long argument about women (*RL:* 255–62), Miriam explains to Hypo what she has learned about women – their art of creating atmospheres ('It's as big an art as any other,' *RL:* 257), their ability to hold several opinions at once 'because they see the relations of things which don't change' (*RL:* 259). She comes close here to Irigaray's view of woman as multiple and Woolf's notion of women's diffuse identity. With her deeper understanding of women, Miriam is now able to spend an afternoon in their world and appear to fit in (*RL:* 268). She again observes the gulf between men and women in English society, but now sees 'the women moving, more and more heavily burdened, towards the heart of life and the men getting further and further away from the living centre' (*RL:* 271). Men are a mass of opinions and ambition; they have no personality apart from that given them by their professional status. Whereas 'a woman can become a waitress and remain herself' (*RL:* 280). In *Revolving Lights*, we see Miriam drawing closer to the world of women, drawn because of her need to preserve loyalty to her mother, yet finding there a world very different from her mother's.

Paradoxically Miriam thinks that she would find her insights about women easier to explain to a man than to a woman because 'The very words expressing it have been made by men' (*RL:* 281). Miriam shows no desire to return to semiotic babble which she equates with her mother's rage and powerlessness. What she wishes to do is expand the language used by men to make it capable of containing and expressing feminine consciousness. She foreshadows Kristeva's approach – that women should enter the symbolic order, not in order to become men, but to disrupt it with their radical insights. Miriam will use men's language, albeit expanded and developed, so that in Woolf's phrase it becomes 'the psychological sentence of the feminine gender,' in order to subvert men's view of women. For Richardson, 'feminine prose' was not the prerogative of women: in her preface to *Pilgrimage* she cites Dickens and Joyce as its practitioners. Woolf herself noted, in her review of *Revolving Lights*, that this new 'feminine' sentence did not belong to female writers: 'Other writers of the opposite sex have used sentences of this description' (Barrett 1979: 191). The difference Woolf perceives between Richardson and male experimental or modernist writers is not one of style, but subject matter: 'It is a woman's sentence, but only in the sense that it is used to describe a woman's mind,' (Barrett 1979: 191). This is the crucial distinction between Richardson, Woolf and French feminists such as Cixous and Irigaray who place the emphasis on the biological imperative of women to write differently.

After her stay in the Oberland, the relationship with Hypo Wilson resolves into a triangle: Miriam finds herself stimulated by contact with Hypo's mind whilst also paying homage to the spirit of the 'womanly woman' in his wife, Alma. This is a neat illustration of Helene Deutsch's argument, developed by Chodorow that, as a result of being mothered by women, women are left with emotional needs that cannot be fully met by men. Chodorow concentrates on the triangle of woman–man–child, but points out that it can equally work, as here, as woman–woman–man. However, this triangle is not the one which is going to satisfy Miriam ultimately. Already, in the restaurant with the Wilsons after a performance of Wagner, she feels out of place with them. The question 'What am I doing here?' (*Dawn's Left Hand*: 166) arises as it has arisen throughout her life, warning her that she has not yet found her true home: 'But though it sounded insistently, it held now a promise, as if of an appointment made towards which, though all her ways seemed blocked, she was invisibly moving' (*D'sLH*: 167). The first indication that Miriam is coming closer to finding her true home is her assertion, against Hypo, of the importance of the inner world over the outer: ' "There's more space within than without," she said. And he had heard, the first clear statement she had found to assert her world against his own' (*D'sLH*: 168).

The second indication that Miriam is moving closer to the heart of her quest is her meeting with Amabel which occurs a few pages further on in *Dawn's Left Hand*. It is Amabel who will confirm Miriam's identity and replace Alma in the emotional triangle. It is Amabel who confers on Miriam something which has eluded her all her life, the Lacanian look of love and approval. Her mother was unable to give her daughter the affirmation she needed because she was trapped by stereotypes of femininity. Her father despised women, so that even though he encouraged Miriam's 'masculine mind', his affirmation of her identity left out a crucial component – the gender bond with her mother. With Amabel, Miriam feels at last recognised for the woman she is: 'The girl's reality appealing to her own, seeing and feeling it ahead of her own seeings or feelings that yet responded, acknowledged as she merged from her reading in herself and the girl . . . the reality she had known for so long alone, brought out into life' (*D'sLH* : 217; ellipsis mine). It is Amabel who confirms for Miriam her earliest memory of being alone in a garden (*D'sLH*: 243), where earlier (*Deadlock*: 124) Michael had failed her. There is great emphasis in the initial stages of the relationship with Amabel on 'the recognising look' (*D'sLH*: 175), on the mirroring and merging of two personalities. Miriam finds herself gazing into Amabel's eyes 'as into a mirror,' (*op. cit.* 188) and sees herself 'reflected in the perceptions of this girl' (*op. cit.* 191). Amabel will act as Miriam's maternal mirror, empowering and valorising her as a woman in a way her own mother could not.

There is a similar moment of the self becoming fully self only when mirrored by another woman in H. D.'s novel *Her* (written in 1927, first published in the United States in 1981). Like Hypo Wilson, Her's fiancé, George Lowndes (modelled on Ezra Pound) sees only Her's social identity: 'He wanted Her, but he wanted a Her that he called decorative. George wanted a Her out of the volumes on the floor' (H. D. 1981/1984: 172). Her finds her true self only through being mirrored by a woman, Fayne Rabb, modelled on H. D.'s friend, Frances Gregg: 'her head . . . was two convex mirrors placed back to back. The two convex mirrors placed back to back became one mirror . . . as Fayne Rabb entered' (*op. cit.* 138; ellipses mine). H. D. describes the moment of self-recognition: 'Her. I am Her. She is Her. Knowing her, I know Her' (*op. cit.* 158). H. D. and Richardson both suggest that a woman finds her true identity not in the male gaze but through being mirrored by another woman. Perhaps then the failure of maternal mirroring in the early stages of development is not such a disaster as psychologists have claimed, provided there is someone at some point who provides adequate mirroring.

There are actual mirrors. Miriam alone in her room turns for recognition to her reflected image and finds written across it a message from Amabel. ' *"I love you ,"* it said' (*D'sLH*: 196). Amabel has superimposed herself on the real mirror, just as she has written herself into Miriam's consciousness (for a useful discussion of this, see Hanscombe 1982: 133–43). Ironically, the discovery of Amabel's message comes at the very moment when Miriam is congratulating herself on her new-found freedom. She is moving out of the room she has shared with Miss Holland in order to concentrate on her writing. 'To sit down unobserved, and endlessly free from interruption, at this little bureau that now could fulfil the promise for which it was bought' (*D'sLH*: 196). She turns to congratulate herself in the mirror and finds Amabel's message scrawled across it. This brings a new problem for Miriam: now that she has formed a relationship how will she be able to reconcile its demands with the demands of her artistic vocation which she has always seen as entailing solitude and detachment? Amabel's knowledge of Miriam has forged a bond between them which may become a burden: 'she was committed for life to the role allotted to her by the kneeling girl' (*ibid.*). When a long letter arrives from Amabel, Miriam has to weigh up the cost of reading it for that will mean the sacrifice of part of an afternoon's work (*op. cit.* 214). Amabel's knowledge of her is affirming but also onerous.

In contrast, Miriam feels that with Hypo Wilson she remains unknown (*D'sLH*: 220). He does not understand the deeper nature of women, seeing them either as submissive disciples or as sex objects. Just as in H. D.'s novel Fayne Rabb helps Her to see George Lowndes in his true perspective, so Miriam's perception of Hypo is heightened by Amabel's confirmation of her identity: 'All this she felt tonight with the strength of two. Amabel was with her, young Amabel, with her mature experience of men, who had confirmed what hitherto she had thought might be inexperience, or a personal peculiarity: her certainty that between men and women there can be no direct communication' (*op. cit.* 223). Now Miriam knows that her consciousness of the gulf between men and women is not simply, as she had feared, 'a personal peculiarity,' but an essential part of a woman's experience in this gender divided world for it has been confirmed to her by another woman.

Nevertheless, Miriam is heterosexual and wants a relationship with a man. Her problem is: how to live in the world if one is physically attracted to men yet unable to live on their terms? In a sense Miriam's situation would have been easier if she had been lesbian. But her relationship with Amabel can only be called lesbian in Adrienne Rich's sense of a lesbian continuum; it is never shown to be genital. Amabel is heterosexual and has a male lover. Yet it is Amabel, not Hypo, who brings about the birth of the woman in Miriam, bearing out Rich's claim that: 'Woman identification is a source of energy, a potential springhead of female power' (Rich 1987: 63).

Hypo's inability to affirm Miriam's identity is made clear during their first sexual encounter: 'Women . . . want recognition of themselves, of what they are and represent, before they can come fully to birth. Homage for what they are and represent. He was incapable of homage . . . But without a touch of it she could not come fully to birth for him' (*D'sLH*: 230; ellipses mine). Lacking this recognition from Hypo, Miriam is caught in an emotional triangle – woman–man–woman. When Hypo tells her she is pretty, it is through Amabel's eyes that she recognises her beauty: 'With her own eyes opened by Amabel' (*op. cit.* 231). Amabel sees the beauty of the individual woman, Hypo sees an object of prey. At their first physical encounter Miriam disarms Hypo's power over her by adopting the maternal role, as she had with Michael. It is the mother within who helps Miriam affirm her female identity in a world of men. This is what Woolf and, to some extent, Jean Rhys searched for all their lives: the internal mother as a protection for the daughter in a patriarchal world.

Amabel overshadows this evening with Hypo: 'over everything that might pass between them the spirit of Amabel would hover, distracting, demanding statement' (*D'sLH*: 242). She tries, and fails, to explain to him what Amabel means to her: 'There was in the whole of her previous experience . . . nothing that could compare with what Amabel had brought. Nothing could be better. No sharing, not even the shared being of a man and a woman . . . could be deeper or more wonderful than this being together' (*op. cit.* 242; ellipses mine). Amabel and Miriam share a wordless communication, outside the symbolic order. It is Amabel who confirms Miriam's inner sense of being and her belief in the importance of the personal life (*D'sLH*: 245). She contributes immeasurably to the dawning of Miriam's feminine consciousness. And this has an effect when the relationship with Hypo is finally consummated. For in this consummation Miriam remains uninvolved: whilst her body is absorbed in 'an unwelcome adventure' (*op. cit.* 257), her mind stays detached from the experience.

The description of this second sexual encounter between Hypo and Miriam is one of the most crucial contributions to the exploration of the feminine consciousness in twentieth-century fiction. Richardson shows the separation between a woman's body and her mind; shows how, while a woman's body may consent to, or even desire, physical union with a man, this does not imply submission to his views. The encounter with Hypo leaves Miriam unchanged: 'within her was something that stood apart, unpossessed' (*D'sLH*: 258). 'He was an alien. To Alma, to any woman ever born he was an alien. That was why last night she had voyaged away alone through the living darkness' (*op. cit.* 263). With the strength of her convictions nourished and confirmed by Amabel, Miriam sees Hypo as 'fatal to the feminine consciousness' (*op. cit.* 264). He is incapable of recognising women 'as a different order of con- sciousness' (*ibid.*). That is why, though her body might yield to him, her mind cannot. She remains detached from her body operating in a male libidinal economy because this is not in harmony with her feminine consciousness. She discovers something about her sexual identity. In sexual relations with a patriarchal man, she cannot be herself.

Here Richardson foreshadows Irigaray who has said:

> It is possible for a woman to come in accordance with the phallic model, and there will never be any shortage of men and pornographers to get women to say that they have amazing orgasms within such an economy. The question remains: aren't they being drawn out of themselves, left without any energy, perceptions, affects, gestures or images to relate them to their identity? (Whitford 1991a: 45)

Significantly, Irigaray connects freedom from the male libidinal economy with love for other women which reinforces a woman's sense of identity. In particular, Irigaray warns, a woman must not give up her love for her mother: 'What we have to do is discover our sexual identity . . . Neither little girl nor woman must give up love for their mother. Doing so uproots them from their identity, their subjectivity. Let us also try to discover the singularity of our love for other women . . . This love is necessary if we are not to remain the servants of the phallic cult, objects to be used by and exchanged between men' (Whitford 1991a: 44–5; ellipses mine). Refusing to give up her attachment to the world of women, an attachment inspired by the initial bond with her mother and continued in her relationship with Amabel, Miriam remains unpossessed by Hypo. It is the heterosexual woman's answer to the unreconstructed heterosexual man.

Not surprisingly, the original of Hypo Wilson, H. G. Wells, disliked Richardson's portrayal of their relationship in *Pilgrimage*. At the same time, recounting their affair from his point of view, he condemns himself out of his own mouth and proves her point about the lack of communication between them. He wanted, he says, 'a sensuous affair', while she 'wanted some complex intellectual relationship and I have never been able to talk to Dorothy . . . she seemed to promise the jolliest intimate friendship; she had an adorable dimple in her smile . . . and then – she would begin intoning the dull clever things that filled that shapely, rather large, flaxen head of hers; she would lecture me on philology . . . while there was not a stitch between us' (Wells 1984: 64; ellipses mine).

Pursuing independence, Miriam will bring up Hypo's child on her own. At the beginning of *Clear Horizon*, Miriam expands on her almost mystical *jouissance* at being pregnant. 'Feeling there, in the very midst of joy and wonder, not surprise but an everyday steadiness and clarity beyond anything she had yet experienced' (*CH*: 282). No one will understand this, she feels. Michael will 'immediately socialize the news in his consciousness' (*CH*: 281); having a child will show to him that she is 'a properly constituted female' (*CH*: 282). As it does. He offers her marriage which seems to her, because of his Judaism, a prison (*CH*: 303). Hypo too sees Miriam 'as reduced to her proper status, set aside to become an increasingly uncomfortable and finally agonized biological contrivance whose functioning, in his view, was the sole justification for her continued existence' (*CH*: 322). Naturally, Miriam rejects Hypo's notion that a woman's sole goal in life is motherhood (*CH*: 331), at least as he and Michael define it.

Miriam is finding it more and more important to establish her point of view even where it conflicts with Hypo's. By the end of the evening with him, she has braced herself to realise 'the truth of their relationship, the essential separation and mutual dislike of their two ways of being' (*CH*: 336-7). His theories can never encompass the whole of reality for her. Sending back a note he has written to her as if to a meekly admiring disciple, she feels vividly restored to her 'sense of the sufficiency of life at first hand' (*op. cit.* 364). She will follow her own view of life, relying on experience rather than theory. The emotional triangle of Miriam–Amabel–Hypo is breaking up but it has confirmed for Miriam the authenticity of the feminine consciousness. She has come to realise that 'the deranging and dehumanizing of women by uncritical acceptance of masculine systems of thought, rather than being evidence against feminine capacity for thought, is a demand for feminine thinking' (*op. cit.* 378). This feminine thinking is what she will now pursue. Her relationship with Hypo has crystallised her aims as a woman writer. Standing, as did Wells, in the Edwardian realist tradition, seen by Woolf and others as an essentially masculine tradition, Hypo writes the kind of 'enclosed' novels which for Miriam leave out a large part of life. 'The torment of all novels is what is left out . . . Bang, bang, bang, on they go, these men's books, like an L.C.C. tram, yet unable to make you forget them, the authors, for a moment' (*CH*: 239; ellipsis mine). Rather than imitating men, she will try to write in a different way.

Miriam cannot, however, see her way clear as a writer until she has solved the problem of what to do about Michael who keeps running to her with his many problems. Motherhood, even if short-lived, has reinforced her determination to be dominated by no one. She has a vision of introducing Amabel to Michael. She realises that her motives are mixed – a wish to shuffle off responsibility for Michael, the urge to satisfy an illusory feeling of power, a desire to show off her friends to one another – yet she cannot help feeling that this meeting is somehow fated. It would also solve the problem of Amabel. Ever since Amabel has come to live with Miriam, the latter has not been able to get on with her writing (*CH*: 354). The marriage of Amabel and Michael will enable Miriam to preserve the detachment necessary for her life as an artist and to pursue her solitary pilgrimage. The triangle has now become Amabel-Miriam-Michael. Of the two, it is Amabel to whom she feels closest. The night before the wedding, Miriam reflects on this closeness: 'Side by side, silent, with the whole universe between us, within us, in a way no man and woman, be they never so well mated, can ever have. In a few hours, Amabel will be isolated for life with an alien consciousness' (*Dimple Hill*: 545). Amabel is still the centre of Miriam's emotional life.

In *March Moonlight*, however, Amabel has a rival. Time spent with the Quaker family, the Roscorlas, has spiritualised Miriam. She is attracted to Quakerism because they do not institutionalise a patriarchal God but allow her space to feminise the divine. Quakerism becomes for Miriam a way of upholding female values while avoiding the type of equal rights feminism she has always distrusted. She tries out another triangle – woman-man-God – in her relationships with Richard Roscorla and Charles, an unfrocked French monk. But again, it is a woman, Jean, who is the emotional centre of *March Moonlight*: 'Jean. Jean. Jean. My clue to the nature of reality . . . With Jean, for me, friendship reaches its centre' (*MM*: 612–13; ellipsis mine). The relationship with Jean is calmer and more spiritual than the one with Amabel, in accordance with Miriam's new spiritual nature. The attraction Miriam feels for Quakerism in *Dimple Hill* and *March Moonlight* is the spiritual equivalent of her artistic creed of withdrawal and solitude. She escapes a conventional Quaker marriage with Charles and returns to London to put her liking for solitude to the test by embracing, finally, the life of a writer.

Miriam visits Amabel and Michael and finds that both have had their identity strengthened in marriage. Michael has found his Jewish home at last. Amabel has exercised her woman's art of creating an atmosphere for their home. Despite this, their marriage is unhappy. Not only does Miriam not acknowledge her share of responsibility in their marriage, she even blames her friends for having discounted the cultural barriers dividing them. Here, the reader may lose some sympathy for Miriam. She has deliberately pushed another woman into patriarchal motherhood for she knew that Michael's main reason for marrying Amabel was to have a son to carry on his Jewish heritage. Her manipulation of her two friends is quite the opposite of what later feminists have defined as the qualities of maternal thinking, that is, humility, acceptance of risk, avoidance of judgement and an open ended attitude to life. Miriam arrogantly closes off two relationships because she is unable to accept the risk they pose to her life as an artist. Her action is anything but open-ended. She rejects any attempt by Amabel and Michael to involve her in a nurturing role in their marriage. For Miriam, a female artist must learn to accept her own egoism; in Hanscombe's words: 'She must accept total responsibility for her own life and none at all for any other life' (Hanscombe 1982: 36). By marrying her two friends off and escaping marriage herself, Miriam has achieved her aim: 'Fully to recognize, one must be alone. Away in the farthest reaches of one's being. As one can richly be, even with others, provided they have no claims' (*MM*: 657).

Pilgrimage ends with Miriam holding the Shatovs' son in her arms, feeling 'the complete stilling of every one of my competing urgencies' (*MM*: 658), a moment of 'freedom' and 'perfect serenity' (*ibid.*). We have, I think, to discount here the knowledge of Richardson's later life, that is, her marriage to Alan Odle and the creation of a new triangle: Dorothy–Alan–*Pilgrimage*, with the book replacing the child in Chodorow's triangle. Though Alan Odle appears briefly at the end of *Pilgrimage* as Mr Noble, there is no indication in the novel that Miriam will have a relationship with him. Richardson's *roman fleuve*, resisting romance, ends very firmly on a vision of the female artist as solitary.

Elaine Showalter is wrong when she states that *Pilgrimage* is unfinished (Showalter 1977/1982: 261). May Sinclair was wrong when she said that nothing happens in *Pilgrimage*. Quite a lot of things happen, leading in the end to a definite resolution. Inspired by loyalty to her mother, Miriam sets out on a quest to find her place in life. In the course of this, she discovers that she can neither fit into society's construct of femininity nor marry a conventionally masculine man. Later she finds all men suspect. She is confirmed in a sense of her identity as a woman and in her belief in the inalienable gulf between men and women by Amabel. Defining herself, both as a woman and an artist, in opposition to Hypo Wilson, she moves on to strengthen her belief in a feminine consciousness and define her creed as an artist.

Miriam's final vision shows her experiencing all the *jouissance* of motherhood while avoiding sexual contact with a man and childbearing in the name of the father. It is, in fact, a highly subversive vision. Miriam long ago entered the symbolic order meeting men on equal terms, not so as to become a man, but so as to disrupt that order. She has achieved her aim. And behind this vision of a woman holding another woman's child in her arms, we are intended to feel, I think, the *jouissance* of the female artist (hence the importance of the word 'serenity'). In *Mrs Dalloway*, Woolf took a woman's activity, that of the society hostess, and used it as a metaphor for the writer's creativity. So here Richardson takes maternity and uses it to describe the work of the female artist. Both writers are rescuing these roles from their functions in the patriarchy and remoulding them to suit the actual experience of women. The ending of *Pilgrimage* is a remarkable foreshadowing and working out of Kristeva's view of art as feeding on rivalry with the mother's *jouissance* ('A New Type of Intellectual: The Dissident' Moi 1986: 297) and her claim that: 'real female innovation . . . will only come about when maternity, female creation and the link between them are better understood' (*op. cit.* 298; ellipsis mine). Unlike many feminists, Miriam does not underestimate the importance of maternity for women, but she finds for herself a maternity that is not coercive.

Dorothy Richardson always maintained, slightly disingenuously, that *Pilgrimage* was a work of fiction, not autobiography. Certainly she is not portraying in Miriam Henderson the young girl that she actually was, so much as the young girl seen by the older Richardson. She believed that the past does not stand still: 'it moves, growing with one's growth' (*MM*: 657). She reworked many things, for example, the relationship with H. G. Wells where Miriam is seen to be less in his power than Richardson really was (Fromm 1977: 263).

Nevertheless, there are similarites between Miriam and her creator. Richardson's parents had hoped their third child would be a boy. Like Miriam, Richardson was brought up as a pseudo-son, being let off the domestic duties her sisters were expected to perform. From an early age she resisted the conventional role for women, returning from teaching in Germany 'convinced that many of the evils besetting the world originated in the enclosed particularist home and in the insitutions preparing women for such homes' (Richardson 1989: 136). Like Woolf, Compton-Burnett and Rose Macaulay, it was to her father Richardson looked for an opening on to the wider world. In 'Journey to Paradise' she describes her family setting off on a journey with their mother 'disquietingly anxious and dependent,' and all of them 'pendant upon his [her father's] omniscience, excited, frightened, and, but for him, lost utterly' (Richardson 1989: 125). She idealised her father, playing down the fact that his extravagance had ruined his family and forced her to earn her own living. And Mr Richardson was only partially helpful to his daughter – like his fictional counterpart, he did not offer to take her to the lectures he attended in London.

While she admired her father's intellect, his judgement and his power, she resented his cruelty to her mother. To a large extent Richardson's sympathies, like Miriam's, lay with her fun-loving mother who taught her daughter to distrust intellectual systems. In 'Data for a Spanish Publisher', Richardson explains that her mother 'unconsciously fostered my deep-rooted suspicion of "facts" and ordered knowledge. From the first I hated, and whenever possible evaded, orderly instruction in regard to the world about me' (Richardson 1989: 132). At the same time, Richardson was afraid of ending up, like her mother, a helpless victim convinced of her own worthlessness. Richardson accompanied her sick mother to the seaside to recuperate, as Miriam does in *Pilgrimage*. She escaped from the sickroom for some fresh air. When she returned to their boarding house an hour later she discovered her mother had cut her throat with a kitchen knife. The account of her mother's death was so painful for her to write that she had initially intended to leave it out of *Pilgrimage* and it was only at her publisher's urging that she added the final chapter of *Honeycomb*.

In addition to her family, Richardson's portrayal, in the figures of Michael and Hypo, of Benjamin Grad and H. G. Wells and their attitudes to women, is essentially true to life. Veronica Grad, the original of Amabel, claimed that she entered into the marriage with Benjamin out of love for Richardson and that the children of the marriage would be Richardson's as well (Fromm 1977: 57). All this is faithfully represented in *Pilgrimage*.

Miriam's artistic credo of solitude and detachment was also shared by her creator. In an article, 'Women in the Arts', published in *Vanity Fair* (1925), Richardson declares that artistic achievement requires quiet and solitude 'in the sense of freedom from preoccupations'. The latter, she says, is almost impossible for a woman to obtain because of her nature which cannot help responding to human need in a way that men do not. Hence, claims Richardson, the absence of 'first-class feminine art'. Certainly Richardson herself found Veronica Grad's demands disruptive (Fromm 1977: 211–12), though she usually managed to put her art first. Her short story, 'Tryst', published in 1941, shows remarkable insight into the psychological burdens of family life on mothers. In 1928 she had an amusing skirmish in the newspapers with Storm Jameson on the subject of bored surburban wives. Richardson was much more sympathetic to the problems faced by these women than Jameson. The conflict between the demands of art and life was one which, unlike Miriam, Richardson never really resolved.

What is omitted from *Pilgrimage* is an account of Richardson's life with Alan

Odle at the time when she was actually writing *Pilgrimage*. But her life continued to be consonant with Miriam's. I have already suggested that life reformed itself for Richardson around a new triangle – woman–man–*Pilgrimage*. Alan Odle was, like the men Miriam meets, a man with whom Richardson could express her maternal instincts. However, after his death, she did not complain of loneliness. In 1952, she wrote to a young woman: 'When one is within it, one is apt to exaggerate the quality of human "belongings", particularly, whether in the case of "love" or of "friendship", or of the two combined . . . The idolators of such things, describing them from outside, fill our literature with falsities. Solitude is neither loneliness nor lovelessness' (quoted in Hanscombe and Smyers 1987: 61; ellipsis mine). Here, Miriam Henderson and Dorothy Richardson, creator and creation, blend into one.

Richardson, of all the writers in this study, comes closest to achieving Irigaray's aim of 'shaking the foundations of the patriarchal order' by rethinking the mother–daughter relationship (Whitford 1991a: 50). Mothers and motherhood are crucial throughout the *Pilgrimage*. It is her relationship with her mother which leads Miriam to be dissatisfied with the world of men and to embark on her discovery of the feminine consciousness. Mrs Bailey, a mother figure, first alerts her to the specifically feminine art of creating atmospheres. Miriam herself has a strong maternal urge and in her relationships with Michael and Hypo disarms their power over her and expresses her creativity by mothering them. She chooses motherhood as a metaphor for the creativity of the female artist. Her long quest is an apt illustration of Cixous's interesting comment that: 'Writers begin as sons, male or female, but later they become mothers when they come to think about what writing is' (Wilcox *et al* 1990: 29).

Miriam renegotiates motherhood for women, taking it outside the patriarchal construct. In so doing, she widens the scope of motherhood and thus provides a parallel, as we have seen, with the theories of Helene Deutsch which were taken up later by Cixous, Kristeva and Irigaray, among others. As Irigaray has said: 'we are always mothers once we are women. We bring something other than children into the world . . . love, desire, language, art, the social, the political, the religious, for example. But this creation has been forbidden for us for centuries, and we must reappropriate this maternal dimension that belongs to us as women' (Whitford 1991a: 43; ellipsis mine). This reappropriation of the maternal is what Richardson succeeds in achieving through her portrayal of Miriam Henderson. We have finally found a writer in the inter-war period able to use her maternal instincts in such a way as to further her vocation as an artist.

Conclusion

Examination of our six writers' treatment of motherhood reveals an extraordinarily rich and varied approach to mothering compared with the inter-war media's one-dimensional view of the role. These writers are reworking the script of the mother–daughter relationship, aiming to redefine patriarchal motherhood to make it consonant with women's actual experience. Recognising that motherhood is not essentialist but represents different things to different women, they question what mothering means and seek to expand the term. Their attempt to recover the maternal inheritance is not simply 'nostalgia' (Jacobus 1995: 2), still less a 're-membering' of the phallic mother (*op. cit.* 16–17); rather it is a quest to find a female identity which will empower them as writers. In their rewriting of Freud's hostile account of mother–daughter relations these authors provide parallels with the work of female psychoanalysts during the inter-war period and anticipate, in some of their most radical insights into motherhood, those of French feminism and American object-relations analysts. They point forward to what feminism is only now beginning to come to terms with: the mother as a creative force and inspirational figure who has been cut off from her daughter by the patriarchy. Far from being a regressive influence which has to be left behind in order for the daughter to enter the symbolic order of language and culture, the mother and the recovery of the mother's voice in many cases frees the daughter's writing. This is noticeably so with Woolf and Rhys.

As we saw in Chapter 1, daughters in the inter-war period often led lives very different from those of their mothers and had different expectations. Because of this, daughters were able to stand back from their mothers and see them as women with their own separate stories. The distance between daughter and mother was naturally exacerbated if the mother died early, as in the case of Elizabeth Bowen and Virginia Woolf, or was particularly unnurturing (the case of Jean Rhys), or was unable to share her daughter's intellectual aspirations (Macaulay, Richardson and Compton-Burnett). Fictionalising the mother–daughter story allowed the daughter to seize control and reshape the relationship in a way that suited her needs. Thus Rose Macaulay creates for herself mothers she can respect and Compton-Burnett diminishes fear of the maternal tyrant by reducing her role to camp. Whereas Bowen's inquisitorial mode points up inadequacies in the most seemingly perfect patriarchal mothers, Dorothy Richardson takes as her starting point the helpless mother and reworks motherhood in such a way as to make it a metaphor for the female artist's power. There is an extraordinary variety of form as well as of theme in these inter-war fictionalisations of the mother–daughter story, from Macaulay's lighthearted wit and Compton-Burnett's implosive decadence through to Woolf's lyrical/elegiac mode and Richardson's 'stream-of-consciousness'.

As daughters, our writers point to the fact that mothering is not a private act but one influenced by the particular socio-cultural context in which it takes place. They are aware of the extent to which their mothers have become entangled in the patriarchal discourse. They show the burdens this discourse places upon mothers (Compton-Burnett, Richardson), the damage it does to mothers who endeavour to uphold the patriarchy's text for women's lives (Bowen), or they get behind idealisations of the patriarchal mother by exposing slips and fissures in her role (Woolf). In Rhys's novels, colonialism is presented as an additional burden on mothers. By analysing the context within which the mother operates, these writers direct their anger not against her but against the patriarchy. Some present the mother's world as a warm, nurturing place, thereby pointing up what is lacking in the patriarchy: Rhys in *Voyage in the Dark* and *Wide Sargasso Sea* and Macaulay in *The World My Wilderness*. Others, notably Woolf, Compton-Burnett and Richardson, openly protest against their society's gender arrangements and the hierarchical power structures of the patriarchal family. Reversing the Demeter–Persephone myth, these daughters try to rescue the individual woman threatened with death in the patriarchal scheme of things. In Woolf's case this involved an attempt to raise up a matriarchy as a counterweight to the power of the patriarchy.

The recreation of the mother in fiction is a way of keeping her close. Our writers claim their right to enter the symbolic on equal terms with men, but not at the cost of the loss of their maternal inheritance. Daughters pick up the pen in order to bridge the gap between themselves and their mothers, fighting against stereotypes of motherhood that hinder their creativity. Writing becomes an effort to understand the mother (Woolf), to repair relations with her (Rhys) or to give her more power than she actually possesses

(Richardson). The mother is not, as in Freud and Lacan, a forbidden place which prevents speech; for writers like Rhys, Woolf and Richardson, the mother *is* the daughter's source of speaking. The work of Rhys and Woolf in particular shows the mother's importance both as protection for her daughter in a patriarchal society hostile to women and as an aid to establishing the daughter's sense of identity. Even in Bowen where the maternal inheritance is abandoned as the daughter takes up her pen and enters the father's kingdom, the haunting sense of loss of that bond with the mother expressed in Bowen's later writing shows how necessary the bond is to the daughter's identity. In many cases the mother–daughter story replaces the romance plot and is presented as more important than the latter for securing the daughter's identity (*The World my Wilderness, The Death of the Heart, The Voyage Out, Wide Sargasso Sea, Pilgrimage*). The maternal inheritance is vital to these women for in a patriarchy the daughter's safety and self-worth depends on the empowerment of the mother as a counterweight to the father. Their identity as writers depends not on cutting themselves off from the mother's world but in trying to retrieve and articulate the mother's voice.

In the context of the maternal and reparative aspects of creativity, Melanie Klein is central. As Janet Sayers explains: 'Klein's discovery of the child's early internalization of its first relation with the mother led . . . to an important shift in psychoanalytic perspectives on art, now understood as stemming not from sublimation of instinct but from wish [sic] to repair relations with others, in the first place with the mother' (Sayers 1991: 226; ellipsis mine). In art, Klein argues in her paper on 'Infantile Anxiety-Situations Reflected in a Work of Art and in the Creative Impulse' (1929), both children and adults seek to make good the damage seemingly done in attacking the mother. So Rhys, Compton-Burnett and Macaulay (in *The World My Wilderness*) use their writing to reach beyond hostility to their mothers.

In many ways, as we saw in Chapter 1, the individual, historical mother could be a hindrance to her daughter's development as an artist, putting obstacles in the way of her education and setting before her the example of the Angel in the House. The striking thing about our six writers is the way in which they overcome these difficulties so that the relationship with the mother is an aid to her daughter's creativity. The mother becomes her daughter's muse, viewed with hatred, longing, love, the figure that animates their writing. For Woolf she inspires an attempt to bring her story into the symbolic. In Compton-Burnett's novels, she becomes a spur to the realisation that motherhood is a role and not necessarily one that is natural for women. In Dorothy Richardson, she is an inspiration to reinvent motherhood outside the terms of the patriarchy. Woolf, Richardson, Compton-Burnett in their different ways seek, in Irigaray's words, 'to shake the foundations of the patriarchy' (Whitford 1991a: 50). They are engaged in a long project, which has not yet found a satisfactory solution, that of altering our way of living so as to undo hierarchical, competitive power relations and instal the egalitarian, nurturing way of life characteristic of the matriarchy as described by Jane Harrison in which women's creativity will be unfettered.

Only one of our writers was a mother in actual fact – and Rhys so distanced herself from the mothering role as to have been hardly a mother at all. Primarily they write as daughters, though this does not exclude them at times, as in the cases of Woolf and Richardson, from also writing as mothers. As daughters they learn to heal themselves from flaws in the mother–daughter relationship through their pen; in a sense the pen becomes their mother. Yet though they write as daughters, through their profound probing of the mother–daughter relationship and its links with female creativity, they have all become our mothers. Their art is a mirror affirming our identities as daughters, mothers, artists. And in turn, as daughters, we must work to keep our maternal inheritance alive.

Bibliography

SELECTED WORKS OF ELIZABETH BOWEN,
IVY COMPTON-BURNETT, ROSE MACAULAY, JEAN RHYS,
DOROTHY RICHARDSON AND VIRGINIA WOOLF

Bowen, E. 1927/1987 *The Hotel*, Harmondsworth: Penguin.
Bowen, E. 1929/1987 *The Last September*, Harmondsworth: Penguin.
Bowen, E. 1931/1946 *Friends and Relations*, Harmondsworth: Penguin.
Bowen, E. 1932/1945 *To the North*, Harmondsworth: Penguin.
Bowen, E. 1935/1976 *The House in Paris*, Harmondsworth: Penguin.
Bowen, E. 1938/1989 *The Death of the Heart*, Harmondsworth: Penguin.
Bowen, E. 1942/1984 *Bowen's Court and Seven Winters*, London: Virago.
Bowen, E. 1949/1987 *The Heat of the Day*, Harmondsworth: Penguin.
Bowen, E. 1962 *Afterthought. Pieces about Writing*, London: Longmans.
Bowen, E. 1963/1988 *The Little Girls*, Harmondsworth: Penguin.
Bowen, E. 1966/1987 *Eva Trout*, Harmondsworth: Penguin.
Bowen, E. 1985 *The Collected Stories*, Harmondsworth: Penguin.
Bowen, E. 1986 *The Mulberry Tree. Writings of Elizabeth Bowen* (ed.) H. Lee, London: Virago.
Compton-Burnett, I. 1911/1971 *Dolores*, Edinburgh: Blackwood.
Compton-Burnett, I. 1925/1952 *Pastors and Masters*, London: Victor Gollancz.
Compton-Burnett, I. 1929/1954 *Brothers and Sisters*, London: Victor Gollancz.
Compton-Burnett, I. 1931/1948 *Men and Wives*, London: Eyre and Spottiswood.
Compton-Burnett, I. 1933/1948 *More Women than Men*, London: Eyre and Spottiswood.
Compton-Burnett, I. 1935/1951 *A House and Its Head*, London: Eyre and Spottiswood.
Compton-Burnett, I. 1937/1961 *Daughters and Sons*, London: Victor Gollancz.
Compton-Burnett, I. 1941/1984 *Parents and Children*, Harmondsworth: Penguin.
Compton-Burnett, I. 1944 *Elders and Betters*, London: Victor Gollancz.
Compton-Burnett, I. 1957/1972 *A Father and His Fate*, London: Victor Gollancz.
Compton-Burnett, I. 1962 'Interview with Miss Compton-Burnett', *Review of English Literature*
  III: 96–112.

Compton-Burnett, I. 1963 *A God and His Gifts*, London: Victor Gollancz.
Compton-Burnett, I. 1971 *The Last and the First*, London: Victor Gollancz.
Macaulay, R. 1916/1986 *Non-Combatants and Others*, London: Methuen.
Macaulay, R. 1920 *Potterism: A Tragi-farcical Tract*, London: Collins.
Macaulay, R. 1921 *Dangerous Ages*, London: Collins.
Macaulay, R. 1922 *Mystery at Geneva*, London: Collins.
Macaulay, R. 1923/1983 *Told by an Idiot*, London: Virago.
Macaulay, R. 1926/1985 *Crewe Train*, London: Methuen.
Macaulay, R. 1928/1986 *Keeping Up Appearances*, London: Methuen.
Macaulay, R. 1950/1983 *The World My Wilderness*, London: Virago.
Macaulay, R. 1956/1978 *The Towers of Trebizond*, London: Fontana.
Macaulay, R. 1961/1968 *Letters to a Friend* (ed.) C. Babington-Smith, London: Fontana.
Macaulay, R. 1962 *Last Letters to a Friend* (ed.) C. Babington-Smith, London: Collins.
Macaulay, R. 1964 *Letters to a Sister* (ed.) C. Babington-Smith, London: Collins.
Rhys, J. 1928/1973 *Quartet*, Harmondsworth: Penguin.
Rhys, J. 1930/1971 *After Leaving Mr Mackenzie*, Harmondsworth: Penguin.
Rhys, J. 1934/1969 *Voyage in the Dark*, Harmondsworth: Penguin.
Rhys, J. 1939/1969 *Good Morning, Midnight*, Harmondsworth: Penguin.
Rhys, J. 1966/1968 *Wide Sargasso Sea*, Harmondsworth: Penguin.
Rhys, J. 1968/1972 *Tigers are Better-Looking*, Harmondsworth: Penguin.
Rhys, J. 1976/1979 *Sleep It Off Lady*, Harmondsworth: Penguin.
Rhys, J. 1979/1981 *Smile Please*, Harmondsworth: Penguin.
Rhys, J. 1984 *Letters 1931–1966* (ed.) F. Wyndham and D. Melly, London: Deutsch.
Richardson, D. 1967 *Pointed Roofs* [1915], *Backwater* [1916], *Honeycomb* [1917], *The Tunnel* [1919], *Interim* [1919], *Deadlock* [1921], *Revolving Lights* [1923], *The Trap* [1925], *Oberland* [1927], *Dawn's Left Hand* [1931], *Clear Horizon* [1935], *Dimple Hill* [1938], *March Moonlight* [1967] in *Collected Edition* 4 vols, London: J. M. Dent and Sons Ltd.
Richardson, D. 1989 *Journey to Paradise*, London: Virago.
Woolf, V. 1915/1981 *The Voyage Out*, London: Granada.
Woolf, V. 1919/1992 *Night and Day*, Harmondsworth: Penguin.
Woolf, V. 1922/1984 *Jacob's Room*, London: Granada.
Woolf, V. 1925/1981 *Mrs Dalloway*, London: Granada.
Woolf, V. 1927/1988 *To the Lighthouse*, London: Grafton.
Woolf, V. 1928/1977 *Orlando*, London: Grafton.
Woolf, V. 1931/1980 *The Waves*, London: Granada.
Woolf, V. 1937/1985 *The Years*, London: Granada.
Woolf, V. 1941/1978 *Between the Acts*, London: Grafton.
Woolf, V. 1953/1981 *A Writer's Diary* (ed.) L. Woolf, London: Granada.
Woolf, V. 1975 *The Letters of Virginia Woolf* vol. 1 1888–1912 (eds) N. Nicolson and J. Trautmann, London: Hogarth Press. And subsequently vol. 2 1912–1922, Hogarth, 1976; vol. 3 1923–1928, Hogarth, 1977; vol. 4 1929–1931, Hogarth, 1978; vol. 6 1936–1941, Hogarth, 1973.
Woolf, V. 1977 *The Diary of Virginia Woolf* vol. I 1915–1919 (ed.) A. O. Bell, London: Hogarth Press.
Woolf, V. 1978a *The Pargiters* (ed.) M. A. Leaska, London: Hogarth Press.
Woolf, V. 1978b *The Diary of Virginia Woolf* vol. II 1920–24 (ed.) A. O. Bell, London: Hogarth Press.
Woolf, V. 1979a '*Anon*. and *The Reader*. Virginia Woolf's Last Essays', (ed.) B. R. Silver, *Twentieth Century Literature*, 25 (3/4): 356–441.

Woolf, V. 1979b 'Virginia Woolf's *The Journal of Mistress Joan Martyn*', (eds) S. M. Squier and L. A. De Salvo, *Twentieth Century Literature*, 25 (3/4): 237–269.

Woolf, V. 1990 *Moments of Being* (ed.) J. Schulkind, London: Grafton.

Woolf, V. 1992 *A Room of One's Own*. [1929] *Three Guineas* [1938] (ed.) M. Shiach, Oxford: Oxford University Press.

OTHER CONTEMPORARY SOURCES AND SELECTED POST-WAR CRITICISM

Abel, E. 1979 'Women and Schizophrenia: The Fiction of Jean Rhys', *Contemporary Literature*, 20: 155–77.

Abel, E. (ed.) 1982 *Writing and Sexual Difference*, Brighton: Harvester.

Abel, E. 1983 'Narrative Structure(s) and Female Development: The Case of *Mrs Dalloway*', *The Voyage In: Fictions of Female Development* (eds) E. Abel, M. Hirsch, E. Langland, Hanover, NH: University Press of New England.

Adams, P. 1983 'Mothering', *m/f A Feminist Journal*, 8: 40–52.

Angier, C. 1990 *Jean Rhys*, Harmondsworth: Penguin.

Annan, N. 1984 *Leslie Stephen. The Godless Victorian*, London: Weidenfeld and Nicolson.

Appignanesi, L. and Forrester, J. 1993 *Freud's Women*, London: Virago.

Armstrong, K. 1996 *The Gospel According to Woman*, London: Fount.

Ashworth, A. 1987 ' "But Why Was She Called Portia?": Judgement and Feeling in Bowen's *The Death of the Heart*', *Critique*, Spring, 28 (3): 159–66.

Bagnold, E. 1938/1987 *The Squire*, London: Virago.

Barrett, E. 1987 'Matriarchal Myth on a Patriarchal Stage: Virginia Woolf's *Between the Acts*', *Twentieth Century Literature*, 33 (1): 18–37.

Barrett, M. (ed.) 1979 *Virginia Woolf on Women and Writing*, London: The Women's Press.

Barthes, R. 1977/1990 *A Lover's Discourse: Fragments*, tr. R. Howard, Harmondsworth: Penguin.

Beauman, N. 1983 *A Very Great Profession. The Woman's Novel 1914–39*, London: Virago.

Beauvoir, S. de 1953/1972 *The Second Sex*, Harmondsworth: Penguin.

Beddoe, D. 1989 *Back to Home and Duty. Women Between the Wars, 1918–1939*, London: Pandora.

Bell, Q. 1972 *Virginia Woolf. A Biography*, II, *Mrs Woolf. 1912–1941*, London: The Hogarth Press.

Belsey, C. and Moore J. (eds) 1989 *The Feminist Reader*, London: Macmillan.

Benjamin, J. 1980 'The Bonds of Love', *Feminist Studies*, 6 (1): 144–74.

Benjamin, J. 1990 *The Bonds of Love. Psychoanalysis, Feminism and the Problem of Domination*, London: Virago.

Benstock, S. (ed.) 1987 *Feminist Issues in Literary Scholarship*, Bloomington: Indiana University Press.

Benvenuto, B. and Kennedy, R. 1986 *The Works of Jacques Lacan*, London: Free Association Books.

Berry, P. and Bishop, A. (eds) 1985 *Testament of a Generation. The Journalism of Vera Brittain and Winifred Holtby* London: Virago.

Bowen, J. 1979 'An Interview with Ivy Compton-Burnett', *Twentieth Century Literature* 25: 165–172.

Braybon, G. 1981 *Women Workers in the First World War. The British Experience*, London: Croom Helm.

Braybon, G. and Summerfield, P. 1987 *Out of the Cage. Women's Experience in Two World Wars*, London: Pandora Press.

Brittain, V. 1933/1978 *Testament of Youth*, London: Virago.

Brittain, V. 1940/1989 *Testament of Friendship*, London: Virago.

Burkhart, C. 1965 *I. Compton-Burnett*, London: Victor Gollancz.

Burkhart, C. (ed.) 1972 *The Art of I. Compton-Burnett: A Collection of Critical Essays*, London: Victor Gollancz.

Chessman, H. 1983 'Women and Language in the Fiction of Elizabeth Bowen', *Twentieth Century Literature*, Spring, 29 (1): 69–85.

Chodorow, N. 1978 *The Reproduction of Mothering. Psychoanalysis and the Sociology of Gender*, Berkeley and Los Angeles: University of California Press.

Chodorow, N. 1989 *Feminism and Psychoanalytic Theory*, New Haven and London: Yale University Press.

Conley, V.A. 1984 *Hélène Cixous. Writing the Feminine*, Lincoln and London: University of Nebraska Press.

Cooper, L. 1936/1987 *The New House*, London: Virago.

Cramer, P. 1993 'Virginia Woolf's Matriarchal Family of Origins in *Between the Acts*', *Twentieth Century Literature*, 39 (2):166–84.

Crosland, M. 1981 *Beyond the Lighthouse: English Women Novelists in the Twentieth Century*, London: Constable.

Davidson, A. 1985 *Jean Rhys*, New York: Frederick Ungar.

Davidson, C. N. and Broner E. M. (eds) 1980 *The Lost Tradition. Mothers and Daughters in Literature*, New York: Frederick Ungar.

Delafield, E. M. 1927/1988 *The Way Things Are*, London: Virago.

Delafield, E. M. 1932/1988 *Thank Heaven Fasting*, London: Virago.

De Salvo, L. 1991 *Virginia Woolf. The Impact of Childhood Sexual Abuse on her Life and Work*, London: The Women's Press.

Deutsch, H. 1944/1946 *The Psychology of Women*, vol. 1, *Girlhood*, London: Research Books Ltd.

Deutsch, H. 1945 *The Psychology of Women*, vol. 2, *Motherhood*, New York: Grune and Stratton.

Diamond, I. and Quinby, L. 1988 *Feminism and Foucault. Reflections on Resistance*, Boston: Northeastern University Press.

Dick, K. 1983 *Ivy and Stevie: Ivy Compton-Burnett and Stevie Smith, Conversations and Reflections*, London: Allison and Busby.

Dinnerstein, D. 1978 *The Rocking of the Cradle and the Ruling of the World*, London: Souvenir Press; published in the USA as *The Mermaid and the Minotaur: Sexual Arrangements and Human Malaise*, New York: Harper Row, 1976.

Du Plessis, R. B. 1985 *Writing Beyond the Ending. Narrative Strategies of Twentieth-Century Women Writers*, Bloomington: Indiana University Press.

Dyhouse, C. 1981 *Girls Growing Up in Late Victorian and Edwardian England*, London: Routledge and Kegan Paul.

Dyhouse, C. 1989 *Feminism and the Family in England 1880–1939*, London: Basil Blackwell.

Edwards, D. 1928/1986 *Winter Sonata*, London: Virago.

Eichenbaum, L. and Orbach, S. 1992 *Understanding Women*, Harmondsworth: Penguin.

Emery, J. 1991 *Rose Macaulay. A Writer's Life*, London: John Murray.

Faderman, L. 1985 *Surpassing the Love of Men. Romantic Friendship and Love Between Women from the Renaissance to the Present*, London: The Women's Press.

Flax, J. 1978 'The Conflict between Nurturance and Autonomy in Mother–Daughter Relationships and within Feminism', *Feminist Studies*, 4 (2): 171–89.

Foucault, M. 1990 *The History of Sexuality, volume I*, Harmondsworth: Penguin.

Freud, S. 1961 *The Standard Edition of the Complete Psychological Works of Sigmund Freud* vol. XIV (1914–1916), vol. XXI (1927–1931) and vol. XXII (1932–36), London: Hogarth Press.

Freud, S. 1977 *Some Psychical Consequences of the Anatomical Distinction between the Sexes* in *On Sexuality* (ed.) A. Richards, vol. 7, Harmondsworth: Penguin.

Friedan, B. 1965 *The Feminine Mystique*, Harmondsworth: Penguin.

Fromm, G. 1977 *Dorothy Richardson. A Biography*, Chicago: University of Illinois Press.

Gardiner, J. K. 1982 'On Female Identity and Writing by Women' in *Writing and Sexual Difference* (ed.) E. Abel, Brighton: Harvester.

Gardiner, J. K. 1985 'Mind Mother: Psychoanalysis and Feminism', *Making a Difference: Feminist Literary Criticism* (eds) G. Greene and C. Kahn, London and New York: Methuen.

Gentile, K. 1991 *Ivy Compton-Burnett*, London: Macmillan.

Gilbert, S. and Gubar, S. 1979 *The Madwoman in the Attic*, New Haven: Yale University Press.

Gilbert, S. and Gubar, S. 1988–9 *No Man's Land: The Place of the Woman Writer in the Twentieth Century*, vol. I *The War of the Words* and vol. II *Sexchanges*. New Haven, CT: Yale University Press.

Gilligan, C. 1982 *In a Different Voice. Psychological Theory and Women's Development*, Cambridge, MA: Harvard University Press.

Glendinning, V. 1977 *Elizabeth Bowen. Portrait of a Writer*, London: Weidenfeld and Nicolson.

Glendinning, V. 1983 *Vita. The Life of V. Sackville-West*, London: Weidenfeld and Nicolson.

Gordon, L. 1984 *Virginia Woolf. A Writer's Life*, Oxford: Oxford University Press.

Grimshaw, J. 1986 *Feminist Philosophers. Women's Perspectives on Philosophical Traditions*, Hemel Hempstead: Harvester Wheatsheaf.

Grosz, E. 1990 *Jacques Lacan: A Feminist Introduction,* London: Routledge.

H. D. 1960/1984 *Bid Me to Live*, London: Virago.

H. D. 1981/1984 *Her*, London: Virago.

H. D. 1984 *The Gift*, London: Virago.

H. D. 1985 *Tribute to Freud: Writing on the Wall, Advent*, Manchester: Carcanet.

Haldane, C. 1927 *Motherhood and its Enemies*, London: Chatto and Windus.

Hall, R. 1924/1981 *The Unlit Lamp*, London: Virago.

Hall, R. 1928/1982 *The Well of Loneliness*, London: Virago.

Hanscombe, G. 1982 *The Art of Life. Dorothy Richardson and the Development of Feminist Consciousness*, London and Boston: Peter Owen.

Hanscombe, G. and Smyers, V. L. 1987 *Writing for their Lives: The Modernist Women 1910–1940*, London: The Women's Press.

Harrison, J. 1903 *Prolegomena to the Study of Greek Religion*, Cambridge: Cambridge University Press.

Harrison, J. 1924 *Mythology*, New York: Longmans, Green and Co.

Heilbrun, C. 1991 'To the Lighthouse: The New Story of Mother and Daughter', pp. 134–9 in *Hamlet's Mother*, London: The Women's Press.

Herman, N. 1989 *Too Long a Child. The Mother–Daughter Dyad*, London: Free Association Books.

Hirsch, M. 1981 'Mothers and Daughters', *Signs*, 7 (1): 200–22.

Hobby, E. and White, C. (eds.) 1991 *What Lesbians do in Books*, London: The Women's Press.

Holtby, W. 1923/1981 *Anderby Wold*, London: Virago.

Holtby, W. 1924/1981 *The Crowded Street*, London: Virago.

Holtby, W. 1934 *Women and a Changing Civilisation*, third edition, London: Bodley Head.

Holtby, W. 1936/1988 *South Riding*, London: Virago.

Holzman, E. 1982 'The pursuit of married love: women's attitudes towards sexuality and marriage in Great Britain 1918–1939', *Journal of Social History*, 16 (Winter): 39–51.

Homans, M. 1986 *Bearing the Word. Language and Female Experience in Nineteenth-Century Women's Writing*, Chicago: University of Chicago Press.

Horney, K. 1967 *Feminine Psychology* (ed.) H. Kelman, New York: W.W. Norton and Co.

Irigaray, L. 1980 'When Our Lips Speak Together', *Signs*, 6 (1): 69–79.

Irigaray, L. 1979/1981 '*Et l'une ne bouge pas sans l'autre*', 'And the One doesn't stir without the Other', transl. H.V. Wenzel, *Signs*, 7 (1): 607.

Irigaray, L. 1993 *je, tu, nous. Toward a Culture of Difference*, transl. A. Martin, London and New York: Routledge.

Jacobus, M. (ed.) 1979 *Women Writing and Writing About Women*, London: Croom Helm.

Jacobus, M. 1995 *First Things: The Maternal Imaginary in Literature, Art, and Psychoanalysis*, London and New York: Routledge.

Jameson, S. 1934/1982 *Company Parade*, London: Virago.

Jameson, S. 1984 *Journey From the North* vol. 1 [1969], vol. 2 [1970], London: Virago.

Jesse, F. T. 1934/1979 *A Pin to See the Peepshow*, London: Virago.

Joannou, M. 1995, *'Ladies, Please Don't Smash These Windows': Women's Writing, Feminist Consciousness and Social Change 1918–38*, Oxford: Berg.

Jung, C. 1986 *Aspects of the Feminine*, London: Ark.

Jung, C. and Kerenyi, C. 1963 *Essays on a Science of Mythology*, New York: Harper and Row.

Kaplan, E. A. 1992 *Motherhood and Representation. The Mother in Popular Culture and Melodrama*, London and New York: Routledge.

Kemp, S. 1990 'But How to Describe a World Seen Without a Self?: Feminism, Fiction and Modernism', *Critical Quarterly*, 32 (1): 99–118.

Kennedy, M. 1924 *The Constant Nymph*, London: Virago.

Kennedy, M. 1936 *Together and Apart*, London: Virago.

Kiernan, R. F. 1990 *Frivolity Unbound. Six Masters of the Camp Novel*, New York: Frederick Ungar.

Klein, M. 1948 *Contributions to Psycho-Analysis 1921–1945*, London: Hogarth Press.

Lassner, P. 1990 *Elizabeth Bowen*, London: Macmillan.

Lechte, J. 1990 *Julia Kristeva*, London and New York: Routledge.

Lee, H. 1981 *Elizabeth Bowen: An Estimation*, London and Totowa: Vision Press and Barnes and Noble.

Lefkowitz, M. 1981 *Heroines and Hysterics*, London: Duckworth.

Lehmann, R. 1927/1936 *Dusty Answer*, Harmondsworth: Penguin.

Lehmann, R. 1930/1982 *A Note in Music*, London: Virago.

Lehmann, R. 1932/1981 *Invitation to the Waltz*, London: Virago.

Lehmann, R. 1936/1981 *The Weather in the Streets*, London: Virago.

Lehmann, R. 1944/1982 *The Ballad and the Source*, London: Virago.

Lehmann, R. 1967/1982 *The Swan in the Evening*, London: Virago.

Leigh, N. J. 1985 'Mirror, Mirror: The Development of Female Identity in Jean Rhys's Fiction', *World Literature Written in English*, 25 (2): 270–85.

Leighton, A. 1989 *Feminist Literary Theory: An Introduction*, University of Hull, Occasional Paper 8.

Leonardi, S. J. 1989 *Dangerous by Degrees. Women at Oxford and the Somerville College Novelists*, New Brunswick and London: Rutgers University Press.

Lewis, J. (ed.) 1986 *Labour and Love. Women's Experience of Home and Family, 1850-1940*, Oxford: Basil Blackwell.

Lidoff, J. 1986 'Virginia Woolf's Feminine Sentence', *Literature and Pschology* 32 (3): 43–59.

Light, A. 1991 *Forever England. Femininity, Literature and Conservatism Between the Wars*, London: Routledge.

Lilienfield, J. 1977 ' "The Deceptiveness of Beauty": Mother Love and Mother Hate in *To the Lighthouse*', *Twentieth Century Literature* 23 (October): 345–76.

Little, J. 1977 'Festive Comedy in Woolf's *Between the Acts*,' *Women and Literature*: 26–37.

Marcus, J. (ed) 1981 *New Feminist Essays on Virginia Woolf*, Lincoln and Nebraska: University of Nebraska Press.

Marks, E. and de Courtivron, I. (eds.) 1981 *New French Feminisms*, Hemel Hempstead: Harvester Wheatsheaf.

Mayor, F. M. 1924/1973 *The Rector's Daughter*, Harmondsworth: Penguin.

Mayor, F. M. 1929/1987 *The Squire's Daughter*, London: Virago.

Melman, B. 1988 *Women and the Popular Imagination in the Twenties. Flappers and Nymphs*, London: Macmillan.

Miles, R. 1987 *The Female Form. Women Writers and the Conquest of the Novel*, London: Routledge.

Minow-Pinkney, M. 1987 *Virginia Woolf and the Problem of the Subject. Feminine Writing in the Major Novels*, Brighton: Harvester Press.

Mitchell, J. 1990 *Psychoanalysis and Feminism. A Radical Reassessment of Freudian Psychoanalysis*, Harmondsworth: Penguin.

Mitchell, J. (ed.) 1991 *The Selected Melanie Klein*, Harmondsworth: Penguin.

Mitchell, J. and Rose, J. (eds) 1982 *Feminine Sexuality. Jacques Lacan and the* Ecole Freudienne, London: Macmillan.

Moi, T. (ed.) 1986 *The Kristeva Reader*, Oxford: Basil Blackwell.

Moi, T. 1985/1990 *Sexual/Textual Politics. Feminist Literary Theory*, London and New York: Routledge.

Moi, T. 1987 *French Feminist Thought: A Reader*, Oxford: Blackwell.

Monteith, M. 1986 *Women's Writing. A Challenge to Theory*, Brighton: Harvester Press.

Neumann, E. 1963 *The Great Mother. An Analysis of the Archetype* transl. R. Manheim, London: Routledge and Kegan Paul.

Nice, V. 1992 *Mothers and Daughters. The Distortion of a Relationship*, London: Macmillan.

Noddings, N. 1984 *Caring. A Feminine Approach to Ethics and Moral Education*, Berkeley: University of California Press.

Oldfield, S. (ed) 1994 *This Working-Day World. Women's Lives and Culture(s) in Britain 1914–1945*, London: Taylor and Francis.

Olivier, C. 1989 *Jocasta's Children. The Imprint of the Mother*, London and New York: Routledge.

Olivier, E. 1927/1981 *The Love Child*, London: Virago.

Orwell, G. 1935/1990 *A Clergyman's Daughter*, Harmondsworth: Penguin.

Plain, G. 1996 *Women's Fiction of the Second World War. Gender, Power and Resistance*, Edinburgh: Edinburgh University Press.

Plante, D. 1979 'Jean Rhys: A Remembrance', *Paris Review* 76: 238–84.

Pugh, M. 1992 *Women and the Women's Movement in Britain 1914–1959*, London: Macmillan.

Rabinow, P. (ed.) 1991 *The Foucault Reader*, Harmondsworth: Penguin.

Rice, M. 1939 *Working Class Wives. Their Health and Conditions*, Middlesex: Penguin.

Rich, A. 1977 *Of Woman Born. Motherhood as Experience and Institution*, London: Virago, London.

Rich, A. 1987 'Compulsory Heterosexuality and Lesbian Existence' (1980) in *Blood, Bread and Poetry. Selected Prose 1979–1985*, London: Virago.

Roe, S. 1990 *Writing and Gender. Virginia Woolf's Writing Practice*, Hemel Hempstead: Harvester Wheatsheaf.

Rose, J. 1992 *Marie Stopes and the Sexual Revolution*, London: Faber and Faber.

Rose, P. 1978 *Woman of Letters. A Life of Virginia Woolf*, London: Routledge and Kegan Paul.

Rosenman, E. 1986 *The Invisible Presence. Virginia Woolf and the Mother–Daughter Relationship*, Baton Rouge and London: Louisiana State University Press.

Ruddick, S. 1990 *Maternal Thinking. Towards a Politics of Peace*, London: The Women's Press.

Rule, J. 1989 *Lesbian Images*, London: Pluto Press.

Sackville-West, V. 1931/1983 *All Passion Spent,* London: Virago.

Sayers, D. L. 1935/1991 *Gaudy Night,* London: Hodder and Stoughton.

Sayers, J. 1991 *Mothering Psychoanalysis*, London: Hamish Hamilton.

Scharfman, R. 1982 'Mirroring and Mothering in Simone Schwarz-Bart's *Pluie et vent sur Télumée Miracle* and Jean Rhys's *Wide Sargasso Sea*,' *Yale French Studies* 62: 88–106.

Schreiner, O. 1911 *Women and Labour*, London: Fisher Unwin.

Scott, B. Kime (ed.) 1990 *The Gender of Modernism*, Bloomington and Indianapolis: Indiana University Press.

Segal, H. 1964 *Introduction to the Work of Melanie Klein*, London: Heinemann.

Shattuck, S. 1987 'The Stage of Scholarship: Crossing the Bridge from Harrison to Woolf', in *Virginia Woolf and Bloomsbury. A Centenary Celebration* (ed.) J. Marcus, London: Macmillan Press.

Shaw, M. 1986 'Feminism and Fiction Between the Wars: Winifred Holtby and Virginia Woolf', in *Women's Writing. A Challenge to Theory* (ed.) M. Monteith, Brighton: Harvester Press.

Shaw, M. and Vanacker S. 1991 *Reflecting on Miss Marple*, London: Routledge.

Shiach, M. 1991 *Hélène Cixous. A Politics of Writing*, London and New York: Routledge.

Showalter, E. 1977/1982 *A Literature of Their Own. British Women Novelists from Brontë to Lessing*, London: Virago.

Sinclair, M. 1919/1980 *Mary Olivier: A Life,* London: Virago.

Sinclair M. 1922/1980 *The Life and Death of Harriett Frean,* London: Virago.

Sontag, S. 1964/1983 'Notes on Camp' *A Susan Sontag Reader*, Harmondsworth: Penguin.

Spurling, H. 1984 *Ivy. The Life of I. Compton-Burnett*, New York: Alfred A. Knopf.

Staley, T. 1979 *Jean Rhys. A Critical Study*, London: Macmillan.

Stern, D. 1976 *The First Relationship: Infant and Mother*, Cambridge, MA.: Harvard University Press.

Stern, D. 1985 *The Interpersonal World of the Infant*, New York: Basic Books.

Stevenson, J. 1990 *British Society 1914–45*, Harmondsworth: Penguin.

Stoneman, P. 1993 'Postructuralism and Psychoanalysis', unpublished paper, University of Hull.

Stopes, M. 1918/1957 *Married Love: A New Contribution to the Solution of Sex Difficulties*, London: Hogarth Press.

Stott, M. (ed.) 1987 *Women Talking. An Anthology from The Guardian Women's Page 1922–35 1951–71*, London: Pandora.

Strachey, R. 1928 *'The Cause'. A Short History of the Women's Movement in Great Britain*, London: G. Bell and Sons.

Struther, J. 1939/1989 *Mrs Miniver*, London: Virago.

Swanwick, H. 1935 *I Have Been Young*, London: Victor Gollancz.

Twentieth Century Literature, 1979 'Ivy Compton-Burnett Issue,' 25 (2).

Tylee, C. 1990 *The Great War and Women's Consciousness* London: Macmillan.

Vreeland, E. 1979 'Jean Rhys: The Art of Fiction', *Paris Review* 76: 218–37.

Warner, M. 1985 *Alone of All Her Sex. The Myth and the Cult of the Virgin Mary*, London: Picardo.

Warner, S. T. 1926 *Lolly Willowes. Or The Loving Huntsman*, London: Chatto and Windus.

Warner, S. T. 1990 *Selected Stories*, London: Virago.

Weedon, C. 1992 *Feminist Practice and Poststructuralist Theory*, Oxford: Basil Blackwell.

Wehr, D. 1988 *Jung and Feminism. Liberating Archetypes*, London: Routledge.

Wells, G. P. (ed.) 1984 *H. G. Wells in Love*, London: Faber and Faber.

West, R. 1918/1980 *The Return of the Soldier*, London: Virago.

West, R. 1936/1992 *The Thinking Reed*, London: Virago.

White, A. 1933/1978 *Frost in May*, London: Virago.

White, A. 1950/1979 *The Lost Traveller*, London: Virago.

White, A. 1952/1979 *The Sugar House*, London: Virago.

White, A. 1954/1979 *Beyond the Glass*, London: Virago.

White, A. 1983 *As Once in May. The Early Augobiography of Antonia White and Other Writings* (ed.) S. Chitty, London: Virago.

Whitford, M. (ed.) 1991a *The Irigaray Reader*, Oxford: Basil Blackwell.

Whitford, M. 1991b *Luce Irigaray. Philosophy in the Feminine*, London and New York: Routledge.

Wilcox, H., McWatters K.,Thompson A., and Williams L. (eds) 1990 *The Body and the Text. Hélène Cixous, Reading and Teaching*, Hemel Hempstead: Harvester Wheatsheaf.

Winnicott, D. J. 1971 'Mirror-Role of Mother and Family,' *Playing and Reality*, New York: Basic Books.

Wisker, G. *It's My Party: Reading Twentieth-Century Women's Writing*, London: Pluto Press.

Young, E. H. 1925/1992 *William*, London: Virago.

Young, E. H. 1930/1984 *Miss Mole*, London: Virago.

Index

Note: Comments on specific works of fiction are indexed under the title of the work with a cross-reference from the author. All points from non-fiction works are indexed directly under their authors.